GIANTS OF GAELIC
FOOTBALL

GIANTS OF GAELIC FOOTBALL

SEÁN ÓG Ó CEALLACHÁIN ∾

Gill & Macmillan

Gill & Macmillan Ltd
Hume Avenue, Park West, Dublin 12
with associated companies throughout the world
www.gillmacmillan.ie

© Seán Óg Ó Ceallacháin 2007, 2008
978 07171 4547 8
First published in hard cover 2007
First published in this format 2008

Index compiled by Cover to Cover
Typography design by Make Communication
Print origination by Carole Lynch
Printed and bound by Nørhaven Paperback
A/S, Denmark

This book is typeset in Linotype Minion and
Neue Helvetica.

The paper used in this book comes from the wood
pulp of managed forests. For every tree felled,
at least one tree is planted, thereby renewing
natural resources.

A CIP catalogue record for this book is available
from the British Library.

5 4 3 2 1

This book is dedicated to the many fine radio sports commentators who, Sunday after Sunday, brought the passion of their art to every household in the land and beyond. They were the great men who are no longer with us. From the initial broadcast of the 1926 All-Ireland hurling championship semi-final between Kilkenny and Galway on the new 2RN (Irish station), the GAA owed a lot to the enthusiasm generated by the radio commentaries provided by P. J. Mehigan, who being a hurler, footballer and athlete of note, brought a great sense of audience participation to the events he covered on air.

The new station was able to make a proud boast: 2RN broadcast running commentaries on sporting events before the BBC did. The 'Beeb' was barred from doing commentaries by its obligation not to broadcast news before 7 p.m., which lasted through 1926. 2RN therefore had this field to itself. P. J. Mehigan was for years the regular GAA commentator for 2RN and died in 1965.

The year 1938 marked the arrival of a young Michael O'Hehir who was to go on and carve a niche for himself as the greatest in the commentary field, especially on GAA games.

Mick Dunne was a statistical genius in his career as a commentator. Tom Rooney was noted for his great passion for Gaelic games, as was also Liam Campbell, an ardent Dub.

I would add my late father, Seán senior, to this list. He launched the first magazine style sports programme on radio in 1932, which initially embraced mostly all the major field games. Eventually he was forced to devote all his time to covering Gaelic games and that helped to popularise the national games still further. Had there been a TAM rating in operation, his Sunday night GAA programme would have had a 99 per cent listenership. Indeed, to miss Seán Ó Ceallacháin on a Sunday night was almost unthinkable, and tantamount to missing Mass on Sunday morning. When he retired in 1953, I took over the programme which goes out on the internet (audio) all over the world. It is now the longest running programme of its kind in the world.

'Don't walk behind me;
I may not lead.
Don't walk in front of me;
I may not follow.
Just walk beside me
and be my friend.'

(UNKNOWN)

CONTENTS

TEACHTAIREACHT
AN UACHTARÁIN

NIOCLÁS Ó BRAONÁIN
UACHTARÁN CLG

Is chúis mhór áthais dom an deis seo a fháil cúpla focal a scríobh ar fhoilsiú an leabhair nua seo.

Seán Óg Ó Ceallacháin has given a lifetime of service to the GAA, from his years as a player of some note to his incredible service as a broadcaster with RTÉ, and of late his contributions to an ever-increasing library of GAA related publications.

In this latest tome, Seán Óg reflects on the careers of some of the greatest players in the history of Gaelic football. Their stories are told in a manner which reflects the author's own great love for and knowledge of the game, and his respect for men who have defined the sport through their heroism and mastery of the unique arts of Gaelic football.

While the book features many who have attained the ultimate glory of an All-Ireland medal—instantly recognisable names such as Matt Connor, Brian Mullins, Enda Colleran and Mick O'Dwyer, it also focuses heavily on many of the greats of the game who have never climbed the steps of the Hogan Stand in September.

Men such as Iggy Jones of Tyrone, Packie McGarty of Leitrim, and more latterly Mickey Kearns of Sligo and Noel Roche of Clare, are still revered within their own counties and remembered fondly further afield for sterling displays, often against the odds and frequently with little silverware to show for their efforts.

Their stories, and those of many other 'Giants of Gaelic Football' are beautifully told in this book that will be treasured by many and will rekindle the memories of the great players and the great occasions that have defined the GAA and Gaelic Football since the Association was founded in 1884.

Happy Reading!

Iúil 2007

RÉAMHRÁ

PEADAR Ó CUINN

Is cúís mhór áthais dom réamhrá a scríobh do'n leabhar nua seo ó Seán Óg Ó Ceallacháin—iar-imreoir, iar-iománaí de'n chead scoth, iar-réiteoir, iriseoir agus fear a bhí dluthbhaint aige le cursaí craolacháin trid a shaol, agus atá go foill. Ba é Sean a thug '... *príomh thortaí an lae ...*' duinn os cíonn leathchéid agus a chuir in iúl duinn cad a bhí ag tarlú ar fud na tire, maidir le peile agus iománaíochta—na deich nóiméid is tábhachtaigh na seachtaine duinn, sna caogaoidí agus sna seascaidí agus, ar ndoigh, go dtí an lá inníu.

As Cumann Lúthchleas Gael basks in the glory of continued growth and success, it is crucial that, from time to time, we are reminded of who makes us what we are. Despite our importance in various walks of national life, without our players we would be nothing; they made us, and still make us, the great national institution we have become.

Seán Óg Ó Ceallacháin was himself a player of very considerable merit, proud to wear the jersey of both his club and his county (and, if folklore has any truth to it, of another county too), proud of his country and its people, and willing to make a difference to Irish life. While hurling was, and still is, his first love, he also played football, he refereed in both codes and he reported on all our Association's games and activities throughout his life. It is entirely appropriate that he should now remind us of those who gave our games their status, created our heroes and became the role models for subsequent generations.

Giants of Gaelic Football is a stimulating read. What makes it different is its balance between those who achieved national success and those who laboured long and hard in their counties' colours, without success—those deprived of the prospect of a winner's medal, by an accident of location. How many players, who could only dream of emulating Packie McGarty's skill and determination over a twenty-five year inter-county career, have won multiple All-Ireland medals (and good luck to them!) and take their place at football's top table, while Packie retired without the rewards he deserved?

How many provincial championships would Declan Browne have won, had he been born in Kerry or Meath, in Dublin or Tyrone, in Mayo or Armagh? How successful would Mick Carley, or Mick Tynan, or Jim Wall, or Peter McGinnity, or about a dozen others in this book, have been, had they been playing with a different county? And why should a 'dual' player like Martin Meally opt to play football in Kilkenny—the home of classic hurling?

Seán Óg writes about men who had a passion for our national 'big ball' game, who played, not for money or other rewards, but for the thrill of a high catch; or the satisfaction of seeing droplets cascading from a net shaking from a 'rasper', as an umpire raises the green flag; or the smack of a ball on the palms of outstretched hands as a kick is blocked by a diving defender; or any of the other skills which make Gaelic Football not just unique, but uniquely Irish. Without exception, these were and are great men; without exception, they deserve this tribute; and without exception, they provided, and some still provide, pleasure to supporters and inspiration to another generation of players. No tribute to such men can be overstated.

In this publication, almost fifty of our finest ever players are recalled and their lives and achievements are celebrated. It is an insightful and revealing work. Great credit is due to its author for his research, but even more for his interest and his enthusiasm, at a stage in his life when he could easily have retired. Had he not written this book, those of us who admire great Gaelic footballers would have lost out. Maith thú, a Sheáin, agus go maire tú go deo.

Iúil 2007

ACKNOWLEDGMENTS

Compiling this book would have been impossible without the kindness and co-operation of old friends and colleagues, most of whom I have listed in my sources. To all who helped in any way, I am extremely grateful. I am especially thankful to my old friend Owen McCann, who read the manuscript and gave freely of his advice and information.

I am very thankful to the staff of the National Library, Pearse Street Library and my local Raheny Library. My thanks to Fergal Tobin and his wonderful staff at Gill & Macmillan, who worked extremely hard to bring it to a successful conclusion.

Rath Dé oraibh go léir.

Seán Óg Ó Ceallacháin
July 2007

PREFACE

When Fergal Tobin of Gill & Macmillan asked me to write this book, I accepted with an appropriate degree of wariness, knowing the pitfalls that would arise from the outset. The number of players historically linked and deservedly accepted as models for a book of this nature run literally into thousands. My brief confined me to a mere fifty or so, and hence my dilemma. I knew immediately the inescapable twin prongs of error that would manifest themselves: the inclusion of too many star players too well known to the public; and the omission of too many who are still cherished as old favourites.

In my defence, I can only plead an enthusiasm for the game of Gaelic football and attempt to placate both sides of the divide.

Writing this book gave me an ideal opportunity to pay tribute to the greats of the game because of honours won on the field of endeavour, while also including players equally proficient in the game's skills but perhaps lacking the rewards that went with them. In that regard I would point to players of the calibre of Gerry O'Malley (Roscommon), Gerry O'Reilly (Wicklow), Mick Tynan (Limerick), Jim Wall (Waterford), Martin Meally (Kilkenny), Mick Carley (Westmeath), Kevin O'Brien (Wicklow), P. J. O'Dea (Clare) and Andy McCallin (Antrim). Naturally, I haven't neglected the all-time greats, those household names who filled reams of newspaper reports and were the subjects of radio and television coverage describing their heroics on the field of play.

So, gentle reader, I have made my choice, knowing that not everybody will find instant favour with the final selection, but *c'est la vie.* I did, however, include the thirty-two counties on this occasion.

KEVIN ARMSTRONG

D own through the years football and hurling have provided
many distinctive players from counties that have not enjoyed
successes at All-Ireland senior title level. Players who have
brightened the scene with their talent have stood tall with the giants
from those counties regularly in the national titles rankings and earned
their places among the all-time greats.

Such a master craftsman from Antrim was Kevin Armstrong. He
paraded his skills in an exciting manner with the best of his era not only
in football but also in hurling. He was an accomplished forward, well
tutored in the skills of both games, a player with the ability to set the
scene alight with his artistry.

Armstrong played many fine games in football at inter-county and
inter-provincial level during a twenty-year senior career that began in
1937. He also found time to add to his exploits on the football field by
producing top-class fare in hurling—again with both county and
province—so much so that he rightly commands a place in the ranks
of the greatest dual players of all time.

He gave great service to Antrim in both codes and also served Ulster
really well in hurling and football in the Railway Cup (now the M. D.
Donnelly inter-provincial championships). Armstrong helped to make
history not once, but twice in football in the Railway Cup. Ulster have
been such a power in the football series in modern times that it is hard
to appreciate that they were striving for a first title in 1942 when they
lined out in the decider against Munster fifteen years after the first final.

The North had a powerful side that year. Team captain John Joe
O'Reilly, who was to go on and lead Cavan to their 1947 and 48 All-
Ireland title wins, Alf Murray, a future president of the GAA, and
Columba McDwyer (Donegal) were among Armstrong's team mates.

The team proved equal to the task by forging a five-point win—the last province to join the title winners rankings.

Armstrong helped Ulster to retain the title in 1943 and four years later entered the record books again when he became the first to bring the trophy across the border after leading the North to victory over Leinster.

Kevin's football skills and consistently high standard of play earned him the reputation as one of the brightest inter-provincials of the 1940s and early 50s. He played in six finals between 1941 and 1950, winning three medals and contributed in rich measure to help provide the foundations on which Ulster have built their now proud record in the series.

He also shone with the county team. A peak was reached in the 1946 final when Antrim, powered by Armstrong and other stars of the time including Paddy O'Hara, Seán Gallagher and Harry O'Neill, threw down the gauntlet in the final to the then title specialists Cavan, who were bidding for an eighth title in succession.

The challengers, who gave a sparkling display of solo runs and clever forward play, not only won more convincingly than the 2-8 to 1-7 score-line suggests, but ended a long famine by regaining the title after thirty-three years. That was a fast, fit and well-drilled Antrim side which made a fancied Kerry work very hard for a three-point win in the All-Ireland semi-final.

Armstrong helped Antrim regain the Ulster title in 1951 when they again mastered the title specialists from Breffni, finishing ahead by 1-7 to 2-3. The Ulster champions put up a very spirited performance in the All-Ireland semi-final against Meath, but again had to settle for second best. The Royals won by two points.

Although an All-Ireland senior final outing did not come his way in football, Armstrong did reach a Liam McCarthy Cup summit. Along the way to that 1943 All-Ireland senior final appearance, the Glens men played their part in adding a bright chapter to the events that spotlight the glorious uncertainty of sport. That year Antrim returned to the All-Ireland senior championship after a lengthy absence and celebrated with not one, but two against-the-odds wins. The second really stands out in a big way.

As World War II dragged its weary way in 1943, Kilkenny visited Corrigan Park, Belfast, as the firm favourites for an All-Ireland senior semi-final against the northern standard-bearers. Antrim had sounded a warning to the Noresiders on their return to All-Ireland fare a few weeks earlier. They entertained Galway at Corrigan Park in an All-Ireland quarter-final, which they won in a remarkable game that produced thirteen goals and only two points, 7-0 to 6-2.

Despite that success, few at the time expected Kilkenny to have anything other than a comfortable semi-final win. But Antrim again rose to the challenge to provide one of the greatest shocks in the history of the championship. In a low-scoring game, they displayed no inferiority complex as they hurled with drive and determination to forge a 3-3 to 1-6 win and so earn the county a first-ever All-Ireland senior hurling final appearance.

They were presented with a tremendous challenge as their opponents, Cork, were striving for a third title in a row and so were well schooled in their own match-winning style. The Rebels also had such potential match-winners in their side as the legendary Christy Ring, Jack Lynch (later to become taoiseach), Con Cottrell and Con Murphy, a future president of the GAA.

The holders played with a breeze in the first half and were a point ahead after only a minute. Soon after, midfielder Noel Campbell put Antrim on level terms amid great excitement. But Cork took control after that and ran out decisive winners by 5-16 to 0-4 before an attendance of 48,843. It is an indication of the interest created by Antrim's march to the final that, at a time when travel was difficult, the game still attracted the greatest attendance to a decider than at any other in Cork's progress to a record four titles in a row from 1941 to 1944.

The northerners came up against a Rebel county team at peak form and had to pay the penalty. Nevertheless, they did well to get so far and ensured their place in the record books with that unique outing in hurling's top match of the year. Antrim had some outstanding hurlers in all departments, notably Kevin Armstrong at right full forward, Sammy Mulholland, also in attack, centre half-back and captain Jimmy Walsh, and Jackie Bateson and Campbell in the middle of the park.

In hurling, as in football, the skilled dual player from Belfast also represented his county at inter-provincial level. Although the Railway Cup competition had been launched in November 1926, Ulster did not make their mark in the series until 1944 when they met Munster in a semi-final at Croke Park. Armstrong was a member of that Ulster side, but it was far from an auspicious beginning as Munster, with many of their great names of that era, had a handsome twenty-point win.

Undaunted, Ulster were back again a year later. They entertained Leinster at Belfast, and in a game of few scores they surprised most by coming out on top by 3-1 to 2-3. Hopes were high as the northerners journeyed to Croke Park to meet the defending champions, Munster, despite the obvious strength of the opposition, which included Cork's Christy Ring, the greatest inter-provincial of all time, Tommy Doyle (Tipperary), Jackie Power (Limerick) and Jim Ware (Waterford). With such a wealth of experienced talent in their side, it is hardly surprising that Munster had a comfortable twenty-point win. Armstrong was at centre half-forward in what was to prove his last appearance in an inter-provincial hurling final. A member of the O'Connell club in Belfast, Kevin won many Ulster senior hurling medals.

All-Ireland medals are by no means the only guideline to greatness in the national games. Mastery in the arts of a particular game and above all consistency in producing top-class fare over a lengthy period are vital factors in the make-up of a player worthy of a place among the greats. Kevin Armstrong measured up superbly to that benchmark, not only in football but in hurling too, despite the fact that Antrim found major successes elusive jackpots in the latter game. He is well entitled to rank as one of the top dual players of all time.

BRENDAN BARDEN

As in most sports many Gaelic games successes at national level are eventually achieved with one extraordinary moment of individual brilliance by an especially gifted exponent of the particular code or by an inspired decision of team management, or both. Séamus Darby's wonderful winning goal for Offaly in the final minutes of the 1982 All-Ireland final against Kerry was a pertinent cameo of his own determined single-mindedness as well as being a tribute to his manager Eugene McGee's foresight to introduce Darby as an impact substitution in the concluding stages of that historic encounter.

The superb contribution of Maurice Fitzgerald and his sublime scoring skills, both in the drawn game and subsequently against Armagh in the 2000 All-Ireland senior football semi-final, were pivotal to the Kingdom's success.

Conor Gormley's famous hand block on Stephen McDonnell's kick as the Armagh man sped goalwards was the final decisive act as Tyrone secured a momentous first senior triumph in the 2003 All-Ireland football final.

Similarly, in the 2006 All-Ireland senior campaign, the switching of Kieran Donaghy to the full forward berth against Longford in the qualifiers was the defining catalyst for Kerry's change of tactics. This ultimately resulted in Donaghy propelling Kerry to successive victories over Armagh, Cork and Mayo on their way to their thirty-fourth All-Ireland senior title.

It could be contended that an equally significant though less well-documented contribution was accomplished by Longford's magnificent defender Brendan Barden in the 1966 National 'Home' League final against Galway. To put this into its proper context one must recall the superb quality of that Galway team which won three successive All-Ireland senior titles between 1964 and 1966.

In the midst of that amazing sequence, the previously unheralded Longford covered themselves in glory as they controlled the match against their more celebrated opponents. Though the first half was of a mediocre standard, Longford showed tremendous speed and determination as they outmanoeuvred and outplayed the westerners to lead at half-time, 0-7 to 0-5. However, the second period produced exquisite football as Galway rose to the challenge in the style of true champions. Halfway through the second half, Galway had fought back to level the contest at 0-8 each. Twelve minutes from the end of this enthralling and heart-throbbing clash came the moment, and the man, to thwart Galway's increased momentum and ensure a surprising but deserved victory for the midlanders.

Speedy Galway forward Séamus Leyden gained possession seventy yards out from the Longford goal. Not once, not twice, but four times did Longford's majestic right half-back Brendan Barden legally prevent the Galwegian from stepping inside him. He continually kept goal side of him, shadowing and tracking his every move as he herded Leyden towards the sideline. Showing the utmost discipline, the Clonguish club man persevered diligently in his task for all of sixty yards, eventually forcing the Galway player to foul the ball. A quick free upfield resulted in Longford corner forward Seán Donnelly being fouled in the danger area. Ace free-taker Bobby Burns, who scored eight of Longford's final tally of nine points, tipped the ball over the bar for the last score of the game and, more importantly, a one-point victory for Longford to earn them their first 'Home' League title in this, their greatest hour.

The National League final proper was a two-legged contest with New York. In the first leg Longford defeated the American side by five points before 8,000 spectators who basked in glorious weather in Longford's Pearse Park on Sunday, 2 October. In the second leg, a week later in Croke Park, though the midlanders lost by a point, they were proclaimed National League champions for the first time on an aggregate score of 1-18 to 0-17. It was the popular opinion of most neutrals that Longford thoroughly deserved to win and that they had earned themselves an eternal place of affection in the annals of Longford history. It must be said that had New York played to their strength and not resorted to strong-arm tactics, the outcome would have been much closer.

The Herculean displays by midfielder Jimmy Flynn, the fantastic input of central defenders Larry Gillen at full back and John Donlon at centre back, and the keen positional sense of talented corner back Séamus Flynn will be long remembered. One must not forget the tiger-ish defending of the pacey Pat Barden (Brendan's younger brother) at left half-back and the solid display of Brendan Gilmore at corner back. The subtle, silken skills of wing forward Jackie Devine embellished the telling contribution of fellow forwards Seán Donnelly, Mick Hopkins, Seán Murray, Jimmy Hannify and expert free-taker Bobby Burns. However, it was the sheer class and the ball-playing skills of captain Brendan Barden that provided the decisive platform for eventual victory.

Two years after their National League triumph in 1968, Longford surprised Dublin in the Leinster championship by three points. In the Leinster semi-final, Meath surrendered their Leinster and All-Ireland titles to a much superior Longford by 0-12 to 0-7.

Mick Hopkins, captain Vincent Daly, Jimmy Hannify and Jackie Devine shone in the Longford forward division. Tom Mulvihill (brother of GAA ard stiurthoir Liam) and Jimmy Flynn controlled the midfield sector. Goalkeeper John Heneghan brought off several outstanding saves, but again it was the consummate brilliance of Brendan Barden, ably assist-ed by his brother Pat, Séamus Flynn and John Donlon, which assured a Leinster final appearance against Laois. From the outset Longford totally dominated the final and in the end they scored a comprehensive 3-9 to 1-4 victory to secure that elusive Leinster senior football title for the first time.

All the starting fifteen plus the substitutes Pat Burke and Mickey Reilly were really magnificent in another red-letter day in the history of Longford football. Team manager Fr Philip McGee, trainer Mick Higgins (a thrice All-Ireland senior medallist with Cavan) and selectors Jimmy Flynn, Mel McCormack, Mickey Kelly, Patsy Reilly and Bertie Allen (a legendary mentor with Barden's Clonguish club) will always be fondly remembered for their Trojan efforts in bringing Longford to their first All-Ireland football semi-final.

Longford faced the might of Kerry, the acknowledged masters of the art of Gaelic football, in the semi-final. The first half belonged to the Munster men as they cruised to an interval lead of 2-7 to 0-6. Five minutes into the second half, Kerry had added a further two points to assume an apparently unassailable lead of nine points. Injury-hit

Longford—their most notable absentee was the masterly Jimmy Flynn—appeared to be completely out of their depth. Then, inexplicably and suddenly, one of the greatest come-backs in the history of Gaelic football occurred, as a rejuvenated Longford side began to play superbly. Outstanding in the air, first to every ball and showing tremendous skill, Longford simply owned the ball.

During this half all the Longford players, in addition to substitutes Micky Burns and Brendan Gilmore, played fabulous football. Tom Mulvihill, Mick Hopkins (another Clonguish man) and Jackie Devine were really awesome as they tormented the Kingdom's defence. It was during this purple patch that Brendan Barden, arguably, played the greatest football of his distinguished career. Once the ball entered Longford's defensive zone, inevitably it was the immaculate fielding or clever anticipation of Barden which impeded any Kerry advance. Most Longfordians and indeed many neutrals will rank Barden's second half display as one of the truly great individual performances ever witnessed in Croke Park.

In the game itself, after Jackie Devine had dispatched a penalty to the Kerry net, there were only eight minutes left. More significantly from a Longford perspective was the now incredible scoreline of Longford 2-10, Kerry 2-9. However, Longford's dream of a first All-Ireland senior appearance was short-lived as their defence started to wilt under incessant pressure, and Kerry ran out the eventual winners, 2-13 to 2-11. The dream had ended but Longford supporters, up to the present day, still salute and celebrate those fantastic Gaelic football ambassadors of the 1966–1968 golden era. As a team, that 1968 championship side were probably at the zenith of their considerable powers. Indeed, many of them turned in scintillating individual performances for several more years. Brendan Barden's display in the Leinster championship replay against Offaly in 1970 was probably his last great performance in a Longford jersey.

In 1938 Brendan Barden was born in the parish of Clonguish that encompasses the village of Newtownforbes, just three miles west of Longford town. He received his early education at Melview Primary School before becoming a terrific juvenile footballer with Clonguish. He made his debut in an adult final in 1957 when his home club was defeated in the county junior championship final by Emmet Óg from Killoe. Two years earlier his impressive club performances had caught the eye of the county minor selectors and he was chosen on the minor team in 1955 and 56—against Louth on both occasions—in the Leinster championship. The press reports of the 1956 match were unanimous: though Longford lost, they had in midfielder Brendan Barden the outstanding player on the field.

In 1958 Brendan joined the Air Corps in Dublin and played with them for the next few years, winning two Dublin senior league titles and reaching two county finals, only to be beaten on both occasions by a star-studded St Vincent's fifteen. Subsequently, he returned to his native Clonguish with whom he won championship medals in 1963, 64, 65, 68, 69, 72 and 73—the first six at centre back and the last one at left corner forward. Those were the halcyon days of the Clonguish club and their many great games with north Longford club Granard St Mary's are deeply ingrained in Longford folklore. Fellow club men Mick Hopkins, Séamus Flynn, Jimmy Flynn and Pat Burke were also fellow county colleagues with the Bardens during that splendid run of inter-county successes. Mick Hopkins and the Bardens were double cousins, and Pat Burke was also a first cousin of Mick Hopkins and the Bardens.

Brendan still has fond memories of great battles against some of the country's best forwards. 'My favourite individual memory is of a league game against Leitrim in Mohill in the early 1960s. I was marking the great Packie McGarty and I kept him scoreless in the first half. Packie, Mickey Kearins of Sligo and Mickey Niblock of Derry were just three of the best opponents I marked during my career. Of course the overall highlights of my time was captaining Longford to success in the league in 1966 and winning Leinster in 1968. On a personal level two of my brothers, Pat and Eamonn, once formed the entire Longford half-back line along with myself in Croke Park. That was a very happy family occasion.'

The Bardens of 2007 are carrying on a proud tradition instigated by one of Longford's greatest footballers when he raised aloft the National Football League trophy in Croke Park on Sunday, 9 October 1966. Brendan Barden, definitely and justifiably, will always be affectionately remembered, not alone in his native Longford but also throughout the length and breadth of Ireland, as a really great footballer.

3 ~

| DECLAN BROWNE

U ndoubtedly, if a transfer market existed for GAA players, the celebrated Tipperary footballer Declan Browne would have more than a few callers to his door. The Premier county may be regarded as one of the minnows of the code, but all concerned with the game in Tipperary are proud to have in their ranks Declan Browne—a football icon. The story of the Tipperary genius was pretty well summed up by *Tipperary Star* sportswriter John Guiton: 'If Browne was a soccer star he would be trying to decide which Ferrari to drive to the supermarket!' For while the Moyle Rovers club man, a native of Clerihan in south Tipperary, has paraded his silken skills in inter-county championship football, he has also enjoyed the distinction of starring in International Rules, helping Ireland to a memorable victory over Australia in November 2004.

Mention the illustrious Declan in any GAA company, and the conversation immediately centres on his loyalty to his native county. It will never be forgotten that he gave unwavering commitment to the blue and gold down through the years at a time when many players of his age and talent would have made themselves available to some of the top counties in the game. It is a measure of his love for his native county that he has soldiered through thick and thin for the cause. Even though he has had his share of injuries, he has rarely missed a league or championship encounter, and continues to be a talismanic figure for his club, Moyle Rovers.

Browne's talents shone from an early age. After representing the county at under-age, he soon made his mark in the senior ranks. As many a right full back can testify, Browne has magical skills. Razor sharp in thought and action, he is renowned for his quick burst of speed and sleight of foot. By no means the tallest of forwards, he has still managed to create nightmares for some of the best-known defensive giants in the game. His shooting is rarely less than impeccable and he can execute points from his right or left boot.

Over his career at inter-county level he has chalked up huge personal tallies, in many cases taking scores from the most impossible of angles. His accuracy from play, frees and penalties has ranked him among the most prolific forwards of all time.

Declan Browne has mass appeal among GAA folk. In essence, he is the complete player, with a most unassuming, self-effacing manner. Colleagues and opponents alike are loud in their praise of one of the most likeable personalities in the game. Perhaps one of the most fitting examples of the high esteem in which Declan is held was minutes after the Tommy Murphy Cup final in 2005.

Tipperary had just beaten Wexford and Browne and his colleagues were beside themselves with the joy of getting their hands on silverware in Croke Park. As Declan was making his way to the dressing room, the Wexford maestro Mattie Forde ran up, gave Declan a congratulatory hug, and with a smile on his face dropped his Wexford jersey into the cup Browne was carrying. Despite his disappointment in defeat, it was a lovely gesture from Forde to a man he revered on the football pitch. Forde, like his colleagues, appreciated that Browne had eventually climbed the steps of the Croke Park podium on a day his dream of winning a national title came through. They were equally delighted that the Tipperary star, a double All Star, was recognised for his brilliance in his selection on Ireland's International Rules team in 2004. Declan, of course, was following in the footsteps of two other celebrated Tipperary footballers, Brian Burke and Declan's club mate Derry Foley.

He was overjoyed when he received the news that he had been chosen on the panel—injury had dealt him a bad blow in 2003 and scuppered his chances of making the games. In an interview in the *Tipperary Star*, Declan spoke of his pleasure at participating in the 2004 series which Ireland won by 132 points to 82. He said: 'It was a great feeling being out on Croke Park winning an international Test. The atmosphere was unbelievable, and it was amazing how well we all gelled together as a team. I was just delighted to get a chance, and it is one of those memories that will stay with me for ever.'

A crowd of 60,515 attended the second Test and enjoyed a real carnival atmosphere. Declan described living like a professional player as being most interesting: 'It was like nothing we are used to at home, and everything goes out the window when you arrive to train. We have made some great friends, and it is wonderful to have the chance to play with some of the top footballers in the country.'

Whether in the green, white and gold jersey of Ireland or the blue and gold of his native county, Declan Browne has acquitted himself with grace and distinction. The Test manager at the time, Pete McGrath of Down fame, readily concurred: 'Declan was an excellent choice and was one of the key figures in the vital matches. No task was too great for him and his contribution from a marksmanship viewpoint was a major factor in our great victory in the series.'

The Moyle Rovers representative has never forgotten his roots. He has never failed to turn out for his club, whether in championship or mere challenge fare, and, not surprisingly, he was a key figure in the club's accumulation of county football titles. What is generally forgotten, of course, is that he was also a talented hurler and played in a number of grades for Tipperary. Not surprisingly, he was an eagle-eyed forward in that code too.

Much sought after for medal presentations and club functions throughout County Tipperary and further afield, Declan is a big hit with budding footballers. His down to earth, humble approach has earned him a legion of friends and admirers in the GAA. In short, Declan Browne is a football legend and a role model in modern times.

4

WILLIE BRYAN

The great Kerry midfielder Mick O'Connell once said of Willie Bryan: 'A great midfield player. He had a head for the game with an excellent sense of position. I would like to have had him as my partner in the middle of the field.' Willie Bryan was 14 years of age when his father brought him to Croke Park to watch Kerry play Dublin in the 1962 All-Ireland football semi-final. The minor curtain-raiser was between Kerry and Offaly which the Munster lads won. It was Willie's first-ever visit to Croke Park and after watching Kerry in action against Dublin in the senior match, the young Bryan was fired with the ambition that he would play some day on the famous sod. Little did he know then that he would fulfil that dream when he opposed the famous Mick O'Connell in the 1969 All-Ireland final.

Willie Bryan was born in the neighbouring county of Laois, being a native of Portlaoise. However, at a very tender age Willie and the family moved to Walsh Island after his father took up employment with Bord na Mona. The first indications of his football potential became evident as a pupil at Walsh Island National School and subsequently at Portarlington Vocational School. On leaving school he obtained an apprenticeship with Bord na Mona as a fitter, and his star-studded career with Walsh Island and Offaly blossomed. He was blessed with a wide repertoire of skills that were backed by an unflinching commitment of whole-hearted endeavour. He was a spectacular high fielder, whilst his ability to read a game, his astute distribution and an almost uncanny positional sense also ranked among his outstanding attributes.

They were never seen to better advantage than in the 1971 All-Ireland senior football final in which Offaly overcame Galway, and again the following year when he turned in a regal performance in helping Offaly to retain the Sam Maguire at the expense of Kerry. Although midfield was his favourite and arguably his best position, such was his versatility that at one time or another he filled all six forward berths for both club and county with almost equal distinction.

Walsh Island, although a small rural club with sparse playing resources, boasts a proud record since it was founded in 1930 and entered a team in the local junior championship. Within two years success came the way of the wearers of the green and white hoops, when they defeated Doon by eight points in the junior championship final. The club took promotion in their stride by winning the premier title at their first attempt, defeating Tullamore in the last final played in the old Ballyduff Park. The title was retained the following year, again at the expense of Tullamore, in the first final played at O'Connor Park.

All Walsh Island's early senior county championship victories came in pairs—1933 and 34, 37 and 38, and 42 and 43. Sharing in all these successes over a span of eleven years was the late and great Bill Mulhall, who was the first Offaly man to play for Leinster in a Railway Cup final. Inevitably, the club's first golden era was followed by a prolonged lean spell. The break-up of the team that brought such glory through the late 1930s and early 40s, coupled with emigration, meant that the club's catchment area encompassed just 128 houses, leaving insufficient resources to maintain senior status on their own. However, in 1970 the Island, led by Willie Bryan, were back in a senior final, this time as part of a parish alliance together with Clonbullogue and Bracknagh under the banner of Eire Og. They lost that final to Gracefield by 1-8 to 0-9 and the new champions nominated John Smith as the Offaly captain for the following year.

Willie Bryan's ambition was achieved when he lined out in his first All-Ireland senior final against Kerry in 1969 and was pitted against the formidable and legendary Mick O'Connell at centrefield. Willie admitted that he was very nervous at the start, not helped by the long delay caused by Kerry, who were slow to take the field. For a week preceding the final speculation had been intense, wondering if O'Connell would be there when Kerry appeared from under the Cusack Stand. Everyone in Croke Park, and the thousands looking in on television, waited. When at last Kerry ran out on to the pitch, the figure of Mick O'Connell emerged to a tumultuous roar from the stands.

Offaly lost that day to a Kerry team that did just enough to capture the title. The great Offaly full back Paddy McCormack felt that it was by no means a great Kerry victory. He said: 'We were led by only three points at half-time and we had the benefit of the strong breeze in the second half and yet we couldn't do it.' Willie Bryan's wonderful display against Mick O'Connell wasn't mentioned by the writers, who saw a virtual unknown outplay the Kerry maestro for long periods.

Offaly lost their Leinster title in 1970 to Meath, but they were back with a vengeance in 1971 and regained the provincial crown at the expense of a good Kildare team. In the All-Ireland semi-final they put paid to Cork hopes on a 1-16 to 1-11 scoreline. Willie Bryan was nominated as captain for the 1971 All-Ireland final against Galway as John Smith was ruled out because of injury. This was a major test for the Walsh Island star. The pressure of the team captaincy was difficult enough, but now the responsibility of trying to win a first ever All-Ireland title for his county only added to his job.

Midfield berths are normally filled by players exceeding the six foot mark where height certainly pays dividends in the battle for control of the centrefield area. Reputations have been built on the ability to out-field opponents, which inevitably can lead to ultimate success. There are times, however, when an exception can defy the rule and in that context the name of Willie Bryan springs readily to mind. Mick O'Connell of Kerry had a great respect for Bryan and the Offaly man's ability to measure up to requirements on the high fielding factor. In the 1971 All-Ireland final against Galway the Offaly centrefield pairing was Willie and Kieran Claffey. They faced Galway's Liam Sammon and Billy Joyce. As events transpired the respective captains, Sammon and Bryan, found themselves marking each other. Both were exceptional sporting players and the duels between them added immeasurably to the exchanges.

The Offaly full back line of Mick Ryan, Paddy McCormack and Mick O'Rourke was giving very little away. The opening quarter started in frenetic fashion and referee Paul Kelly had his hands full. The weather had taken a turn for the worst, which didn't help matters. But the tensions eased as the game continued and the standard improved all round. Séamus Leydon had Galway's two goals, but the reliable Matt Connors, a gifted free-taker, scored Offaly's crucial winning goal on a 1-14 to 2-8 scoreline. Winning an All-Ireland senior title is a big event in a county's history. Winning a title of such magnitude for the first time can put the achievement beyond belief. Willie Bryan never viewed the role of captain as being one of great importance, but merely as someone who tossed for ends. It was only years afterwards that he appreciated the importance of the role.

He certainly hadn't time to think about it very much with the bedlam that followed when the Croke Park arena was engulfed with Offaly supporters when the final whistle sounded on 26 September 1971. Offaly had taken its place in GAA history as being an All-Ireland senior football title-winner—and under the captaincy of Willie Bryan. The victory gave the Faithful county a terrific lift and the homecoming on that Monday night brought out the crowds in their thousands. But there was much more to come for Willie Bryan and the footballers of Offaly. At that time you measured your greatness by the high standards set by Kerry. Your education wasn't complete without first achieving the coveted accolade by defeating the Kerry trend-setters. And 1972 was to prove the year of fulfilment in more ways than one for the Offaly footballers.

Offaly retained their Leinster senior football championship title in 1972. They beat Cork in the All-Ireland semi-final 1-18 to 2-8. Tony McTague was captain. Willie Bryan was still in his favourite position at midfield, partnered by Nicholas Claffey. Kerry were their opponents in the final. Offaly had fond memories of their last meeting with Kerry. That was in a National League game in Tullamore late in November 1971. Offaly won the game decisively. In the eyes of the Offaly men that was a mini All-Ireland and was to prove a major milestone on the road to the second All-Ireland success in 1972.

It has to be said that Offaly were by far the fitter team that November day against Kerry, so they were not carried away by that win. Willie Bryan put it down as a psychological result nevertheless. 'We now realised that where Kerry before seemed to be able to put the Indian sign on Offaly teams, this one was in an entirely different category.'

Offaly and Kerry finished level, 1-13 each, in their first meeting on 24 September 1972 before 72,032. The attendance for the replay was 66,136, which was a record for a drawn replay.

Mick O'Connell was told after the game that had he gone for the winning point himself in the closing stages of the drawn match, Kerry would have won it. O'Connell opted instead to pass the ball to a forward closer to the goal, but who was quickly dispossessed by the Offaly defenders. Offaly won the replay by 1-19 to 0-13, the heaviest defeat

Kerry ever suffered in an All-Ireland final. For Willie Bryan, the last fifteen minutes of the replay saw him at his brilliant best. He dominated the midfield sector to such an extent in this period that he was acclaimed afterwards as the match-winner by the *Irish Press*. 'Bryan the Brave' read the deep banner headline over Pádraig Puirseal's account, while the *Evening Herald* ran the headline, 'Offaly the Great'. Each headline told the story of an extraordinary achievement.

Willie Bryan expressed this view: 'We were not accepted as All-Ireland champions by many people after our victory over Galway in 1971. It was necessary for us to defeat the Kingdom to prove the point. The fact that we did it so comprehensively in the end could have left no doubt at all in anyone's mind about our entitlement to be styled true champions.' The fact that Kerry had an intimidating replay record at All-Ireland level (Kerry lost only one All-Ireland replay—against Galway in 1938) didn't unduly worry Offaly. Willie did express the view that if they had not been All-Ireland champions and had not beaten Galway, it could well have been a different matter.

All-Ireland triumphs during the barren years were restricted to two junior hurling victories in 1929 and 32, both of which were achieved against Cork. A further thirty-five years were to elapse before another All-Ireland title came Offaly's way, this time in football, when a brilliant minor side, captained by Ferbane's Seán Grogan, overcame Cork by 0-15 to 1-11, a game which brought Offaly a first national title in any grade of football.

This victory was to mark a turning point in Offaly's fortunes on the playing field, for the 1964 minors were to provide the nucleus of the All-Ireland winning senior teams of 1971 and 72. Foremost in this illustrious company was Willie Bryan from Walsh Island, a player who occupies a special place in the Faithful county's GAA annals.

Walsh Island enjoyed a second golden era and Willie Bryan made a contribution to the club's record-breaking six Offaly senior football championships in a row, 1978–1983, although by then his best days were behind him. Indeed he started only in the 1978 final, but in the following years he made a number of substitute appearances.

Bryan reaped a rich harvest of achievements during his playing career, for with the exception of a National League medal, he has won every honour that the game had to offer. In addition to the Offaly championships won with Walsh Island, he collected four Leinster SF

medals, the Leinster club championship in 1979 and 80, Carroll's All
Star awards in 1971 and 72, a Railway Cup medal at full forward for
Leinster in 1974, and a Texaco award in 1972.

More important than all these mementoes, however, is the reputation for sportsmanship and fair play that Willie Bryan carried into his
retirement. He was never known to intentionally foul an opponent
throughout his long and distinguished playing career.

5

PETER CANAVAN

During his playing career Peter Canavan became known as 'Peter the Great' — hardly surprising that, as Peter Canavan's silken skills, guile, deft distribution and finishing technique marked him out as a footballer to stand tall with the greats of the game in any era.

The gifted footballer, who gave tremendous service to Tyrone, was also in a special class as a team leader. He was a sportsman to his finger-tips.

More than O'Neill county supporters rejoiced when in 2003 he led the county to their long-hoped-for first All-Ireland senior football title and was at last assured of not joining the ranks of outstanding footballers who failed to win the game's premier medal.

It had been a long wait for the Errigal Ciaran club man, who had had many disappointments in a distinguished senior career stretching back to the early 1990s—disappointments like the All-Ireland senior final of 1995 (Tyrone's first in nine years), when a late equalising point against Dublin was disallowed, and the Dubs edged home by the minimum margin.

Canavan's contribution to that Tyrone effort was huge. Not only did he sparkle in general play, but he finished with an impressive 0-11, all but a point of his team's total.

Three years earlier he was in the Tyrone team that had hopes of a first National League title dashed in the final by neighbours Derry. But those set-backs were put firmly in the shade in the autumn of Canavan's career when he bowed out of the game with not one but two All-Ireland senior medals.

There are many keen followers of football and hurling who regularly attend schoolboy matches, not only because of the appeal of the games but because they can prove valuable pointers for the future prospects of young players. Those who made it to Croke Park on an April afternoon in 1989 for the Tyrone-Mayo All-Ireland Vocational Schools final— curtain-raiser to the league 'home' decider between Cork and Dublin— could not have failed to have been impressed by the budding skills of Peter Canavan.

Peter captained Tyrone in fine style with his clever play at centre half-forward, and also served early notice of his finishing powers by ending the game as the leading marksman on either team with five points. There was ample evidence in that final that the O'Neill county youth had the potential to go on and carve out a big reputation for himself in the premier inter-county grade.

There were other early pointers in that direction, such as the day that Canavan scored 2-3 in an All-Ireland under-21 final at Mullingar in 1990 but still finished on the losing side against Kerry. The following year Peter enhanced another memorable scoring achievement in a final by leading Tyrone to a first national triumph. That was when his leadership, clever football and, above all, his lethal finishing expertise made him a brilliant match-winner in the All-Ireland under-21 final. Finishing expertise? He scored a superb 2-5 as Tyrone took a handsome winning revenge over Kerry at Newbridge for that final defeat the previous year.

Those were heady times for Tyrone and Canavan in the under-21 grade. He made history again in 1992 when he led the county to a successful defence of the All-Ireland under-21 title to become the first to captain two national championship-winning sides in the grade.

Leadership, cultured football, finishing of the highest standard— what a cv for the maturing young man to carry forward from his form- ative years in inter-county football!

However, as the years rolled on during his senior career, it began to look as if the top prize would elude him. But the old saying that 'every- thing comes to him who waits' was to be eventually realised during a golden era in the early years of this century.

Before the pinnacle of senior football was achieved, Canavan earned another famous first as a captain with the scoring touch. He rifled over six points as he led his county to victory over Cavan at Clones in 2002 for their initial National League title. That was to prove the stepping-stone on the road to a truly wonderful period for the county. The National League title, with Canavan again in a familiar role as team-leader, was retained in a show-down with Laois at Croke Park in 2003. The promise of a first All-Ireland title loomed brightly again and Tyrone enhanced the prospect by qualifying for the final, but with a doubt hanging over their champion competitor. Canavan had badly damaged ankle ligaments in the semi-final win over Kerry five weeks earlier and for a time it was feared he would not be fit for the showpiece game. But after intense treatment he led the team from the throw-in against the defending champions Armagh in the first final featuring counties from the one province.

Not only that, he was instrumental in getting the side off to a very good start, a start that did much to lay the foundations for their success. During that period he scored five points from frees to help the challengers to an interval lead of 0-8 to 0-4.

Peter did not appear for the restart, but the Tyrone players showed their maturity by battling on with spirit, determination and plenty of ability. Canavan returned to the fray with about ten minutes remaining to give his side a real boost. He got through much valuable work as Tyrone defended their lead with skill and drive to eventually turn a dream into a reality with a 0-12 to 0-9 win.

Peter had good reason to feel well pleased not only with the breakthrough, but also with his contribution to the overall success story. He was by far his county's leading marksman for the campaign with a thundering 1-48 (51 points) from the eight-game run.

Canavan promised to continue playing with Tyrone the following year. Their All-Ireland crown was lost in a quarter-final with Mayo, but Canavan still soldiered on. At 34, an age when many a footballer had long traded his football boots for the role of spectator, Canavan was back again in 2005 in a central role in the biggest game of the Irish sporting year.

What a challenge that Sam Maguire Cup tie presented to Peter the Great and his colleagues with Kerry, holders at the time of the national crown, providing the opposition.

The teams provided a pulsating game, with Tyrone slow to get off the mark. They were 1-3 to 0-3 in arrears at the end of the first quarter, but the Ulster men got their game together steadily after that, and coming up to the interval, up stepped Canavan for a vital score.

Owen Mulligan won possession and cleverly sent on to Canavan, who expertly beat the Kerry goalkeeper with a ground shot. That gave

Tyrone a 1-8 to 1-5 lead at the interval and they went on for a famous 1-16 to 2-10 win, a fitting finale to the career of Peter the Great.

'Great' is a much over-used word in sporting matters. But it certainly applies to Peter Canavan, who has not only won every major honour in the game, but will be remembered especially for the high-quality football and sportsmanship with which he brightened the scene for so long.

| MICK CARLEY

Even now, some three decades after he brought his footballing career to a close, gaels far and wide still talk about Mick Carley. One of the greatest players of his generation, the Tyrrellspass colossus was a sportsman of exceptional talent whose place in Westmeath GAA history is an honoured one. Mick's career spanned almost a quarter of a century, during which time he enjoyed remarkable success at club level. While success wasn't as forthcoming at inter-county level, he was a regular in the early 1960s at midfield for Leinster, with whom he garnered his most prized possession, two Railway Cup medals, in 1961 and 62.

On both occasions Mick played at centrefield, and in 1962 he partnered the great Des Foley on a day the legendary Dub was uniquely a member of the winning teams in both codes. Although football was part and parcel of everyday life for Mick during his childhood years, he claims that Michael O'Hehir was his earliest influence. 'I remember going to my uncle Ned's house every Sunday to listen to Michael O'Hehir on the wireless. I hadn't been all that interested in football before then, but Michael's commentaries soon changed all that. I loved the excitement of it all and dreamt of playing in Croke Park someday myself,' Mick reflected. After completing his primary education at Tyrrellspass National School, he attended St Mary's CBS, Mullingar, where his immense footballing talent came to be noticed.

As a first year, he used to look up to a Leaving Cert student named Frank O'Leary. Frank, whose father was a locally stationed garda superintendent, was St Mary's star player at the time and went on later to enjoy a distinguished inter-county career with Westmeath, Kerry and Mayo. Mick didn't leave St Mary's empty-handed as he won a Leinster Colleges senior 'B' medal in 1955, at the expense of St Peter's College,

Wexford. Around this time he played on a successful under-17 championship winning team, Kilbeggan.

Mick's adult career began in earnest in 1956 when he broke on to the St Mary's intermediate championship team. Two years later, he won an intermediate championship memento with the Bridge before embarking on a new career with the mental hospital, later known as St Loman's, Mullingar. His career blossomed in the blue and white and he was an inspiring figure on their county senior championship winning teams of 1961 and 63. A few years later Mick joined the Downs, then an emerging force in senior football. He played with them for seven years, winning five senior county championships in 1968, 69, 70, 72 and 74.

In the two latter years he captained the teams. He also captained the Downs to the provincial club final in 1973, but the black and ambers lost heavily in the Leinster final to Dublin kingpins St Vincent's, Des Foley et al. In 1975 Mick returned to his native Tyrrellspass (a club hadn't existed in the village when he first started playing), where he played out the remaining years of his career. He was prominent with them both as a player and as a manager, guiding them to intermediate and Feis Cup successes. In more recent years he has been involved in under-age coaching at the club. At inter-county level Mick made his senior debut in 1957 and remained an integral member of the Westmeath set-up for almost twenty years. He had the distinction, shared by only two others (Mattie Coleman in the 1930s and Séamus Conroy in the 70s) of lining out for both Westmeath minors and senior teams on the same day in the Leinster championship on 11 May 1958. Louth (then the Sam Maguire Cup-holders) provided the opposition for Westmeath in the two games, and Mick played both matches at full back.

Mick's performances for his county in those early years were of such quality that he was selected to play for Leinster in the Railway Cups of 1961, 1962 and 1963. By then he had developed into a top-class midfielder, and it was in this position that he recorded his greatest achievements. In the finals of 1961 and 62, Leinster defeated Munster and Ulster respectively, but Ulster exacted revenge in the 1963 decider. Mick also had the honour of being selected on the Rest of Ireland team which took on the Combined Universities in 1961. In 1966 he was selected for a tour of the US on a team of talented players drawn from the strong footballing counties of that era. These games were known as the

Cardinal Cushing Charities Games. This writer was secretary of the Cushing Games committee which selected the players for that prestigious trip.

I can categorically state that Mick Carley was an instant hit with the gaels of New York, Boston and Hartford and fully justified his selection with eye-catching displays at midfield. In the mid-70s Mick's inter-county career drew to a close. Looking back on it now, his biggest regret is that Westmeath failed to make the breakthrough following their narrow defeat to a star-studded Kerry team in the National League semi-final of 1969. On that day in Croke Park, Mick and his club mate from the Downs, Dom Murtagh, firmly established themselves as two of the best midfielders in the game.

'That was definitely our best chance,' he said. 'If we had beaten Kerry that day, I'm sure we would have gone on to greater things. That Westmeath team included a good few members of the minor team which lost the All-Ireland final to Kerry in 1963, and it had great potential. Unfortunately, the potential was never fully realised and this, coupled with bad organisation, resulted in us making little or no headway.' Strangely, Mick blamed himself for losing the same game to the Kingdom. 'I wasn't fully fit for that match and to this day I'm convinced we would have won it had I been able to stay with Mick O'Connell in the second half. Dom had been doing very well against O'Connell in the first half and I had been faring OK against Dinjo Crowley. However, the management instructed me to mark O'Connell in the second half and I just wasn't able for him. If I hadn't been smothered with the flu for three weeks beforehand, I'm certain it would have been a different story.' That particular game against Kerry was a game Mick Carley preferred to forget.

What then was his finest hour in the maroon jersey? 'It would definitely have to be a National League game against Leitrim at Cusack Park,' he opines. 'I can't remember the exact year and a lot of people won't remember the game I'm referring to, but I couldn't put a foot wrong in it. Everything I attempted seemed to come off.'

Even though Mick's many years of loyal service to the maroon and white of Westmeath didn't yield tangible rewards—all he has to show for his efforts are two O'Byrne Cup medals from 1959 to 1964—he takes immense pride from having played with some highly talented individuals. 'It's a mystery to think that we didn't get anywhere with some great players, among them Georgie Keane and Brian Kavanagh (Rosemount), Paddy Cooney (St Finian's), Dessie and Tommy Dolan, Mickey Scanlan, Jimmy Nugent (all Athlone), Dom Murtagh and Christy Corroon (the Downes), Pat Buckley (Maryland), and Jim Fallon and Pat Bradley (St Mary's).'

As for the best players Mick has played against, he singles out Paddy Doherty of Down for special praise. 'Paddy Doherty was the best player I've ever seen or played against,' he remarks. 'He was a brilliant half-forward who had everything a footballer could wish for. Another player from the great Down team of the 1960s I had great admiration for was Jim McCartan. He wasn't far behind Doherty in terms of football ability.'

Nowadays, Mick considers himself just an ordinary football supporter. He takes a keen interest in the affairs of Tyrrellspass, with whom his son Michael won a senior championship medal in 1999, when the navy and blue won the Flanagan Cup for the first (and to date the only) occasion. He also keeps a close eye on how Westmeath are progressing but wouldn't consider himself an avid follower. The county has come on by leaps and bounds since Mick's playing days ended.

Michael 'Spike' Fagan was selected to represent Ireland in the Compromise/International Rules series against Australia in the 1980s. The county itself won a minor All-Ireland in 1995, an under-21 crown four years later, and ultimately a Leinster senior title came to the Lake county in 2004. These teams produced a new generation of heroes for success-starved Westmeath fans, including the county's first All Star, midfielder Rory O'Connell, who was honoured in 2001 when Westmeath reached the All-Ireland sFc quarter-final (and could have easily gone further), while Des Dolan (a son of Dessie from Mick's era) and John Keane (similarly, a nephew of Georgie) got their All Star statuettes when the Delaney Cup was finally won in 2004.

However, few if any Westmeath gaels aged 40 or more would dispute that Mick Carley merits the title of 'Westmeath's greatest footballer', and he was selected on the Team of the Millennium in 2000. He was undoubtedly the first name pencilled on to that particular team sheet, as he had been during his playing days decades earlier.

7

ENDA COLLERAN

I will always remember Enda Colleran with deep affection as a great footballer, a brilliant games analyst and a very good friend. I had no hesitation in nominating him as my *Sunday Game* football analyst during my stint presenting the popular TV sports programme in the early 1980s. I was particularly impressed with Enda because of his football exploits, twice captain of the famous Galway football team which won the famous All-Ireland three-in-a-row in the mid-60s. He had many fine qualities and I enjoyed his company greatly. He was always a very modest individual and his clear-headed analytic summing up of team performances during his TV appearances made him a highly esteemed figure.

He was born to be a great footballer. Football was in his blood and he sprang from a distinguished Colleran family tradition. His father and uncle were fine footballers and his three brothers, Gerry, Gabriel and Séamus, had worn the maroon jersey in some grade or other. Enda made an instant impact during his schooldays in St Jarlath's College, Tuam, winning a Hogan Cup medal in 1960. Significantly, included in that great team were a number of players who were destined, like Enda, to be stars of the future. They were Johnny Geraghty, Pat Donnellan and Séamus Leydon. When Galway won the All-Ireland minor football title in 1960, beating Cork 4-9 to 1-5, the team was captained by Seán Cleary who, with Christy Tyrrell and Noel Tierney, were to aspire to the great three-in-a-row power block of the mid-60s, undoubtedly created by the foundation already laid by the All-Ireland and Hogan Cup successes in 1960.

Enda Colleran's defensive career was being fashioned very positively and his first baptism came in 1961 when he was chosen on the senior team to play Roscommon in a National League game in Tuam. He filled

the left corner back spot and emerged as a defender of note. The man
of the match was Mattie McDonagh, who was flanked by Cyril Dunne
and Pateen Donnellan. Enda was enjoying his football and began to
take his training very seriously. He realised that fitness was very much
a part of the football armoury when opposed by fleet-footed forwards.
Indeed, he spent much of his playing days doing extra bouts of training in order to maintain the high standards he set himself.

In 1962 Galway faced old rivals Roscommon in the Connacht final, a
game which was to have an extraordinary sequel. Galway dominated
the first half with their forwards, Mattie McDonagh, Brian Geraghty,
Cyril Dunne and John Keenan very much to the fore on the scoring
sheet. Fifteen minutes into the second half, Galway led 2-7 to 1-4 and
looked out and out winners. Then fate stepped in when the crossbar
was broken. The culprit was Roscommon goalkeeper Aidan Brady, who
jumped up and caught the bar as a Galway point sailed over. It took
local officials a full ten minutes before they could replace it.

The stoppage brought a complete transformation in the game's
outcome. Whether it was the tongue-lashing the Roscommon players
suffered during the delay or perhaps Galway still felt they could pick up
the action where they left off, remained the big question. But it was
Roscommon who responded the quickest to the challenge. They took
over complete control and went on to win a game they had looked liked
losing, 3-7 to 2-9.

Galway and Enda really came of age in 1963 with victories over Mayo
and Leitrim to capture the Connacht title. Munster champions Kerry
were raging favourites to go all the way against Galway in the 1963 All-
Ireland semi-final, but the Kingdom came up against the well-drilled
and superbly fit Connacht champions and went down in a close battle,
1-7 to 0-8. Enda Colleran, Noel Tierney and Seán Meade were rock-like
in the Galway full back line and conceded very little, while Pat
Donnellan, Séamus Leyden and Mick Garrett were the other quality
players who were most prominent.

The All-Ireland final against Dublin produced a terrific game in
which Dublin committed grand larceny by snatching the title with a
last-minute goal. Galway were favourites going into the game and were
living up to their pre-match rating, leading by two points with minutes
remaining, when disaster struck. Dublin launched a final all-out effort.
The ball reached the Galway end line. Dublin's Simon Behan chased it,

rounded his marker and passed to the in-running Gerry Davey, who punched it home for a shock Dublin victory.

Enda had his heart set on winning a first-ever senior All-Ireland medal, and to lose it by that last-minute score was heart-breaking. He made a very pertinent point about losing teams later when he was quoted as saying: 'There's no place for losers when you are beaten in a major championship test. I'll remember the 1963 final. When referee Eamonn Moules [Wicklow] blew the final whistle, the Dublin supporters ran on to the pitch in high elation and rushed through the Galway players. For that reason, I believe that the losing team should also be brought to the rostrum and honoured in some way.' I thoroughly agreed with Enda and I believe the day is not far off when the GAA will reach a decision to do just as Enda suggested. I must say that Galway's problem in that 1963 final was a lack of forward finish. They failed to put scoring chances away, but that wasn't easy against a no-nonsense Dublin defence which included Leo Hickey, Lar Foley, Bill Casey and Mick Kissane. A lack of experience could have been another factor on a day when Galway played great football. All that was to change in the space of twelve months.

Galway's prospects of capturing an All-Ireland title looked bright starting off in 1964. They had a tough battle against a highly motivated Sligo team, but Mayo provided a weak test in the Connacht final. John Donnellan captained the Galway team that year as Dunmore had captured the county championship crown. He was an ideal leader, strong on the ball, tenacious in the tackle and renowned for his wise ball distribution. The big test came when the Tribesmen faced Meath in the All-Ireland semi-final. The match was a cracker. It can be safely said that the match made Galway into a force to be reckoned with. Meath had beaten Leinster title-holders Dublin very comprehensively in the provincial final and many fancied their chances.

Galway looked mighty in their win over Mayo, so two great contenders faced each other in the penultimate stage of the 1964 All-Ireland championship. The game lived up to all expectations. Enda Colleran viewed the game as a chance to win a first All-Ireland senior medal and was determined to do so. His performance at corner back was commanding. He nipped in and secured possession of breaking balls in the danger area, and cleared them to safety. The game was marked by brilliant scores from both sides. One Galway goal in particular was memorable. It started from the Galway defence. Noel Tierney fielded brilliantly, booted the ball upfield to Mick Reynolds out near the Hogan Stand. Reynolds punted ahead to Seán Cleary on the halfway line. Cleary soloed forward and kicked to Mattie McDonagh, who collected and burst his way past a couple of tackles towards the Meath square. Burly Dinny Donnelly of Meath came across and stopped him, but the Ballygar man managed to kick the ball to the roof of the net. It took just four kicks of the ball to rattle the Meath net. Meath turned up the heat in an exciting second half to get back on terms. A pointed 50 from Mick Reynolds restored Galway's lead, and Seán Cleary, cool as a cucumber, stole in and pointed to clinch victory for Galway.

Kerry were Galway's opponents in the All-Ireland final and they were very determined to make amends for their semi-final defeat by Galway the previous year. However, the Connacht men were unstoppable and ran out clear winners by 0-15 to 0-10.

Moylough had won the Galway county title in 1965 and Enda Colleran, on foot of a marvellous display for his club, was named the Galway team captain.

Sligo once again went very close to toppling Galway in the 1965 Connacht final, which Galway won 1-12 to 2-6. Ulster champions Down were Galway's opponents in the All-Ireland semi-final, played in atrocious weather conditions at Croke Park. In a low-scoring first half, Down led 0-4 to 0-3 and they produced the more solid football in the early stages of the second period. Enda, playing a captain's role at corner back, admitted feeling apprehensive when the player he was marking knocked over a few points at the start and was quoted as saying, 'I assessed the situation and changed my tactics. Down were storming our goal for all of the second half and I found that no matter where I went, the ball seemed to fall into my hands. I seemed to be in the right place all the time, and made all the right decisions.' Enda, in one particular advance, foiled a possible goal. Seán O'Neill had the ball and was coming in at speed. Paddy Doherty moved into the full forward position. Enda had two options: one was to stay with his own man, Brian Johnston; the other was that Seán O'Neill would pass the ball to Doherty. He took the chance and ran for Doherty, nipped in from behind and whipped the ball from him and cleared it upfield—a possible goal prevented.

Colleran's display at corner back on that occasion was the finest and best seen at All-Ireland level in many years. He inspired his team mates in every sector of the field and their response was profound. Down, floundering under the pressure, shot costly wides, and at the end of a hard-fought contest Galway emerged the winners by 0-10 to 0-7.

It was Galway versus Kerry again in the All-Ireland final, their fourth major game in three years and, surprisingly, this clash turned nasty. Kerry departed from their previous direct approach and adopted a more physical style which boomeranged. If it was Kerry's intention to put Galway off their game, it simply did not work. Kerry ended up having two players sent off (Galway lost one player). The more important sequel was that Galway collected the coveted Sam Maguire Cup on a 0-12 to 0-9 scoreline. Captain Enda Colleran brought Sam back to the West for the second successive year. 'The West' was very much 'awake' again.

In 1966, led again by their captain Enda Colleran, Galway won their third All-Ireland football title in a row when they easily beat Meath by 1-10 to 0-7, and Enda joined the unique small band of players who have captained back-to-back All-Ireland winning teams. When his football career came to a close, he found another outlet for his talents which would keep him occupied and maintain his fitness level. His close friend Máirtín Newel suggested playing a bit of rugby with Corinthians club, one of the best in the province. He had never taken a rugby ball in his hands, but the training was invaluable to both of them and he enjoyed the work-outs. The club asked both to play in the Thirds team. Enda said: 'Our arrival coincided with a revival in the first team and we were lucky enough to be there when Corinthians won the Connacht League and Cup.'

They were quickly invited to play in the Seconds and a short time later they were promoted to the First team. They had the pleasure of playing against many renowned international stars and Enda got great satisfaction playing against Wanderers at Lansdowne Road and scoring twelve points. Kevin Flynn was at outhalf for Wanderers and Phil McNaughton was in the centre. Enda usually played at full back and found the ball handling and kicking skills acquired from Gaelic football invaluable. He also found kicking a rugby ball easier off the ground than a Gaelic ball. The rugby ball sits up and you can really hit it. He took most of the penalty kicks and ended up top scorer for

Corinthians. He said rugby is a player's game and he did not realise how enjoyable it was to play until he tried it.

Enda was a supreme Gaelic football corner back. He was fast, had a safe pair of hands and was rated one of the longest kickers of a dead ball in the game. He never resorted to rough house tactics and never out-stepped the canons of good sportsmanship. After all his successes on Gaelic fields, his selection on the Team of the Century in 1984 gave him great satisfaction. He was honoured again in 2000 when he was chosen on the Team of the Millennium and joined his illustrious county star, Seán Purcell, who was also honoured on both selections. Both were stars in their own right.

8

PAT 'RED' COLLIER

Football has down the years been enriched by many distinguished players, footballers whose skill and all-out endeavour established them as drawing cards in their own right. Forwards have generally set the standard in this regard because scores win matches and well-worked goals and points are out on their own in setting the pulse racing and earning special places for finishers in the esteem of followers. However, many defenders have also earned their place in this select company of footballers. Pat Collier, or 'The Red' Collier, as he was affectionately known, occupies a high rating in this exciting company.

Collier was one of the leading personalities and one of the most popular footballers during a senior career with Meath that enlivened most of the 1960s. His non-stop effort, fearless approach and genuine ability at the back in top-flight competition earned him many admirers throughout the length and breadth of the land.

Only one All-Ireland senior medal came his way in the Royal colours, but it was a case of quality rather than quantity. By 1967 he was an established member of the Meath senior team and it was no surprise to keen followers of the game when his high-quality football contributed that year to the return of the Sam Maguire Cup to the county.

Collier was a hard-working right half-back when Meath's hopes of a first All-Ireland senior football title in twelve years were ended in 1966 by an all-powerful Galway side that completed in that game the county's only sequence of three senior championships in succession. Meath took that set-back firmly on the chin and bounced back in impressive style to reach the final a year later. Collier was in his then familiar right half-back position for their meeting with Cork, who in 1966 ended Kerry's eight-year reign in Munster. They had high hopes of a first title in twenty-two years after retaining the provincial title and qualifying for the Sam Maguire Cup tie at the expense of Cavan.

Meath and the Rebel county provided a tense and exciting game that held interest all through although it yielded just one goal. But what a decisive score it proved! The Munster champions enjoyed so much territorial advantage in a low-scoring first half that they should have been further ahead at the interval than by 0-4 to 0-1. They did not help their cause by shooting eight wides. Nevertheless, the outlook still appeared bright for the Leesiders starting the second half. However, Meath possessed character as well as skill and they lost no time in proving that they were in no mood to allow a first title in twenty-three years to easily pass them by.

Right full forward Paddy Mulvey and full forward Noel Curran quickly reduced the arrears with points from play. Then with the half six minutes old came that vital goal, a neat overhead flick by Terry Kearns. Kearns had started the game at midfield, but was moved to centre half-forward after twenty-one minutes. Mattie Kerrigan, who had started at centre half-forward, flighted the ball in that led to Kearns's goal which put Meath ahead by 1-3 to 0-4. It was the turning point of the match and the Royals were never headed after that, although they still had to fight a strong rearguard action after that with Collier, Bertie Cunningham and Pat Reynolds providing a solid barrier at half-back.

A week later Collier had a splendid game when Meath beat New York at Croke Park in the first 'World Cup final'. There was no All Stars selection at that time, but had there been one, the Meath half-backs would all have been front runners for places.

Collier took some time to make the right half-back position his own. He was called up to the county senior team in a tournament game late in 1961 and played many solid games in the No. 2 spot for three seasons. However, the Stamullen club man was moved out to right half-back in 1964 and the move certainly proved the start of a great era not only for Collier but for the game of football. He quickly took to his new surroundings to go on and establish a deserved reputation as one of the best ever in the position.

Indeed, he lost no time at all in making a powerful impact at No. 5. The Leinster final of 1964 against Dublin demonstrated that point in striking fashion. Collier was masterly from first to final whistle and his dependable football not only contributed richly to Meath's first title in ten years, but also earned him the 'man of the match' award. There could hardly have been a better way than that to announce his arrival in a comparatively new position in a major game. He won a second Leinster senior medal two years later, and of course added another provincial souvenir on the way to that All-Ireland senior medal.

Like so many down the years, Collier graduated to the premier grade from the minor ranks. He had a bitter sweet experience in 1962 when he won a Leinster junior medal. However, he subsequently made his senior championship debut and so was no longer eligible for the junior ranks. As luck would have it, Meath went on to win the All-Ireland junior title. The tenacious Royal county defender was also honoured by Leinster in the Railway Cup, but an inter-provincial medal eluded him.

Meath's All-Ireland title win of 1967 opened up an amazing new vista for the county that few could have anticipated at the time. In late October of that year the then newly crowned All-Ireland champions met an Australian selection in a Gaelic football game at Croke Park before 23,419 spectators. The game proved an enjoyable affair. The visitors were allowed to lift the ball directly from the ground and they finished good winners by 3-16 to 1-10. Collier in his customary right half-back berth was one of Meath's brightest stars. There was an unexpected sequel to the match when Meath were invited to visit Australia in 1968. The invitation was accepted and Meath went on to blaze a new frontier for Gaelic football by touring Australia in March. They played five games in nine days at various cities including Perth, Melbourne and Sydney, and won them all. Collier proved very popular with enthusiasts down under with his whole-hearted brand of football.

However, he was by then accustomed to turning on the style outside this country. He had put his talents on parade at Wembley Stadium during the era of Gaelic games there that extended from 1958 to 1976. He also won many admirers in the US when he played there in the long since suspended Cardinal Cushing Games.

Meath had some outstanding players during the sixties. However, there is little doubt that 'Red' Collier was in a special class, not just in Meath but nationally at the time and was one of the exciting exponents of the game who kept football booming in that decade.

| MATT CONNOR

Many Gaelic games enthusiasts, especially those with long memories, contend that football forwards of the modern era do not match those of the past when it comes to consistently finding the target. Whatever about the merit or otherwise of that point of view, there is little doubt that there is a case for lamenting the number of wides that are commonplace in match after match at present—this, too, at a time when training for games at both club and inter-county level is more intense and more 'professional' than at any other time in the past.

History has certainly provided many forwards who were accurate marksmen. Matt Connor of Offaly proved to be one of the best ever in any era in this regard. His skills and artistry shone brightly in inter-county and inter-provincial football throughout the first five seasons of the eighties. He was an exciting and outstanding personality in the game, a superb bachelor of the scoring science, a master of the free kick, an outstanding footballer and a great sportsman.

His short senior inter-county career began against Meath in a National League game at Tullamore in March 1978 and came to a premature end as a result of a serious car accident on Christmas Day 1984. During that all too limited spell the Faithful county forward provided many talking points as he enhanced match after match with his brilliance in general play and an amazing consistency in finding the target in spectacular fashion.

It is no mean achievement for any footballer or hurler to top an annual scoring chart for all games in a single year. It is something special, however, when a player fills that position for five years in succession. Connor did just that between 1980 and 1984, and with flair and a finishing technique that ensured he chalked up superb totals each year. This was at a time when the game was rich in exceptional forwards with the ability to notch up impressive individual match returns.

It is hardly surprising, then, that the man from Offaly set up national records that still dominate the charts. In his inaugural season in the premier position in the nationwide scoring chart, he became the first in football or hurling to score more than 200 points, goals and points combined, in league, championship, inter-provincial, challenge and tournament games. He finished 1980 with 22 goals and 135 points (201 points) in 29 games—a then new record. It is one that not only still stands today but is likely to continue to command the No. 1 position well into the future.

That games total also says much for the way Matt Connor maintained his scoring expertise over a demanding and lengthy annual programme— a schedule, furthermore, that stands out prominently at a time when we hear so much nowadays about the demands on inter-county players.

During his years in under-age competitions Connor displayed much of the exciting potential that blossomed so brilliantly in the senior grade. He won Leinster under-21 medals in 1977 and 78. He was also prominent with Walsh Island, helping the club to their Leinster title wins in the 1978 and 79 seasons, and he also scored a goal in each provincial final. So, very few within the county at least could have been surprised when he was called up to the Offaly senior county team in that game against the Royal county early in 1978.

The dashing finisher did not waste much time either in finding his scoring touch in spectacular style. There must surely have been many, apart from Offaly fans, who sat up and took notice of the newcomer when he helped himself to a splendid 3-2 against Limerick at Askeaton in a league tie soon after joining the team. There were many noteworthy returns by the Offaly sharpshooter after that. Kerry got a real insight into his superb finishing in 1980, when they were at the peak of their power. Connor scored a majestic 2-9 (0-6 from frees) in the All-Ireland senior semi-final of 1980, but the Kingdom still overcame that scoring tour de force to go on to the All-Ireland final and chalk up a third Sam Maguire Cup win in succession. That return brought the Offaly man's score for the entire championship season that year to 5-31 (46 points) in only four games for what ranks as his best annual return in a championship season.

However, there was better fortune for Connor—and Offaly—two

years later when the counties met in the All-Ireland decider. That was the game in which substitute Séamus Darby's last-gasp goal snatched a record five senior titles in succession from Kerry's grasp just as their supporters were about to celebrate a unique event. His goal gave the Faithful county a 1-15 to 0-17 win.

Full forward Connor left his stamp on the success. He chipped in with seven valuable points (six from frees) to win his only All-Ireland senior medal. His cool, unflurried and poised approach ensured turning the key in the door to vital scores from frees. In short, he was the supreme master of the art.

Matt Connor chalked up many splendid scores during his career. One of the best was his first goal in that unsuccessful 1980 All-Ireland semi-final bid against the Kingdom. After about twenty minutes a splendid movement involving midfielder Tomás Connor and full forward Vincent Henry put Matt in possession. He carried the ball well, beat a tackle from Mick Spillane and then sent an unstoppable shot past Charlie Nelligan in the Kerry goal—a classic.

Not unexpectedly, Connor's stylish football and scoring flair did not go unnoticed by the All Stars selectors of the time. He was honoured three times and, remarkably, in a different position each year. He was chosen at right full forward in 1980, left half-forward in 82, and centre half-forward in 83.

Although he won only one All-Ireland senior medal, Matt still reaped a rich reward in football. In addition to those All Stars trophies and the All-Ireland medal, he helped Walsh Island to five county senior titles between 1978 and 1983, won three Leinster senior souvenirs with Offaly and made six appearances with Leinster.

However, the eastern province went through a lean spell during the Offaly forward's time on the side. How ironic, then, that just a few months after his serious accident Leinster regained the inter-provincial title after eleven years.

Connor's outstanding talents and finishing technique also found favour in 1984 when the Ireland-Australia International Series was revived as part of the Centenary Year celebrations.

Matt Connor was in action in the National League a few weeks before his accident, adding to his scoring returns and boosting his record to an amazing 82 goals and 600 points (906 points) in 161 games. The Offaly man, then, was truly an exquisite expert of the scoring art.

10

SEÁN FLANAGAN

Seán Flanagan was unique in many ways. He was truly a leader of men and he applied that principle throughout his playing career. A strict disciplinarian, he brooked no nonsense from his playing colleagues. He never suffered fools gladly. He led by example and expected those around him to follow suit. He was one of the finest corner backs in football. When he captained the Ireland team for the inaugural exhibition game against the Combined Universities in 1950, I had the privilege of refereeing that match. Both teams were brimming with household names, and the standard of football served up by both was intensively high. Seán Flanagan kept driving his men to greater effort and chastised those he felt were not responding to his urgings.

I was not spared either. He reproached me on a couple of occasions, complaining that I was penalising his team unduly. I pointed to the packed stands. There were immediate cries of 'put him off, ref, put him off', which I ignored. I said, 'Seán, those people over there are enjoying this match because it is brilliant. You keep playing the football and I will do the refereeing, okay?' He just smiled and went about his business. I had no more complaints.

The match was a real thriller and the football displayed elevated the contest to one of real passion. Seán led his Ireland players to a very decisive victory, 1-12 to 2-3, before a huge crowd. It was remarkable that the game was contested in true championship fervour, despite the fact that it was billed as an exhibition match.

Seán figured on the four Ireland winning teams from the outset of the series (1950 to 1953). All the major stars were chosen—Seán Purcell, Billy Goodison, Seán Quinn, Con McGrath, Bill McCorry, Tony Tighe, Batt Garvey, Brian Smyth and Peter Donohoe, to mention some. But the Combined Universities were bedecked also with star players who would have easily made the Ireland team: among them P. J. Duke, Jim Brosnan, Pádraig Carney, Peter Solan, Edwin Carolan, Mick O'Malley, Hugh McKearney and Billy Kenny. It was the quality of the players appearing on both selections which helped to make the series so exciting. Naturally, the composition of the teams changed from time to time and there were always plenty of super stars to fill the respective teams.

Seán Flanagan was a product of the famed St Jarlath's College of Tuam who captured eight successive Connacht Colleges titles (1932– 1939). He captained the last of that successful run in 1939. He entered Holy Cross College in Dublin that year and remained there until he graduated in 1942 with first place in his degree.

Delving into Seán Flanagan's storied sporting background really astonished me. I was aware of his prowess as a highly competent footballer, but I had no knowledge of his other sporting interests. I didn't know that he was a very good soccer player. He played minor football with Mayo in both 1939 and 1940. As an undergraduate in Clonliffe College in 1940, he played with a very impressive Mayo team which hammered Kerry in the All-Ireland semi-final. Sadly, Mayo were without their entire half-back line for the final against Louth and that proved costly.

That trio of Seán Mulhern, Joe Carroll and Seán himself were prevented from playing because of college rules. Ironically, Seán was playing soccer in the field adjacent to Croke Park when the Mayo minors took the field for the All-Ireland final against Louth. The Leinster men won the title by 5-5 to 2-7. Seán claimed that playing soccer proved very useful in later years when he trained with the Mayo county team.

Seán joined the very reputable Seán McDermott club in Dublin during his holidays from Clonliffe College, and joined up with great stars Eddie Boyle, Mick Connaire, Paddy McIntyre, the Robinsons, Tommy Banks, Jimmy Coyle and many other household names. He continued to play with 'Seans' after he left Clonliffe.

In 1943 Seán McDermotts qualified to play UCD in the Dublin senior championship final and were ahead in the closing minutes when they conceded a soft goal in injury time. He teamed up with UCD the following year and that was the start of his career as a corner back, a position which helped him achieve and fulfil most of his playing objectives. He said: 'We walked away with the Sigerson Cup, walloping UCC in the final at Croke Park. I captained the 1945 side and we easily won the final in Belfast. We won the Dublin senior league quite easily, but we were down 2-2 to 0-1 after the first ten minutes. I strolled up the field and said: Right lads, time to play a bit. We won easily at the finish.'

In February 1943 Seán was apprenticed to the law firm G. J. Quinn and a new aspect of his life took shape. G. J. was one of the famous Quinn brothers of Old Belvedere Rugby Club fame along with Frank, Paddy and Kevin, who won the Leinster Senior Cup seven times in a row.

He developed an interest in rugby through Gerry Quinn and went to a number of matches, including the wartime Irish xv games where he first saw Jackie Kyle in action. He considered the Ulster star a genius and met him personally through Gerry Quinn. Kyle was a very modest person and Seán claimed he was the only sportsman he had ever asked for an autograph.

He had another interest—cricket—again through his great friend Gerry Quinn, whose later death affected him very much. Over the years Seán watched most of the great cricketers at county or test level in places like Bombay, Jamaica, Lords, Sydney, Hobart and Barbados as well as various county grounds in England.

Seán Flanagan started his own practice in November 1947 in Ballaghadereen. He played no club football during that period. He wrote to the County Board resigning from the team. He was contacted by board officials, who asked him to reconsider his decision and make himself available for the 1948 season. Mayo easily beat Kerry in the 1948 semi-final and were very determined to beat the holders, Cavan, in the final. However, they were defeated by Cavan in the All-Ireland final. Only one point separated the teams with Cavan edging it 4-5 to 4-4.

Mayo, however, won the 1949 National Football League title, but were beaten by Meath in the All-Ireland semi-final that year. Meath, led by Brian Smyth, captured the Sam Maguire, beating Cavan in the final. Following Mayo's defeat in the All-Ireland semi-final a canvas took place within the county to change the rule giving the captaincy of the senior team to the nominee of the county champions. A strong case was made for Seán to be made captain. The change was approved and Seán Flanagan from Ballaghadereen Junior Club assumed the important role of team leader.

Immediately after being told the good news, Seán called a meeting with the Mayo Board chairman, Dr Jim Laffey, who was told that he had only one function to perform for the team, and that was to keep the County Board away from the team until the day that Seán Flanagan presented the Sam Maguire to his native county. That command was to upset a number of people, especially the County Board's reverend president at the time. He came storming into the training camp where the Mayo players were having lunch. When Seán saw him coming, he immediately stopped him entering the dining room and asked the cleric if he had received a message from the county chairman. There was something muttered about Seán's attitude. Seán said, 'Look, Father, this is not easy for me either, but the chairman's warning included you. Now please leave, and I will see you when I have the Sam Maguire in my possession.'

Naturally, his strong words sparked off plenty of resentment within the board management. He was accused of being an arrogant so and so, and others claimed he was a bully and a dictator. But Seán wanted the respect of his players and he didn't want his authority undermined or his preparation undone by events outside his control. It is highly significant to stress that Mayo have won only three All-Ireland senior football titles (1936, 50 and 51). In the latter two years the team was captained by Seán Flanagan. It should be pointed out that Mayo have not won an All-Ireland senior title since 1951.

Armagh were unable to upset the popular favourites in the All-Ireland semi-final, which Mayo won 3-9 to 0-6. So it was on to Croke Park for the All-Ireland against a very good Louth side. Mayo had been building up strength with new blood from the 1947 and 48 teams. There were three great additions to the 1950 side in Seán Wynne, Mickey Mulderrig and big John McAndrews. Mayo set the pace and were coasting along in front 1-3 to 0-1 when Billy Kenny was injured and was stretchered off. He was a very important figure-head at centre forward and the attack was to suffer from his absence. Once again the presence of Seán Flanagan was to add immeasurably to the composure of the Mayo defence. Louth gained in confidence and long-range deliveries from Seán Boyle kept the pressure on the Mayo backs. The Connacht champions hung on, cheered by a big Mayo following in the 76,174 attendance, to carry off the Sam Maguire Cup for the first time since 1936. Flanagan had achieved his objective and his promise to the Mayo people.

The following year he joined the elite band of footballers who captained their respective teams to win back-to-back All-Ireland titles when Mayo beat Meath 2-8 to 0-9 to win their third All-Ireland crown. He led Connacht to victory in the Railway Cup series and also captained the Rest of Ireland to beat the Combined Universities. The only set-back that year was losing the National Football League final to Meath.

Seán won his second league title in 1954 when Mayo easily crushed Carlow. Significantly, Dr Pádraig Carney was brought back from America for both the semi-final and the final. The US -based doctor had a wonderful game and played a leading role in that 1954 league success.

In Brian Carty's book, *Football Captains (The All-Ireland Captains)*, Seán Flanagan contributed this piece on the role of a team captain: 'The performance of a team at its best is far greater than the sum of the individual abilities of fifteen players. I believe a captain can contribute. Some have certainly done so. Before the start of the 1950 championship season, I gathered the forwards together and told them that no team in Ireland would score more than ten points against us, giving them a scoring target minimum. We achieved it.' And to those entrusted with the task of promoting Gaelic games, he advised: 'Catch them young, treat them gently. No player to play any other grade while still a minor. Under-21s not allowed to play senior. Not enough care is taken with young talent. For one Dermot Earley, thousands have been murdered by too early promotion. The games are physically tough, so bones need to be mature. It is too early to break a young person's heart. Mayo has a sad history here.'

(Interviewed in November 1992. Seán Flanagan died in February 1993.)

11

BILLY GOODISON

Billy Goodison was numbered as one of the great all-time centre backs in football. Growing up in Wexford town in the 1940s and 50s, football and hurling were so much a part of the ritual. He graduated to become one of the great centre half-backs of Gaelic football. To many, during his playing days, Billy was a boyhood hero. He was the greatest in County Wexford, the regular centre back on provincial and Ireland teams in the days when Gaelic football was the chosen sport of the youth of the GAA supporters in the Model county. He made a vivid impact on football during his playing career and was always viewed as a ready-made filler of the important centre back berth.

Paradoxically, he was not easily called to mind by the rank and file because he was never on an All-Ireland winning team. Billy, however, was not just another player. Wexford during his era may not have been around long enough in the championship to attract such attention as other leading counties, but he still managed to capture the imagination of the entire country. He may have been small in stature for a central defender, but as was so often described, he leaped for the high ball as if he had a spring in his boots, often out-fielding taller opponents.

There was so much to his game—beautiful fielding, and long, accurate deliveries with either foot. His reading of the game and positional play stamped him as a player of very high quality. His memorable fetching of a high ball and his pin-point distribution typified all that was good about Gaelic football during that era.

Born in Wexford town, it was on the streets that Billy learned his footballing skills, which he developed on the small green areas at the north end of the town. Volunteers, the greatest club football side ever to emerge in the county, rejoiced in his talent and that of countless young men born in the infant years of the Free State. In one local

Left to right: Brendan Barden (Longford captain), referee Paddy Hughes (Louth) and John Timmons (Dublin captain), await the result of the coin toss before the 1965 Leinster senior football final. (*Ray Donlon, Longford*)

Tipperary footballer Declan Browne (*second from right*) shares a few moments with old friends.

Kevin Armstrong (Antrim) played against Cork in the 1943 final, but never had the thrill of winning an All-Ireland medal.

4 September 2005: Declan Browne (Tipperary). Tommy Murphy Cup final, Wexford v Tipperary, Croke Park, Dublin. (*Sportsfile*)

September 1971: Offaly captain Willie Bryan lifts the Sam Maguire after his side defeated Galway in the All-Ireland football final, Croke Park. (*Sportsfile*)

8 October 2006: Errigal Ciarán captain Peter Canavan is carried aloft after the W.J. Dolan Tyrone senior football championship final replay. Errigal Ciarán v Carrickmore, Healy Park, Omagh, Co. Tyrone. (*Sportsfile*)

19 November 2006: Peter Canavan (Errigal Ciarán) in action against Niall McCusker (Ballinderry). AIB Ulster senior football championship semi-final at Casement Park, Belfast. (*Sportsfile*)

Mick Carley (Westmeath), one of the greats in football for many years with both county and province.

Dashing Galway corner back, Enda Colleran, who captained his county to All-Ireland success in 1965 and 1966. (*Sportsfile*)

Enda Colleran in action against Dublin 1963, as Mattie McDonagh awaits developments. *Left to right*: Dessie Ferguson (Dublin), Mickey Whelan (Dublin) and John Timmons (Dublin).

Seán Flanagan (Mayo captain) *third from right*, with the
Sam Maguire trophy, surrounded by fans after the 1950
All-Ireland final win against Louth.

A unique picture. Three great All-Ireland winning captains. *Left to right*: Jimmy Murray
(Roscommon), Enda Colleran (Galway) and Seán Flanagan (Mayo), all from the province
of Connacht. (*Eoin McCann*)

The stylish Matt Connor (Offaly), in action against Meath, July 1981. (*Sportsfile*)

newspaper interview, Billy was quoted as saying: 'We had no gear, no boots or stockings, and the knicks we had were made from flour bags by our mothers. Our difficulty was finding a football and one club ball was in service for years, and that ball of leather panels and its tube and lace, was a hell of a lot more difficult to handle and kick than the football of today.'

His career with Wexford began at the tender age of 16 and the first of a whole series of sporting frustrations had begun. Three times Wexford played Louth in the Leinster senior championship and three times the Slaney men went down in finals. At the time Billy held a unique record, as he so often told in later years: 'But I have one record in that respect that is unlikely to be beaten. I was the only minor to play in a Leinster final in Croke Park as a married man.'

The irony of all that was that he progressed immediately from minor to senior status. In those years his club, Volunteers, were at the peak of their power and he developed into their greatest player, while through-out his career he filled the centre half-back position regularly. He helped Wexford to success in the Leinster League in 1945 before going on to beat Offaly in the Leinster final. Billy Goodison firmly believed that Wexford should have won the All-Ireland final that year. In an inter-view he dismissed the episode simply: 'Things went wrong. But I won't blame anyone or any set of circumstances. It's now part of history.'

Wexford lost the All-Ireland semi-final to the great Cavan team that boasted such men as P. J. Duke, Tony Tighe, big Tom O'Reilly, the 'Gunner' Brady, J. J. Stafford, Mick Higgins, Simon Deignan and Peter Donohoe. He always considered Mick Higgins as the best man he ever played against. Cavan lost the All-Ireland final to Cork, while Wexford went to the Mardyke on the first Sunday in October of 1945 and gave the newly crowned champions a lesson in Gaelic football in the National League series.

Billy once told with gusto of the single blemish on his career. In 1944 in a league game in Tullamore against Offaly, he was sent off in the wrong by his good friend, referee Bill Delaney of Laois. In punching a ball clear he came in contact with his immediate opponent who feigned injury. Wexford were nine points in arrears at the time when they lost Goodison. So incensed were his colleagues at his dismissal, that their reaction was only amazing. Wexford's blood was up at what they considered a very unfair decision by the referee.

Goodison, now sitting on the subs bench, was truly fascinated watching the play and later remarked: 'Nicky Rackard, Paddy Kehoe, Jim Coady, Jackie Culleton—the lot of them proceeded to steamroll the opposition into the ground. I never had a thrill like it. There were Wexford people who left the match at half-time who were astonished to learn later in pubs in Carlow that we had won by a few points.'

Billy continued to play in the county colours until 1957. The team also figured in the Leinster football final of 1953 against Louth, when many of the minors that had been in opposition thirteen years earlier again confronted each other. Louth were the victors once more.

In the meantime Billy tried his hand at hurling. There had been an upsurge in the game in his native county in the wake of the inter-county success, and in his unusual role at corner forward won junior and intermediate medals with Faythe Harriers. Eight years earlier, in 1945, he had assisted Volunteers in the final of the junior hurling championship.

Billy had a fine record of service with Leinster in Railway Cup games and played on the Ireland team in 1950 and 52. Having once been offered a soccer contract with English club Arsenal, he decided to stay on in Wexford with his family and friends, which at the time he felt was the right decision. Having enjoyed such a wonderful career with his club, Volunteers, and his county, he went on to referee the 1955 All-Ireland senior football final between Kerry and Dublin. The national papers the following day were loud in their praise of his handling of such an important match. He also refereed the Football League final involving Dublin and New York.

Rarely included in the bar stool debates about the greatest foot-ballers of all time, Goodison still qualifies as one of the top centre backs of his era. After his death people stood in silence as his funeral passed along his beloved John Street, the home of the Volunteers. There was one final round of applause for their favourite son.

12

TONY HANAHOE

Tony Hanahoe's role in Dublin's great run of All-Ireland successes in the 1970s can never be underestimated. And it was amply exemplified in one of the greatest team performances in the 1977 All-Ireland semi-final against Kerry.

The match reports the following day correctly highlighted a couple of incidents which marked the basis for that great success. In both instances the input of Hanahoe was unmistakable. My match report in the *Evening Press* made reference to the two passages of play which involved the genius of the Dublin captain. In the fifty-sixth minute of the breath-taking action, I mentioned that Brian Mullins, from a quick free, sent the ball to Anton O'Toole. Kerry's Ger O'Keefe and Jim Deenihan tackled O'Toole, and the ball broke out to Tony Hanahoe. He in turn swiftly passed the ball to Dave Hickey who cracked it to the Kerry net. Minutes later came the crucial goal, this time from Bernard Brogan. Hickey, coming in quickly on a solo run, punted the ball to Hanahoe. Flying in on a support mission came Bernard Brogan. Hanahoe delayed a couple of seconds and then coolly passed the ball into the space in front of the in-rushing Brogan, who collected it and crashed it home. It all happened in the space of six minutes near the end of a classic encounter. Both moves featured the extraordinary perception of Hanahoe to read a situation that was about to happen.

Back in 1964 Tony came on to the Dublin team at a time when triumph and its trappings were still a happy, colourful and vibrantly fresh memory for the Dubs. A year earlier Dublin had beaten Galway in the All-Ireland final. There was, one felt, a reasonable squad of good men around to suggest that Dublin might be an impressive force in the immediate years ahead. It was not to be. Ten years on, in a first round championship match against Wexford at Croke Park, Tony was still on the Dublin team. And one was inclined to wonder why.

Looking back on it now, that 1963 All-Ireland victory over Galway was a climax in Dublin's football fortunes—and a sudden full stop. It was the last brave flourish of a team which had been created in the early 1950s and which with excellent replacements and changes from time to time had come back from the All-Ireland defeat in 1955 to win in 1958 and 63. Yet, through the darkest hours of Dublin's misery and long years in the wilderness, Tony Hanahoe, in the company of Jimmy Keaveney, Paddy Cullen and Gay O'Driscoll, battled on with courage in a lonely struggle. Extreme hopes are always born in extreme misery. When Jimmy Keaveney dropped out of the Dublin squad in 1972, one had to believe then that it was only a matter of time before the other three, Cullen, Hanahoe and O'Driscoll, would follow him.

An interesting note about that Wexford-Dublin championship meeting in 1974 was the fact that it was demoted to the lowly status of a curtain-raiser, and indeed the quality of the entertainment that afternoon hardly justified even that status. Dublin won but not in any remarkable manner that would suggest they had much hope of beating favourites Louth in the second round at Navan. But Navan on a brilliant sunny day marked the day that manager Kevin Heffernan gambled heavily on Jimmy Keaveney at full forward. A very reluctant Keaveney had yielded to the persuasive Heffernan to come out of retirement and once again teamed up with Hanahoe, Cullen and O'Driscoll. It should be said that it was on that sunny day that Tony Hanahoe finally came into his own.

A win over Offaly in a very tough competitive game, followed by a success over Kildare and then Meath in the Leinster final, was the culmination of a very demanding run of victories. They had now a championship kicker in Keaveney. They had developed a new format of training and there was a whole, new physical, psychological and managerial approach to team-building. The new organisation was orchestrated by Kevin Heffernan with the assistance of Donal Colfer and Lorcan Redmond, his two co-selectors. Tony Hanahoe now had new men around him, eager, willing, ready and able to co-operate with him. These same young men, just names when they played against Wexford, now began to emerge as exciting personalities in their own right.

Perhaps for the first time, one became conscious of Brian Mullins, David Hickey, Anton O'Toole, Bobby Doyle and Robbie Kelleher. For

Tony Hanahoe, just as it was for Paddy Cullen, Jimmy Keaveney and Gay O'Driscoll, it was now a new ball game, and all four wanted their share in it. Those five games in Leinster saw the start of the huge momentum of the mighty Dubs and the magic they were to demonstrate in their bid for football's most coveted prize, the Sam Maguire Cup.

In the All-Ireland semi-final of 1974 Dublin came up against Cork, the holders. According to Tony Hanahoe, the whole Dublin team was very psyched up for the match against the reigning champions. None of the players had ever been involved at that level. The captain of the Dublin team, Seán Doherty, was a steward on Hill 16 when Billy Morgan was presented with the Sam Maguire in 1973.

One of the Sunday papers, according to Hanahoe, 'was callous enough to put up the names and faces and say, on an individual basis, how could Dublin be expected to beat Cork?' That was like waving a red flag to a bull when the Dublin players read the piece. Naturally, there were always plans and team tactics drawn up by Heffernan, Colfer and Redmond and discussed with the players. The plans worked. Dublin started at a furious pace against the Cork champions, and they never stopped running, swinging the ball around with telling affect. Cork were totally unsettled and were rocked back on their heels. They never recovered the initiative.

Dublin defeated Galway in the 1974 All-Ireland final in a dour match, the highlight being the brilliant penalty save by Paddy Cullen to deny Liam Sammon a possible team victory. Dublin were to contest two major finals the following year, but lost both. They were shocked by a young Kerry in the 1975 All-Ireland final and by Meath in the National League final.

Tony Hanahoe was never a demonstrative person. If he was set a target or given an instruction by Heffernan at the start of a match, he carried it out to the letter. He was one of the most unselfish players on the field of play. When he was asked to play a roving role, he did so. It was part of the team plan and Tony accepted it as a duty to the other players.

The 1976 All-Ireland final against Kerry was a perfect example. Tony was the team captain that year, nominated by Heffernan. It was felt that Tim Kennelly was the pivotal power at centre back. If he could be taken out of position, it would open up the Kerry defence for the Dublin forwards. Heffernan and Hanahoe saw the wisdom of the plan. The bottom line was that Hanahoe was being asked to sacrifice himself. Some of the other players might have had reservations about such an instruction—certainly not Tony Hanahoe. Such was his commitment to the team that he hardly considered it a sacrifice. Dublin beat Kerry that year by seven points, the same margin that Kerry had inflicted on Dublin the previous year.

The 1976 victory over Kerry gave particular satisfaction to captain Tony Hanahoe. In the years when the capital county won Sam in 1942, 58, 63 and 74, Dublin had been open to the age-old charge: 'Ah, yes, but could you beat Kerry?' That old chestnut was finally buried. But the master stroke which resulted in the very mobile Kennelly being out-manoeuvred by Hanahoe was one of the cardinal ploys which helped Dublin's winning game plan. It must be said that the successful 1976 team was by now a very mature force; but so too was the mighty Kerry side. The great rivalry built up over the years has led to a very competitive edge to the exchanges whenever they meet. Both teams enjoy it thoroughly.

Looking back on his playing history, Tony could remember being on the panel in 1964 and 65, but was not pushed enough to make the county team, so he opted out in 1966. It was the nature of things that he would find himself available again when the provincial championships started in 1970, and he remained on the side in 1971 and 72. But 1973 held no options for him so he again dropped out. The saga involving the return of Kevin Heffernan to the manager's role in 1973/74 held out much better prospects for him, so he was back in business. It must be said that Heffernan and Hanahoe were very close. Hanahoe always represented the solid face of the team.

Heffo's stewardship had guided Dublin successfully to a long sought-after All-Ireland title in virtually his first year in the position. When Jimmy Grey persuaded him to take over the job, Kevin did stress that it would take at least three years to achieve his objective. He succeeded in just one. It had taken a lot of very hard work, taking the Dublin team to a level of greatness unparalleled in the county's history. His period in charge was one of total commitment, and it was now a case of mission accomplished, and he wanted to opt out. But in stepped Jimmy Grey again and persuaded him to change his mind. There were still more laurels to be won by the team he had fashioned.

Speculation was fairly rife after Dublin beat Kerry in the 1976 All-

Ireland final that Heffernan would bow out. Tony Hanahoe and, I suspect, Jimmy Grey were perhaps the only ones who had the information that it was a definite fact, but they kept their powder dry.

One month after the 1976 All-Ireland victory, the team, substitutes, Lorcan Redmond, Donal Colfer and Jimmy Grey sat down to dinner in the Gresham Hotel. It was a light-hearted occasion, but there was a serious air to the table talk as well. Near the end of the meal Kevin Heffernan made the major announcement. He was stepping down from the coaching position. His basic reason for the decision was that he could no longer afford the time or the demands of the job after three years of involvement. Few could disagree with the sentiments expressed. They all knew that the manager's job was a very demanding one. It really was a full-time occupation.

Later in the evening the name of Tony Hanahoe was being mentioned as a possible replacement. It was felt that he was the most dependable, forthright and clear-headed individual capable of replacing the master craftsman. The matter was finally addressed later that week. Tony accepted after Donal Colfer and Lorcan Redmond pledged their support as long as it was needed.

In 1977 Tony Hanahoe was now the team manager, team selector, team captain and a busy solicitor in his profession. He had willing helpers and advisers in Colfer and Redmond which was important. It didn't take Tony very long to lay down his marker when the 1977 championship got under way. It was a lesson he had learned from his predecessor.

Perhaps one of the most extraordinary decisions ever taken by a team captain was his own closely guarded secret. Three weeks before the 1977 All-Ireland senior semi-final against Kerry, he got married but did not tell any of the players about the wedding. He actually turned up for training in the normal way that very morning. The pressures on the Dublin captain from the media, newspapers, radio and television for the Kerry game reached a frightening intensity. Training sessions had to be moved to various venues away from the public eye. The build-up for that final was unprecedented.

Former Kerry GAA star Jimmy Deenihan made a very strong case for his native county. A young team, he said, it would easily have the measure of the older Dublin side. He was sharply reminded by the well-known columnist Con Houlihan of the old South African proverb, 'You should never criticise the alligator's mother before you cross the river.' Dublin beat Kerry in one of the best exhibitions of Gaelic football ever seen at Croke Park. Not alone did the players do their captain proud, but they did themselves and the county proud. Tony completed the job when he led his team to victory against Armagh, a victory sparked off by a brilliant individual goal from Jimmy Keaveney in the opening stages. Dublin never looked back after that.

After an eighteen-month lapse, Kevin Heffernan made his appearance on the bench again with the Dubs. Galway were their victims again in 1983 when the Dubs grabbed the glory of All-Ireland success with twelve players. In 1986 the fairytale ended when the team selectors resigned, to close the greatest chapter of Dublin's football history.

Tony Hanahoe carved a historic niche for himself, becoming only one of five players who led their respective counties to back-to-back All-Ireland successes.

13

KEVIN HEFFERNAN

I played against Kevin at club level; I played with him on Dublin football and hurling teams. And being a near neighbour, I have managed to survive the countless times we have discussed the fortunes of the county during its trials and tribulations.

Kevin Heffernan is, and will always be, a pragmatist. During our argumentative sessions he would always strive for the high road. He is, and always will be, unrelenting and stubborn perhaps in his viewpoint. He is convinced that he is always right.

That is the hallmark of a great player, a great team manager and a very human person. He never suffered fools gladly and once he had set his sights on an objective, he worked hard towards its final execution.

I hold him in very high esteem. He was a brilliant footballer, but his greatness was fully exemplified when he was appointed Dublin football team manager in the early 1970s.

Kevin Heffernan's birthplace was Marino and his club was St Vincent's. During his career he won an All-Ireland senior football championship medal, one junior All-Ireland football medal, 3 National League medals, 4 Leinster senior championship medals, and 7 Railway Cup football medals. He was chosen at left corner forward on the Team of the Century. He has won 15 county senior titles in football, 6 county senior hurling medals and numerous tournament and challenge awards. He captained Dublin in their 1958 All-Ireland win over Derry, but his greatest achievement was to take a Dublin team floundering in the bottom regions at senior football level and lead them to All-Ireland glory and universal acclaim.

Kevin would wince when he attended Dublin matches and watch them slump to defeats against opposition regarded by him as being very poor championship contenders. He was a brilliant competitor on the football field and at his zenith could destroy the reputation of any of the leading defenders of his day. Without purpose or any real backbone or commitment, it looked to him that Dublin football would be consigned to many years in the doldrums of the game. It was difficult for him to believe that Dublin would never again produce the players that had made Dublin teams very much feared at top level—the Foleys, the Freaneys, Jim Crowley, Snitchie Ferguson, Mickey Whelan, Jimmy Lavin and John Timmons, who had all fanned the flames of greatness on Dublin teams of the past.

Unfortunately, apathy, lack of spirit and the absence of any aspirational tendencies had completely enveloped the county team, leading them to the ignominy of relegation to the lower regions of league football.

Kevin had sampled the good times and the bad during his own playing career. The one that stuck in his craw the most was the 1955 defeat at the hands of Kerry. It probably was the match most talked about and written about ever at All-Ireland level.

Dublin had earned the appellation of the 'football machine' following their triumphant rampage through Leinster and culminating in the defeat of Meath on a 5-12 to 0-7 scoreline. They had beaten Meath in the National League earlier that year. Most of the scribes (myself included) had installed Dublin as firm favourites for ultimate honours. It was an extraordinary year for football. Both All-Ireland semi-finals ended in replays in which Dublin beat Mayo and Kerry beat Cavan, and so the scene was set for the most eagerly awaited All-Ireland for years. It was labelled the 'Dublin machine' versus the 'catch and kick' style of Kerry.

Everyone waited with great anticipation for the forthcoming duels between Ollie Freaney at centre forward and Kerry's centre back John Cronin, and Kevin Heffernan's full forward duels with Kerry full back Ned Roche. A new attendance record of 87,102 packed Croke Park, but the entrance gates were broken down by the thousands who were clamouring to see the great clash of styles. The park was jammed with over 90,000 spectators, some of whom never saw the battle on the field of play.

The performance of the Dublin team in their two great contests with Mayo in the All-Ireland semi-final gave credence to the belief that the city men had blossomed into a powerful force. Midfielders Marcus Wilson and Jim McGuinness dominated the centre of the field and the

Dublin forwards had the space and speed to grab the vital scores. Kevin Heffernan, as he did in the Leinster final, roamed at will in quest of the ball, putting the Mayo defence under great pressure. The change in tactics helped to overcome a gallant Mayo team in a great contest.

The build-up to the Kerry and Dublin All-Ireland final put unbelievable pressure on both teams. Kerry had no injury problems. Dublin did have problems which were played down. Marcus Wilson cried off through injury. Jim McGuinness badly twisted his knee in training. Norman Allen, who could fill any role on the field was rushed to hospital for an appendectomy. Heffernan conceded that the injuries to Wilson and McGuinness had a major bearing on the 1955 outcome. McGuinness was given a knee injection, a major decision which certainly affected his performance. He had to withdraw at half-time. The reshaped midfield seemed to affect the whole rhythm of the side, and the Dublin forwards were caught in a vice-like grip by a very astute Kerry defence.

But what surprised me, and indeed other commentators at the time, was the decision taken to leave Kevin Heffernan on the full forward mark, despite the fact that his roaming tactics had formed the basis of the team's victories in previous matches. Kerry's instructions to Ned Roche were to follow Heffernan everywhere. The Dublin decision played into Kerry hands, as it closed down the Heffernan threat. It must be said that Heffernan's best position was at corner forward. The switch to full forward was taken for the Meath Leinster final and it had worked brilliantly. Even with that source curtailed, the failure of the Dublin forwards to finish off good scoring chances was one of the prime factors in losing to a very sound Kerry team, who played their own brand of direct football. On the day they fully deserved their reward. However, Dublin argue to this day that the loss of such high-calibre players as Wilson, McGuinness and Allen proved too great a mountain to climb against the Kerry strength, plus the bad misses by the normally accurate Dublin forwards.

I can categorically state that Kevin Heffernan had to get a painkilling injection for an ankle injury before the game, which was not mentioned in the pre-match summaries. It wasn't mentioned either in the post-match inquest. It may well have been the reason why the Dublin star remained around the Kerry square and not as a roving attacker. It was a well-kept secret and never made the public domain.

Ollie Freaney told me that he always enjoyed playing against Kerry teams. They played hard but fair. A good friendship developed between the two counties over the years as well. That was to manifest itself many years later in an extraordinary way. The lessons learned in 1955 were put to good use by Heffernan when he captained Dublin to victory against Derry in 1958.

Dublin won the All-Ireland again in 1963 when they beat Galway. Filling a selector's role for that success was Kevin Heffernan. He was still active with his club, St Vincent's. Dublin had easily beaten Down in the All-Ireland semi-final, but Heffernan felt that the attack still needed an experienced forward. His choice was Dessie Ferguson who filled the role that Heffernan himself had advocated. It was a master stroke. Ferguson played a very vital part in forging a narrow 1-9 to 0-10 victory.

Perhaps the most important stage of Heffernan's involvement with Dublin came about in a remarkable way. The fortunes of the city men slumped to a very low level after the 1963 All-Ireland victory, and Dublin football languished in the doldrums for a period of ten years. Changes took place at board level with the appointment of Jimmy Grey as county chairman. He was a former All-Ireland hurler and played in goal in the 1961 final against Tipperary, who won by a point. Jimmy was also a sub on the 1955 All-Ireland football final team.

Grey took over as chairman in 1973 and he had plans. Dublin had to be restored to its proper place at the top of the football ladder. I was writing a 'Dublin' column in the *Evening Press* at the time. I phoned Jimmy Grey and enquired about his quest for a new manager. He told me that he had put a proposition to Kevin Heffernan and was waiting for a response. Kevin was at that time very much involved with St Vincent's. My column on the following Wednesday had a bold head-line, 'Heffernan to take Dublin manager's job?' I knew Jimmy Grey wanted Heffo for the job, so I thought I would give the idea a little push. Jimmy was waiting to inform the County Management Committee if Heffo had accepted the position. When my story appeared on the Wednesday, it certainly put the cat among the pigeons.

Heffo took none too kindly to my scoop as he had a number of matters to sort out before committing himself. But Jimmy Grey sub-sequently got his man. The chairman and secretary Jim King got the backing of the Dublin County Committee to break the traditional arrangement for managing a county team. A three-man selection team was put in place. Donal Colfer (Synge St) and Lorcan Redmond (St Margaret's) were chosen. Both had played for the county and they represented the south and north side of the county respectively. A basic objective was agreed to restore Dublin's football pride. To achieve that aim, it was necessary to select twenty-five players who would have the will, character and commitment to pursue that aim vigorously, and achieve its maximum potential within a three-year period.

Heffernan knew the type of player needed for such a mission and he had willing partners in Colfer and Redmond, who were on the same wavelength. They set about developing a team by (1) improving individual skills; (2) achieving maximum fitness; and (3) developing field tactics best suited to their particular team and Dublin football generally. As the weeks and months sped on, the players spent long sessions dealing with various subjects relating to team-building and developing team unity. A lot of hard grafting in training and in matches transformed the players into a solid unit. There were no excuses, no complaints about the rigorous timetable that the players had to endure.

The players chosen were physically endowed. The hard slog in Parnell Park in all kinds of weather every Tuesday, Thursday and Saturday by no means helped in maintaining normal domestic bliss among the married players, or the single men either. Heffernan was ruthless in his approach to training. Planned holidays had to be revised. Some players hated the demanding routine but accepted it as part of the process. A player from the southside of the city was held up in traffic getting to Parnell Park. When he rushed up to Heffernan, after getting togged out, and explained his reason for being late, he was told to get dressed and not to be late for the following Thursday. He wasn't.

I have tried at times to analyse the mind of Kevin Heffernan when he agreed to take over the Dublin senior football teams at the start of the 1973–74 league. I doubt if he would have taken the job unless he firmly believed that it was not a lost cause. He must have seen a ray of sunlight somewhere. Kevin summed the situation up as he saw it: 'It was an exercise in communications. It has always been my belief that there's a way that Dublin fellows should play football. Generally, Dubliners are astute players with plenty of speed and good ball control. These are the things that should be exploited. So it became a matter of meshing these things into a total commitment.'

Frankie Stockwell of Galway, a brilliant full forward like Heffernan, said of the Dublin football revolution, after Dublin's defeat of Galway in the 1974 All-Ireland final: 'Kevin Heffernan has one of the shrewdest brains in football. It's got to be handed to him; he's achieved miracles with the Dublin team.'

To put matters in proper perspective, following the win over the reigning champions Cork in the 1974 All-Ireland semi-final, and the final against Galway, Heffo commented: 'I couldn't over-praise the players for their commitment to training and to playing the type of football I've been talking about and, indeed, to their exercise of it on the field of play.'

During the team-building stages Heffernan, Colfer and Redmond made a decision to maintain an open approach with the players at all times. They also insisted on having the right to justify any changes or alterations in front of the players. It didn't go down well with some of the players when Bobby Doyle was omitted from the 1975 final against Kerry. A player approached Heffo and said Doyle should be on the team. Heffo replied: 'Look, I would drop my own mother if I thought she was not worth her place.' But then Heffernan always listened to the problems of the players, or matters relating to their job or domestic situation. He always had an ear for those who needed support in matters outside the training ground or the field of play.

Losing to Kerry in the 1975 All-Ireland final was a huge set-back. But the reaction of Heffernan and his two co-selectors to the result spurred them to move swiftly to rectify the obvious weakness. Most of the attention was given to the defence. They had conceded a record total of 10 goals and 33 points in the previous four games in the 1975 campaign. In the 1976 championship series, the Dublin backs allowed the opposition only one goal and 35 points in the four matches prior to meeting Kerry.

Dublin reached the 1976 All-Ireland final against Kerry fully primed to atone for the set-back at the hands of the Kingdom the previous year. They also had a completely new half-back line of Tommy Drumm, Kevin Moran and Pat O'Neill, a line of immense solidarity. It is now history that Dublin laid the Kerry bogey by taking the Sam Maguire Cup for the first time since they beat Kerry in 1934. It can be said that Dublin blended power, elegance and creativity to add a new dimension to their game.

Heffernan rightly paid tribute to the work of his two fellow selectors, Donal Colfer and Lorcan Redmond, who were to remain with him for twelve years. The team became known as 'Heffo's heroes', but it was built on the great friendship which existed between the three mentors. No dissension ever arose over the selection of a player. The Dublin team which had come from nowhere to win that 1974 All-Ireland final had performed an unparalleled feat in the recent history of GAA games.

The team went on to compete in six successive All-Ireland finals, winning three. It was to be known ever after as 'The Dubs', who had started out in 1974 as no-hopers and were to become one of the best teams in the history of the game. Kevin Heffernan launched his career in team management in 1974 and closed it successfully in 1983 when the famous 'defiant dozen' defeated the fourteen men on the Galway team in a remarkable All-Ireland final.

One of the great characters who figured on that team was corner back Mick Holden from the Cuala club in Dalkey. He was the joker in the squad and the only player that Heffernan allowed to stretch his patience. Before the Dublin players left Parnell Park after their final work-out for the 1983 All-Ireland final, Heffernan said that if any player found it difficult to sleep before the big game, they could have a sleeping pill. 'Hands up those who would like one.' Not a hand was raised. Then, surprisingly, Mick Holden's hand was slowly raised. The players left the dressing room and Heffernan turned to Holden and said, 'You know, of all the players in this squad, you are the one man I thought didn't need a pill.' Holden replied, 'Ah, it's not for me, Kev. It's for my mother. She cannot sleep a wink before these big matches.' Heffernan's response was unprintable.

14

MICK HIGGINS

O n the Monday morning after the 1952 All-Ireland football final when Mick Higgins led Cavan to their fifth All-Ireland senior title by beating Meath, the *Irish Independent* was fulsome in its praise of the Cavan captain. 'It is not often that an All-Ireland turns out to be such a triumph for an individual but without him, and the apparent indifference with which he ambled up to every free, the result could well have been different.' On the following Friday, the same news-paper nominated him as 'Sports Star of the Week'. Later, in December of that year, he was awarded 'Sportsman of the Year'. Higgins, who was born in America, lived in Mayo and played minor football with Kildare, was now a true blue Cavan hero.

Between 1933 and 1952 Cavan won five senior All-Ireland titles and were beaten finalists on four other occasions. In their greatest period of provincial dominance, sixteen Ulster titles were also secured. During that era the Breffni men produced marvellous footballers. Those All-Ireland winning captains, Jim Smith, Hugh O'Reilly, John Joe O'Reilly (twice) and Mick Higgins, fell into the category of the greatest. But Cavan supporters of that time will enthusiastically proclaim Higgins as the best centre half-forward of all. Former Kerry half-back Jackie Lyne, who played against Higgins in the famous 1947 All-Ireland final in New York's Polo Ground, had no doubt about the veracity of this. 'Mick was the greatest centre half-forward I ever faced bar none.'

When Mick was a small boy, his parents returned from America to Ireland firstly to his mother's place in Kilnaleck, Co. Cavan, before moving to Kiltimagh, Co. Mayo, where his father was born, then back to Kilnaleck to complete his primary school education. Future Cavan star forward Peter Donohoe was a fellow primary school pupil. Tony Tighe made his appearance when he started playing football with

Mountnugent in the U-14 county league. Interestingly, when the Cavan senior football team became famous for their unique brand of forward play, the names of Higgins, Donohoe and Tighe were all involved in their magnificent attacking division.

Mick made his debut for the Cavan junior team in 1942, and the following year he looked a real prospect for the senior panel for the Ulster championship. They beat Monaghan in the provincial final and Higgins felt very much at home when he lined out at centre half-forward against Cork in the All-Ireland semi-final. He made a solid contribution to his side's 1-8 to 1-7 winning scoreline.

In the 1943 All-Ireland final against Jimmy Murray's marvellous Roscommon team, the two counties finished level at 1-6 each. Roscommon won the replay, with the bulk of the credit going to their great midfield partnership of Liam Gilmartin and Éamon Boland.

Roscommon were one of the best football forces at that time in Connacht and they were to prove that very forcibly when they again provided the opposition for Cavan in the 1944 All-Ireland semi-final. Roscommon hammered the Breffni men by 5-8 to 1-3, a result that did little to improve Cavan's morale, despite the fact that they were still the driving force in Ulster.

In 1945 Cavan defeated Fermanagh in the provincial final. They scraped through their All-Ireland semi-final against Wexford, only to come up against old rivals Cork in the decider. Once again luck didn't go Cavan's way and they went down by four points, 2-5 to 0-7. An Antrim side which included Harry O'Neill, George Watterson, Seán Gallagher, Kevin Armstrong, Seán Gibson and Paddy O'Hara shocked Cavan in the Ulster final that year. One of the great duels in that game was between Cavan's Phil 'Gunner' Brady and Antrim's Harry O'Neill. Antrim was the only county to measure up to Cavan in that period of Ulster football. Antrim performed very favourably in the All-Ireland final that year, but they were muscled out of it by the more physically endowed Kerry men.

In 1947 events were taking place on the GAA front which were eventually to make football history. For the three previous years, Canon Hamilton of Clare had been making strenuous efforts at Congress to have the All-Ireland football final played in America. Because of the potato blight which affected the country's stable food, thousands of people had to emigrate to the States. He argued that it would be a great psychological boost to generations of Irish Americans, who might never see the 'auld country' again, in the centenary year of 'Black 47'.

At the GAA Congress of 1947 it appeared that opinion on exporting the All-Ireland football final to America was building up against the move, and Canon Hamilton sensed it too. During an adjournment in the debate he began canvassing delegates for their support. He produced a letter from an exiled priest, stating how privileged he would be if the All-Ireland final would take place in the US. When Congress resumed there was now strong vocal support for the motion. General secretary Padraig Ó Caoimh and Tom Kilcoyne, secretary of the Connacht council, were sent to New York to make preliminary investigations. They reported back to the Central Council, a vote was taken, and by 20 votes to 17, council decided to play the All-Ireland in the Polo Grounds in New York. That decision meant one thing: the winners of the All-Ireland semi-finals that year would earn the trip and the historical game of a lifetime in the Big Apple. Cavan faced Roscommon in their All-Ireland semi-final and won 2-4 to 0-6.

The Munster final that year brought Kerry and Cork together and it promised to be one of the most competitive and vigorously contested finals of all time. Weeks before the final, it rained incessantly, although on the day of the match the weather was fine. But the Cork Athletic Grounds, which lay below the level of the River Lee, began to show signs of wear and tear as the game progressed, a factor, according to Éamon Young, that was to prove the greatest possible help to Joe Keohane and the Kerry man's 'roguery'. With just five minutes remaining, Kerry were ahead by two points when one of their defenders conceded a penalty. If it was converted, Cork would be in the All-Ireland semi-final with every chance of capturing the Sam Maguire in the Polo Grounds. Referee Simon Deignan (Cavan) duly placed the ball on the centre of the fourteen-yard line as Kerry's Bill Casey was receiving treatment for an injury. Éamon Young told me that it was during those moments that Joe Keohane perpetrated the most appalling 'robbery' in the history of Gaelic football.

Said Youngie: 'Lazily and with innocence written all over that honest face, Joe ambled out of the Kerry goalmouth, put his foot on the ball and got into a nice cosy chat with Jim Ahern, who had been delegated to take the Cork penalty kick. And why not? They were the best of friends. I suppose Joe knew that Jim Ahern had never missed a penno.

He also knew that Ahern had a kick like a mule and no goalkeeper, even of the calibre of Danno O'Keeffe, would stop the ball.' They chatted away—Jim ready to take the kick and Joe standing happily there with his foot on the ball. Bill Casey was pronounced fit to resume. Referee Deignan finally indicated that the kick be taken. Jim Ahern, settled himself to take the kick, behind him most of the Cork team, including Éamon Young.

Jim Ahern struck the ball. To the astonishment, dismay and utter fury of every Cork supporter in the vast crowd, and the Cork players on the pitch, there was a numbing shock. Instead of the anticipated rock-et that should have hit the Kerry net, the ball trickled harmlessly along the ground and straight towards the welcoming hands of Danno O'Keeffe. He gathered the ball gratefully and dispatched it downfield. Thus ended Cork's hopes of making the transatlantic trip to America.

To this day Éamon Young—and he laboured the point vehemently to me—swears that by the time that kick came to be taken, the ball had been pressed at least three inches into the mud by the solid boot of Joe Keohane. While that chat was going on Joe, he claimed, had been forcing the ball deeper and deeper into the mud. 'Pure villainy,' says Éamon, though he admitted he would have done exactly the same if the opportunity had presented itself to him.

Naturally, Joe Keohane disclaimed all knowledge of the incident cited by the Cork star, and was actually visibly disturbed that he should be accused of such a foul act. He suggested that the ball had become sodden and encrusted with mud and the extra weight forced it into the heavy, yielding ground. 'Jim Ahern, when he was taking the kick, most probably dug his foot deeply into the ground to compensate for the appalling conditions, and that may have been the cause of his poor penalty attempt.' Continuing, the great Kerry full back said: 'I may have inadvertently placed my foot on the ball before the kick was taken, but to suggest that the ball had been stamped into the ground is ridiculous. Had this been the case, how could I have got away with such a manoeuvre when all the Cork players, bar the goalkeeper, were crowded around the goal area? Remember these were intelligent men, very experienced footballers and most of them All-Ireland medal-winners who were wise to what one could or could not get away with on a football pitch. There was even a future prime minister of Ireland among them [Jack Lynch]. I was also under the close scrutiny of 25,000 Cork supporters. And

Cork people are deservedly credited with being a crafty, brainy breed. It would be difficult for me to pull the wool over their eyes. If my explanation is still unacceptable, will someone please tell me how a simple Kerry man like myself could fool the said 25,000 people, plus the Cork team, including a future taoiseach, in the broad daylight of a Sunday afternoon in an open field.'

And there you have it. Who do you believe? Éamon Young, that stalwart Cork midfielder on that famous occasion told this writer that Keohane admitted to him quietly, 'It was not very sporting, I admit, Éamon, but I could see the Manhattan skyline.' Mick Higgins, who was a great friend of the wily Kerry man, recalled a comment he made after the two counties were returning from a tournament game in England, when he said: 'The next time we meet will be in the All-Ireland final in New York. I have no doubt about that.' Keohane's prediction wasn't made lightly, but it was prophetic.

As events subsequently turned out, Kerry easily defeated Meath 1-11 to 0-5 in their semi-final, and so the most talked about All-Ireland football final of all time was to be contested by Cavan and Kerry. It meant a return to the land of his birth for Mick Higgins, 3,000 miles from home and among three generations of the Irish diaspora.

Both counties trained diligently for the epic battle between the best two sides in the land. Cavan had an extra edge in training as they worked out a little longer than the Munster men, who travelled by sea to New York. The bulk of the Cavan team flew out.

The heat was oppressive and the game was played on a rock hard pitch which belonged to the New York Giants baseball team. Referee for the game was Martin O'Neill (Wexford), who was also the Leinster provincial secretary. The Mayor of New York, Bill O'Dwyer, a native of Bohola in Mayo, threw in the ball. Simultaneously, every household in Ireland with a wireless set crowded around it as they listened intently to Michael O'Hehir's exciting commentary from so far away. Radio Éireann's decision to cover the 1947 final, the first live outside radio broadcast they had undertaken, came in for high praise from listeners all over the country.

Kerry totally dominated the opening quarter. The Kerry star in attack was undoubtedly Batt Garvey. He followed up a Gega O'Connor point with a smashing goal in the tenth minute. The prospect of a very one-sided game looked on the cards when Eddie Dowling got through for another Kerry goal and it was 2-1 to 0-1. Midway through the first half Cavan were eight points in arrears and badly needed an inspirational score. The Breffni men, cheered on by their fans, suddenly came to life. The Cavan selectors moved P. J. Duke to wing back from midfield. Mick Higgins was now in full stride and his opportunistic goal inspired the team. The great forward understanding which had been built up saw Cavan at their brilliant best. Swift hand-passing between Higgins, Peter Donohoe, Tony Tighe and Joe Stafford opened up gaps in the Kerry defence for scores. Cavan had turned the game around and at the interval led 2-5 to 2-4.

The combination of extreme heat (98°F), unfamiliar humidity and the rock hard pitch slowed up the action and the quality of the football after the interval. Cavan restarted the closely fought exchanges very positively. Their fitness and youth began to pay dividends. They were ahead 2-8 to 2-7, but Kerry were still very much in the match. The game's three concluding scores came from the Breffni men. First, the unerring boot of Peter Donohue gave Cavan a two-point advantage, before the magnificent Mick Higgins, coming downfield on solo runs, cracked over a brace of brilliant points. Kerry had a chance of saving the game, but sub Tim Brosnan crashed the ball off the crossbar in the final minute.

When the final whistle sounded, Cavan had achieved GAA history. They became the first county to capture an All-Ireland crown outside Ireland. They had also completed a league championship double, as they had beaten Cork in the league final earlier in the spring.

Michael O'Hehir made his own piece of history with a superb running commentary of that 1947 final. Adding immeasurably to the excitement was his plea to the cable company: 'Give me five minutes more, please. Don't pull the plug.' Someone heard his plea though the commentary went six minutes over its time. O'Hehir had saved the day, much to the enjoyment of his countrywide listeners.

Cavan joy could not be contained as they celebrated the most famous All-Ireland victory of all time. Peter Donohue captured the imagination of the New York scribes. He was dubbed the 'Babe Ruth' of Gaelic football by Arthur Daley of the *New York Times* and Don Parker of the *Mirror*. It was a rare honour indeed to be compared with the star of American baseball.

Cavan retained their All-Ireland crown the following year when they defeated a really great Mayo team which included Seán Flanagan,

Paddy Prendergast, Éamon Mongey, Pádraig Carney, Tom Langan and Peter Solan. This was a very competitive match with the outcome in doubt until the final whistle. Cavan were holding on to a one-point lead when Mayo were awarded a scorable free. The shrewd Mick Higgins, standing on the Cavan goal line, realised the likely trajectory of Pádraig Carney's kick and blocked it. He went off on a solo run, retaining possession, knowing that the final seconds were ticking away, and he held on to the ball until referee J. Flaherty (Offaly) blew the final whistle. Mick Higgins had won back-to-back All-Ireland titles. Mayo's brilliant defender Seán Flanagan, in an after-match comment, said: 'The secret of that great Cavan team was their ability to create scores for one another. The main plank in their success was due to Mick Higgins and Tony Tighe. We never got to grips with them.'

Cavan were going for three in a row when they faced Meath in the 1949 All-Ireland final, but this time the challenge was a really tough one. Meath had the best-drilled, best-balanced and, more importantly, the most compact combination at that time. In Mícheál O'Brien, Paddy O'Brien and Kevin McConnell, Meath possessed the finest full back line I have seen in Gaelic football. They also had forwards of the highest calibre in Frankie Byrne, Peter McDermott, Mattie McDonnell and Paddy Meegan. No matter how hard Cavan tried, they were unable to match the brilliance of the Leinster champions, who won by a clear four points.

When the sides met again three years later little had changed. The old rivalry of the neighbouring counties was as keen as ever. The meeting was highlighted by the inclusion of the Cavan-born Maguire brothers, Liam, Des and Brendan. Liam and Des played with Cavan, while Brendan lined out with Meath. Before the throw-in the three brothers met in the centre of the field and shook hands. This symbolic gesture was in recognition of the historic fact that in the history of the GAA they were the only brothers to play against each other on All-Ireland final day. But it really was the exceptional performance of the Cavan captain, Mick Higgins, who was chaired off the pitch after a fantastic display of point-taking and general all-round brilliance that brought Cavan's fifth All-Ireland success and Mick's third title.

SÉAMUS HOARE

Goalkeepers in any field game are in a class of their own. The men in the last line of defence are often said to be guardians of the loneliest position on the field of play.

Be that as it may, football has had a rich vein of these heroes of rearguard action. Pick any era at random and you will find goalkeepers featuring prominently—men who time and time again proved their mettle in one of the most exciting positions in team sports.

Some blazed magical trails over short periods only to fade from the scene. There were others, however, whose mastery of the art and consistency ensured that they gave long service before eventually bowing out. Séamus Hoare belonged to the latter category, having guarded the Donegal net at senior inter-county level from the mid-fifties through to the late sixties. The north-west county did not win an Ulster senior title during his long tenure between the posts, but that doesn't take away the Letterkenny man's right to rank up there with the best-ever in the position in any county or era.

His excellent instant reflexes were backed up with coolness, good judgment and a swift and deliberate clearance in the face of many a serious examination, and he came through with the highest possible marks, not just with Donegal but also during a lengthy spell as Ulster's No. 1 in the Railway Cup (now the M. D. Donnelly inter-provincial series).

Hoare played his part in writing a historic chapter in the senior football annals of his county. Donegal have been so prominent in the game in modern times and frequent visitors as well to Croke Park of late that it is hard to realise that they did not actually contest a provincial senior decider until 1963.

Hoare contributed to earning that breakthrough with a semi-final win over defending champions, Cavan, who were then still a real force in the game. Not only that; Donegal's speedy, clever and purposeful display forged out such a handsome win against the one-time title specialists (4-5 to 0-6) that the nation sat up and took notice.

The prospects of a long-awaited first title looked encouraging in the build-up to the Breffni Park showdown with Down, despite the fact that the Mourne county had a strong framework of survivors from their All-Ireland title-winning squads of 1960 and 61. However, the north-west county failed to come up to expectations and were well beaten, 2-11 to 1-4, although Hoare was still one of their stars.

Hoare's top-class goalkeeping that season did not go unnoticed by the Ulster selectors. They called him up for the 1964 Railway Cup and his performance was such that he began a very successful and long sojourn between the posts for the province.

The goalkeeping giant from St Eunan's club, like so many more down the years in Gaelic games, graduated to the premier ranks from under-age competitions. The budding skills that were to blossom brightly with Donegal and Ulster earned him a place in goal in the now long-suspended Colleges' inter-provincial championships. He stepped up then to senior championship action with the county team against Monaghan in 1955 and it says much for his expertise and, above all, his consistency in this demanding role that he went on to give fifteen years' great service to the county.

Hoare made his second appearance in an Ulster senior final in 1966 in a match that commands an extra special place in the annals of live television coverage of the national games. That final at Casement Park was the first-ever provincial football decider televised live. The telecast was by the BBC in the North and was relayed to a countrywide audience by RTÉ.

Donegal had much to encourage them in their bid to take revenge over Down for their defeat three years earlier. They had racked up an impressive number of goals on the way to the final, recording nine from their impressive wins over Cavan and Fermanagh. They also had a much more experienced side compared with that in 1993, with the majority of that side still to the fore in the team for Casement Park.

However, the game did not live up to expectations. There was too much petty fouling throughout, although the match did end with an exciting final ten minutes as Donegal moved up a gear on their earlier display in an all out bid to save the day.

They had squandered some good scoring chances earlier on and in the final stages found the Down defence in a miserly mood when it came to providing opportunities for scores, and they lost by 1-7 to 0-8.

Donegal, with Hoare again keeping a sound goal, recovered so well from that defeat that they earned a place in the 1967 National League semi-final for the third successive year. Beaten by Kerry in the 1965 and Longford in the 1966 semi-finals, their third outing, against Galway, who the previous September completed their only treble of All-Ireland senior titles, commands a special place in the folklore of Donegal football.

It looked like a welcome change of fortune for the Ulster county when they led by three points after twenty-five minutes, and they were then awarded a penalty kick. Because a stiff wind was blowing across the pitch, the ball moved after the referee's whistle and was then handled by the Donegal kicker. As a consequence the referee then awarded a free out to Galway, who went on to chalk up a three-point win.

The cool and competent Hoare was on duty in all three games. He was there on another famous first for Donegal in 1965 when the county won the Dr Lagan Cup (a then all-Ulster division of the National League) for the first time and followed on by retaining the trophy over the next two years.

Séamus was one of a talented group of footballers who carved out a golden spell for Ulster in the 1960s in the Railway Cup. The North regained the trophy in 1963 after a three-year interval when they had another of the all-time great goalkeepers, Thady Turbett (Tyrone), on duty. He won his second inter-provincial medal that year.

Hoare took over in the No. 1 position in 1964 and won three Railway Cup medals in succession. He was still on duty when a year later Connacht spiked Ulster's bid for a fifth successive title in the final. However, it was just a stop light on the road as Ulster were back again in 1968 to regain the title with the Donegal goalkeeper again on duty.

The final that year against Leinster was his last and there can be no disputing the fact that he made a major contribution to that golden era, a contribution that, furthermore, earned him a place apart as the first Ulster goalkeeper to win four Railway Cup medals. Brian McAlinden (Armagh) equalled that record in 1979, 80, 83 and 84.

Hoare also gave great service to St Eunan's and guarded the net in their county senior championship wins of 1960, 67 and 69—further strong evidence of how he maintained the highest standards at club and county level over a lengthy period. A player in any position had to have something extra special to do that!

16

EUGENE HUGHES

O ne footballer or hurler does not make a team, but it is nevertheless true that a particular player can prove a vital influence
in turning the key in the door to important successes. Such a
player was the versatile Eugene Hughes, whose ability to scale the
heights in a variety of roles, allied to his mastery of the arts of the game,
established him as one of the foundation stones of a great era for
Monaghan football.

Monaghan struck it rich in a ten-season campaign from 1979 to 88,
during which they won three Ulster senior titles and joined the ranks
of National League title-winners. Hughes was a consistent star of that
era with his quality play, ranging from defence to midfield, and in a
number of roles up front. A player of great skill, he gave whole-hearted
commitment in every game he played. Not only that, he also found
time to make his mark as a capable hurler with the county team.

When Monaghan lined out against Donegal at Clones in the 1979
Ulster senior final, they were bidding for their first title in forty-one
long years. They ended the barren spell with a good all-round display
of football, with Hughes at right full back, one of the architects of the
1-15 to 0-11 win. Kerry proved far too good for the Ulster champions in
the All-Ireland semi-final—they powered to a 5-14 to 0-7 win—but it
says much for the resilience of the Monaghan men that they quickly
bounced back to achieve a rare Croke Park victory.

That was in the now suspended Ceannarus Tournament final
against Roscommon, in which Hughes illuminated the November
gloom of 1979 with a majestic display at right full back. He was only
back a few weeks from a testing US tour with the Bank of Ireland All
Stars—he played in all four games on the tour—but such was
his enthusiasm and drive that he worked non-stop from first to final

whistle. The Castleblayney Faughs club man popped up all over the place at the right spot at the right moment to provide the type of inspiring play that helped to lift his team and send them confidently on their way to a famous 1-12 to 1-7 win. He even scored a point. The performance was the best possible way for Hughes to herald his Bank of Ireland All Stars award a few weeks later at right full back, and with it ranking as the first from the county to earn such an honour.

Eugene Hughes, widely known as 'Nudie', was 24 a few days before that eye-catching display against Roscommon in the Ceannaras final. He played minor and under-21 with the county and was still eligible for the under-18 ranks when he made his senior inter-county debut at right full back.

After their return to the top in Ulster in 1979, Monaghan looked on course for bright days in the 1980s. But fate is fickle and things did not work out in the early years as hoped and generally firmly expected. Indeed, at the start of 1982 Monaghan were in danger of relegation to Division IV of the National Football League. Seán McCague, who was team manager in 1979, was reappointed to the post in 1982 and under the guidance of the man who was later to become president of the association, their fortunes improved.

A major breakthrough came in 1983 when Monaghan, with Hughes a bright ace in the forward pack, beat the then newly crowned National League champions Down at Newry by 0-9 to 0-4 in the Dr McKenna Cup (an all-Ulster knock-out competition) final. Less than a year later Monaghan were on another rare Croke Park visit to meet Meath in the final of the Centenary Cup. That tournament was part of the celebrations of the GAA centenary year. They lost that game by two points but put that experience to good effect to get back to headquarters about a year later to sip at the sweet cup of success following a gripping encounter with Armagh in the National League final. During the march to that historic game Hughes, at times as a third midfielder and at others as an orthodox forward, left his imprint prominently on the successful run-in, and also hit some valuable scores. Monaghan beat Armagh by 1-11 to 0-9 for a first-ever national senior title. Although left full forward Hughes scored only a point in the game, he still made a huge contribution to the success with his creative and tireless play.

More glory came the way of the county that summer. Hughes was a truly commanding figure with his intelligent play in a one-sided 2-9 to o-8 win over Derry at Clones that brought the Ulster crown back to the Farney county after an interval of six years. He was supremely on his game all through that contest and also chipped in with a brace of points. It was a case of so near and yet so far for Monaghan in their All-Ireland semi-final against Kerry, then at the height of their power and also the defending champions. The game went to a replay.

When the teams first met, Monaghan played early on like seasoned All-Ireland campaigners. They were in no way overawed by their famed opponents and had the better of the first half exchanges, thanks in no small measure to an attack orchestrated in splendid fashion by Hughes. The Northern attacking force varied their game from short passing to long through kicks. Kerry did not register their first score until the sixteenth minute, and Monaghan might have been further ahead than 1- 5 to 1-1 at the break. The Kingdom stepped up their scoring rate in the second half. Eleven points were popped over as compared with Monaghan's five scores, 1-4. The defending champions looked to have secured a late winner with a point from Michael Sheehy, but in the tension-laden concluding minutes up stepped Monaghan right half-forward Eamonn McEnaney, displaying ice-cool nerve and accuracy, to send over the bar and tie the game at 2-9 to Kerry's 1-12. The Ulster county lined out in the replay with high hopes of a first final outing since 1930, but they were well beaten, 2-9 to 0-10.

That set-back still could not dull the memories of Nudie's football during the year when it came to All Stars selection time, and few could have been surprised when his selection at left full forward earned him a place in a small band of footballers honoured in defence and attack.

Monaghan lost their league title in a final show-down with Laois in 1986. Two years later Eugene Hughes won his last Ulster senior medal and it was surely appropriate that he marked the occasion with a 'man of the match' display against Tyrone at Clones. This was one of the versatile forward's best-ever performances. He scored the only goal of the game in the first half, and helped himself as well to three points to finish top scorer for either team.

In addition to his scoring flair, Nudie in the No. 13 jersey provided many classic touches in general play, created opportunities for his colleagues and all in all proved a real thorn in the O'Neill county defence. This was a display to savour from the Castleblayney man and a key factor in shaping the 1-10 to 0-11 win. Hopes of an All-Ireland final outing were later ended by Cork, who had a somewhat surprisingly comfortable eleven points to spare at the final whistle. But, as was the case three years earlier, Hughes still found favour with the All Stars later that year at left full forward for his third award, a tribute to the consistently high standard of play the Monaghan man maintained over a lengthy period.

Understandably, the cultured football of Hughes was not overlooked by Ulster in the Railway Cup. Here, too, he served the province both as a defender and as a forward. It was in his early position of right full back that he won his first inter-provincial medal in 1980. Three years later at right half-back he collected a second medal. In centenary year 1984 he helped Ulster to a successful defence of the title from the left full forward berth.

In what was a busy time for Monaghan on the inter-county front, Eugene also found time to contribute to club competitions with Casleblayney Faughs. He won county championship and county league medals with the club and was also a driving force when Castleblayney captured the Ulster club title in 1986. In addition, he joined the ranks of county senior medallists in hurling also with Castleblayney Faughs.

Eugene Hughes, then, undoubtedly commands a proud place in the annals of Monaghan football, and also in that large company of players who have proven their ability as champion competitors in a number of positions.

17

IGGY JONES

It is a cliché in Gaelic games nowadays to say that 'the school boys of today are the seniors of tomorrow', but it is still true none the less. The exploits of one-time college and minor hurlers and footballers scaling the heights in top-class competitive, senior competitions are prominently featured in the history of the national games. Many names spring to mind, but not many scored 3-4 in an All-Ireland under-age final and went on to prove a dazzling star of senior inter-county competitions for some ten seasons.

That briefly encompasses the career of Iggy Jones of Tyrone who, without doubt, must be included in the ranks of those great players who did not get among the All-Ireland senior championship medals.

Ireland, like the rest of the world, was struggling to recover from the ravages of World War II when St Patrick's, Armagh, and St Jarlath's, Tuam, ushered in a new era in Gaelic games when they met at Croke Park in 1946 in the first All-Ireland Colleges' senior football championship final. Jones lined out at centre half-forward for St Patrick's, while at midfield for the western college was another who was also to go on to grace the game at senior level, Seán Purcell.

The final was an epic encounter and proved a personal triumph for Jones from Dungannon. The lightly built nine and a half stone forward gave one of the best individual performances by any player in any game with his speedy, incisive and clever football, his dazzling solo runs and, above all, his expert finishing technique.

Jones really came into his own in the second half. Things did not look all that bright for the northerners at the interval when they trailed by 2-3 to 0-6, but what a transformation after the change of ends! The Dungannon youth, who scored four points in the opening half, turned the game completely around with a superb treble of goals, all after defence-splitting solo runs from midfield, to power St Patrick's to a thrilling 3-11 to 4-7 win. It was an all-round performance of sheer brilliance from Jones and one worthy of the historic occasion that the final was.

But then he had earlier provided plenty of evidence of the maturing talents that were to grace so many games as a senior. From 1927 to 1956 the Colleges' council promoted inter-provincial championships and Jones played with Ulster for three successive seasons, 1943 to 1945. The individual championships were played in 1946, 47 and 48. The inter-provincial championships ended in 1956, and a year later the individual colleges' tests were revived.

Back to Iggy Jones of the zig-zagging and spectacular solo runs, and on the way to that All-Ireland Colleges' medal he scored three goals in the semi-final win over St Mel's, Longford. It was an indication of just what a special talent he was that a few months after his All-Ireland Colleges' medal win he was called up to the senior team for the Ulster championship. That marked the start of a twelve-year career with the county senior side, a career during which he played many outstanding games with Tyrone and also represented Ulster in the Railway Cup.

However, Jones had a long wait for his first Ulster senior medal. But when it came in 1956 at the expense of defending champions Cavan at Clones, it was well worth the wait. It was always an occasion at that time for any county to beat the Breffni men, then the dominant power in the North, in a championship game, let alone a provincial final. Tyrone scored five goals in impressive wins over Derry, runners-up for the 1955 title, and Monaghan, on the way to that first provincial final appearance in fifteen years.

Despite their good form, the general opinion—at least outside the O'Neill county—was that this latest bid for a first provincial senior title would prove a bridge too far. But what a surprise awaited the doubters! Tyrone not only showed no signs of big game nerves from the throw-in, but had the ball in the Cavan net after only a couple of minutes. Despite that bright start they managed just one more score before the interval—a point—to lead by the minimum margin at the end of a low-scoring half.

Tyrone improved greatly after the change of ends. They took the game to their more fancied opponents with flair and determination, conceded just one point and finished more convincing winners than even their most ardent supporters could have expected at 3-5 to 0-4.

Not surprisingly, Jones, who lined out at right half-forward, made an outsize contribution to the success. He was in fine form all through, cleverly setting up scores for his team mates. Well into the second half, he scored his side's third goal, one that really convinced everyone present that a new era had dawned up North. Jones finished with 1-1.

The Ulster final had provided Tyrone with a really encouraging build-up, then, for their senior championship debut at Croke Park against Galway in the All-Ireland semi-final. Hopes of another historic breakthrough by the O'Neill county were not realised. But they made a bonny fight of it in a thrilling game that kept over 50,000 spectators enthralled until the final whistle, with Galway edging through in a low-scoring encounter by 0-8 to 0-6.

Jones provided one of the highlights of the game. He went off on a dazzling second half solo run right through the Galway defence from the right wing and was only foiled of a goal by an alert Jack Mangan in the Galway goal. The fast, elusive and light Tyrone finisher punched the ball forward, but was deprived of what would have been the winning goal by a great save by Mangan.

Tyrone's brave bid was enhanced by Galway's achievement in beating Cork in the final, a game in which the western full forward Frankie Stockwell scored a then individual record for an All-Ireland final, 2-5. Jones had made his mark nationally before Tyrone's Ulster title breakthrough—so much so that he was honoured by Ireland in 1954.

In 1950 the GAA began a new series of representative games between Ireland and the Combined Universities for the Dr Ryan Cup. The Tyrone ace, who stood up so well to the hurly-burly of inter-county football with his nine and a half stone frame, was chosen at left full forward for Ireland—no mean achievement when you consider that his team mates included such well-known stars of the time as Stephen White (Louth), Tadghie Lyne (Kerry), Mal McEvoy (Armagh), Tom Dillon (Galway) and Jack Mangan (Galway). How ironic, then, that team mates of 1954 were to prove central figures in that dramatic moment provided by Jones and Mangan in the All-Ireland semi-final two years later!

Tyrone retained their Ulster title in 1957 with good wins over Armagh, Donegal and Derry, but the master of the solo run missed the final with an injury. He was back in the attack for the All-Ireland semi-final against Louth, but once more hopes of a Sam Maguire Cup outing were unsuccessful. Another Ulster medal eluded Iggy Jones during the rest of his playing career with Tyrone. But he still played many a good game with the county and Ulster. He also had his successes on the local front and helped Dungannon Clarkes to four county senior titles. He was also secretary of the club for a lengthy spell.

18

MICKEY KEARINS

'I remember my first Railway Cup game against Leinster in Ballinasloe in 1963,' says Mickey Kearins. At the start, as I was moving into position before the ball was thrown in, I noticed my direct opponent Paddy McCormack [Offaly] digging a hole along the ground with his boot.

'You're young Kearins from Sligo?' he asked. 'I presume you expect to go back to Sligo this evening.'

'Hopefully,' I said.

'Well,' he said, 'you have a fair chance of making it back if you don't pass that mark.'

Mickey passed the mark several times without mishap and proceeded to score four points from play.

It's amazing how that particular story has made the rounds, and I have heard it associated with Mick Lyons of Meath, Martin Quinn, also of Meath, Joe Keohane of Kerry, Gunner Brady of Cavan and Seán Doherty of Dublin, just to mention a few. But according to honest Mickey Kearins it was just a story. During his playing years I have always admired Kearins as a quiet-spoken footballer with all the talents and up there with the former greats, John Joe Lavin, Nace O'Dowd and the famous Colleran brothers.

Born in 1943 in Dromard, which lies between Sligo and Ballina, Mickey, after his primary school days, spent three years in St Muredach's College in Ballina, after which he went to work with his father in the cattle business. He was chosen on the Sligo minor football team in 1960 and performed very creditably at midfield against one of Galway's best players, Seán Cleary. Galway had a raft of other great players that year in Noel Tierney, Johnny Geraghty, Séamus Leydon, Christy Tyrell and Gerry Prendergast, all of whom went on to achieve

All-Ireland greatness later. Encouraged by his father, a former hurler and footballer with Sligo, Mickey quickly made it on to the Sligo senior team in 1961 and was chosen two years later on the county championship squad. He was picked for his first National League outing against Cavan in Ballymote.

He was very favourably mentioned even though opposed by the great Gabriel Kelly. His first senior provincial championship blooding was against the reigning champions, Roscommon. Sligo lost by a point following a last-minute Roscommon goal. The defeat came as a great disappointment for the young Kearins, who apart from scoring several valuable points, thoroughly enjoyed all the excitement and pressure involved on that occasion. He got marvellous encouragement from such well-known team colleagues as Cathal Cawley, Pat Kilgannon, Joe Hannon and Bill Shannon.

It was extraordinary how quickly he made progress in the football ranks considering he went straight from winning a junior county title with St Patrick's in 1964 to senior level. There was no intermediate grade in Sligo at the time, so he went automatically to senior status in 1965.

Mickey made a very valid point when he emphasised the importance of the Railway Cup series for weaker counties. Their prospects of winning All-Ireland or even provincial titles are minimal. The numerous players figuring on the so-called weaker teams find great satisfaction and, indeed, pride when they are chosen for their province. The honour of representing their county when chosen for their province gives them a marvellous incentive to justify their selection. He said: 'It's a great occasion for players who are with weaker counties who never get the chance to play alongside good players from stronger counties. When I started in the 1960s, just imagine the thrill it was for me to play in the same forward line as the Galway lads of the three-in-a-row team. They always took me into the game. The Galway lads were very easy to play with. Whoever was in the best position got the ball.'

Mickey's inter-provincial record for Sligo is, of course, unsurpassed in his native county, where representative honours are rare. He played for thirteen consecutive years for Connacht with Dermot Early and the lion-hearted Gerry O'Malley. During those thirteen years he won provincial honours in 1967 and 69. Over his senior career he played in three forward berths, right and left half-forward and in his latter years at full forward. His scoring feats were mind-boggling at times.

Mickey played inter-county football for seventeen years starting in 1961 and finishing in 1978, and rarely did his standards drop. Indeed some of his scoring feats continually grabbed the newspaper headlines. In a drawn Connacht final against Galway around 1971, he scored fourteen points (five from play), and the nine placed balls included two from 45s and one from a sideline kick. Former great Galway star Jack Mahon, writing in his book, *The Game of my Life*, stated: 'I was present that day and regard it as the finest display of scoring artistry I have ever seen. The points from play were scored with both feet. Over the years I have seen marvellous scoring achievements from such as Mikey Sheehy, Paddy Doherty, Larry Tompkins, Tony McTague, Brian Stafford, Cyril Dunne, Martin McHugh and Jimmy Keaveney, but none to cap that one.'

Examples of Mickey Kearins's scoring sprees took place in Croke Park against the Combined Universities in 1973, for instance, when he scored twelve points, all from placed balls; on another day in Hyde Park against the same opposition he scored thirteen points, four or five of which were from play.

Being a marked man every time he lined out for Sligo or the province made Mickey very aware of his responsibility and his duty to the county. He admitted that he met a number of hard men who set out to stop him one way or the other. He felt that the opposition in Connacht was always fair, but outside the province he did meet some who were not. Naturally, being the county's sharpshooter brought its own problems for Mickey. Generally, he was singled out for special watching and that meant having opposing defenders breathing down his neck most of the time. Did it worry him? 'I got used to it and prepared myself for it. There were always great half-backs on most teams and I found Brian McEniff of Donegal always a handful. He would stick with you like a leech and rarely did anything out of turn. He was a great competitor and I would rate him as one of the best in half-back play.'

Sligo's lack of major successes could be attributed to a lack of interest in the game by some players once they reached senior inter-county level. The fault lay mainly in the attitude of some players towards training sessions. Around the 1960s and early 70s Kearins himself was a training fanatic when he was very much involved with the game. 'In those early years I trained at least four times a week. I used to train in the morning, often at six or seven o'clock, depending on my work. I'd run three or four miles in a field and that serious training lasted for ten years. I never practised much at place kicking, nor did I take a few practice pots at the goal before the game started.' He wasn't superstitious either or had any fads about his gear as some players had. He was naturally nervous before every match because the team depended on him for scores from frees and from play. Pointing his first score in a game was important to him; it helped to set him up for the remainder of the match. He admitted having poor games if he started a match badly and that tended to upset him.

He had no doubt that Seán Purcell of Galway was the greatest player he ever saw. Seán was immense. He could play well in any position on the field. Some players had the ability to score from the dead ball spot, or outfield opponents, or place balls to advantage for team colleagues. Purcell was a master of every skill. He rated Mick O'Connell of Kerry on a par with Purcell.

He feels that playing both soccer and Gaelic football has tended to obstruct the progress of both codes in former years. Some of the county players who played soccer earlier in the day were turning out in the evening for Gaelic matches. They wouldn't lift the ball and pass it around but preferred to play it on the ground. That pattern has changed for the better nowadays. More importantly still, there is a far better atmosphere prevailing among players at training sessions now than in his day.

In 1965 the Association of Gaelic Sports Journalists became involved in the Cardinal Cushing Games, a charity group set up in New York by John 'Kerry' O'Donnell. The committee was asked by O'Donnell to pick a selection of players to travel to New York to play against a New York team. The proceeds of the games would go to the Cushing charities. Guidelines were set out which would govern the selection of the players: (1) to honour players who had given outstanding service to Gaelic games; (2) to include deserving players whose chance of a US trip with their counties were slight; and (3) to give representation to all four provinces.

Among the football contingent was Mickey Kearins of Sligo, who was a unanimous choice to make a first trip of a lifetime to the Big Apple. This writer was nominated to travel as the journalists' representative. The 1965 panel was something special, being the first to be chosen. We were put up in the Manhattan Hotel on 8th Avenue. The first series of games took place on the Sunday we arrived and they were a sell-out, attracting a full house to Gaelic Park. The net gate receipts were over 20,000 dollars. The excitement generated by the visiting players was unique. Mickey Kearins, who gave an exhibition of free-taking and all-round skills, was the hero of the day, playing a leading role in the visiting team's success.

When the game was over, Mickey was surrounded by Sligo well-wishers, seeking news of home and their families. He told me later: 'It was unbelievable out there. The excitement was like a Connacht final. They really took the game to heart and the home team didn't stand on ceremony. They wanted to win the game at all costs and that made it exciting. I was lucky that my free-taking was good. I think I lost only one chance, which didn't make any difference to the score at the end.'

The Sligo star really enjoyed his first visit to the States. During the interval of the first game, Mickey and the players met Senator Bobby Kennedy and his electioneering party. The following day the group was taken by coach to Washington DC and the Senate, after which they were brought to Arlington Cemetery; wreaths were placed on the grave of President John Kennedy. Every one of the visiting players felt it was one of the most exciting periods of their lives. They presented John 'Kerry' O'Donnell with a specially inscribed trophy on the eve of their departure for home in his eatery on 8th Avenue. It took him completely by surprise and he was genuinely touched by the gesture.

Mickey took up refereeing club games before the end of his playing career. His first major assignment was the 1978 Sligo county final. His main achievements in that field were refereeing four Connacht finals, a National Football League final, two All-Ireland club finals and a Railway Cup final, plus an All-Ireland senior football semi-final.

But he much preferred playing the game. He used to train with his club, St Patrick's, two evenings a week when he was refereeing, and it helped to keep the weight down. He claimed the All-Ireland semi-final between Dublin and Cork was one of his toughest matches. 'I sent Keith Barr off that day. He was involved in an incident five minutes earlier and he ran thirty or forty yards to get involved in the second incident. There was an awful lot of off-the-ball stuff that day and it was very difficult to control the game. But the goal Barr scored in the 1992 Leinster final against Kildare was the best I have ever seen.'

He sent Colm O'Rourke of Meath off in a National League game. 'It was an incident just after half-time when he got a heavy shoulder while in possession of the ball. It knocked the ball out of his hand, but instead of trying to retrieve it, he came after me. The play had moved to the other end of the field, but he followed me the whole way down, talking "friendly" to me all the way. I had to send him off.'

Mickey became involved with the Meath man again when he was doing the sideline during the 1988 All-Ireland final between Meath and Cork over a line ball decision. Colm felt that Mickey gave the wrong decision at that time. Mickey knew, having seen the replay of the decision on television that night, that he had committed an error of judgment. I can say, as a former referee, that match officials have to make instant decisions, some of which may not always be correct. We are human, you know?

He opted out of officiating at matches because he felt he was not getting proper backing from the board officials, which disappointed him. He didn't take up golf because it was too time-consuming. He admitted that international soccer was a big interest. On business trips to Britain he would take in games at Old Trafford and Ellen Road. In 1974 he travelled to the European Cup final in Paris. But his biggest sporting thrill remains a vivid memory—winning his first Sligo senior football championship title with St Patrick's, Dromard. And that would do nicely.

| JOE LENNON

Down, as bright as the flaming red jerseys they wore, pulverised Kerry in the first eight minutes of the 1968 All-Ireland football final at Croke Park to lay the foundation of a two-point victory, 2-12 to 1-13. The game in the second half was to prove something of an anti-climax, despite the gallant but fruitless uphill battle of the losers. Eight minutes after the throw-in, Down led by the astonishing, most intimidating margin of 2-3 to 0-1 and so feeble was the opposition, particularly at centrefield, that it seemed the Mourne Mountains would be looking down from their lofty eminence on the Macgillicuddy Reeks at the end of the hour. When Down put over four more points to lead 2-7 to 0-5 at the interval, the Kerry followers must have abandoned any hope of a recovery.

Six minutes after the restart there was still a yawning gap of eight points between the teams, but Kerry were now in charge. It was baffling that Down, whose mastery was not in the slightest degree exaggerated in the first half, could slump, almost disintegrate. Writing in the *Irish Independent* the following day, John D. Hickey commented: 'It would of course be impossible to pontificate on the point, but in my opinion Down's decline was primarily due to the fact that team captain Joe Lennon pulled a leg muscle early on and in the interest of the team did not resume after the interval. Lennon had performed with such distinction that he looked every bit a man about to turn in another "blinder" in the second half.'

Joe Lennon, captain of that 1968 Down team, actually pulled a ligament in his knee ten minutes before half-time and it was gradually getting worse. He told me, 'I could have played on and suffered the consequences, but I felt I would be letting the team down, playing to half my strength. Admittedly, I was stuck to my seat on the bench as our lead began to dwindle, but I knew we had the capacity and commitment to hang on for that famous victory.' Joe was always a quick healer, a family trait, and after a cartilage operation in Birmingham, was back in action within six weeks and a day. He was on the Down team that won the 1967/68 National League title and emerged as top scorer in the New York game at Gaelic Park.

Lennon's sporting career had taken many twists and turns before he stepped up on the Hogan Stand to accept the Sam Maguire Cup from GAA President Séamus Ó Riain after the 1968 victory over Kerry. He led his county to their third All-Ireland success, having played on the double winning teams of 1960 and 61. He was 13 years of age when the family moved from their home in Poyntzpass, Co. Armagh, to a farm in Lisnabraque, Co. Down. Only a few miles were involved in the move for Joe, but it was to open up new horizons for him and his family.

After leaving St Colman's College, Joe spent six years as a meteorologist before becoming a student again at Padgate College in Lancashire, where he qualified as a secondary school teacher. He became the first Irishman to obtain a first class honours diploma in physical education at Loughborough Training College, where he presented 'Coaching Gaelic Football for Champions' as a thesis for his diploma. Later he was the first Irishman to get an M.Sc. in recreation management at Loughborough. He was also a founder member and first President of the Physical Education Association of Ireland. Joe took up a job in Fermanagh and played with the Irvinestown club. He was promptly chosen on the Fermanagh team at a time when he was ignored by the Down selectors. He gave a superlative performance at midfield against Derry's brilliant Jim McKeever in the Ulster championship and that quickly caught the eye of the Down selectors. He was recalled to duty with Down the following year. His job as a meteorologist took him to the Persian Gulf and he spent two years in Bahrain.

While working in the Gulf, Joe became very proficient at badminton, having taken up the sport at Loughborough College. He would most certainly have become an international player, but a letter from home informed him that Down were going through a traumatic spell and that he was badly needed. Joe told me that he wrote back to his mother adding the line, 'I'll be home soon, back on the Down team and we will win the All-Ireland.' His mother kept the letter and presented him with it late in 1960 when the Down men overpowered Kerry in the All-Ireland final.

Joe, who captained Down in 1968, told me the following story: 'In 1968, I brought the Sam Maguire Cup to Poyntzpass for a few days and left it in Mickey Waddell's shop window. A fanatical Armagh supporter, who was also the local milkman, would not deliver milk to my relations, the Lennons of Poyntzpass, until I took the cup away again.'

Holding a first class honours diploma in physical education from Loughborough College looked a very impressive parchment, but when Joe approached the GAA to convene meetings to plan coaching courses, they were slow to react. A meeting was subsequently held on the morning of the Down-Kildare National League final and even though Joe was involved as the captain of Down, he made it his business to attend. His was the dominant voice at that meeting. He still collected the National League trophy from President Séamus Ó Riain later that day after Down had defeated Kildare in a well-contested decider.

I gave Joe Lennon plenty of airing on RTÉ at the time as he explained the benefits of proper coaching and training. There was a great response to the programme. The kind of fitness and coaching that Joe envisaged was only in its infancy at the time. But judging from the strides that coaching has taken in the interim, it only goes to prove that Joe was a man well ahead of his time.

Lennon can be compared to a number of famous names who made history following their exploits on the football and hurling fields, but whose recollections of past deeds quickly fade relatively soon after the event. This applies particularly in cases where time has dimmed the memory of the achievement. Joe, the holder of three All-Ireland senior football medals, could only single out one of his scores in his first All-Ireland final appearance in 1960. Kerry's Mick O'Connell is another star who has to search his memory in quest of particular match snippets which he has promptly forgotten. There are other players too whose recollections of a major involvement on the playing field quickly disappear in a matter of days after the event.

Lennon's sporting career had taken many twists and turns before he was cast in the role of a star player. He had a brilliant mind and his academic pursuits sparked off growing concerns about the lack of proper coaching and fitness practices in our national games. In 1963 he produced his first book, *Coaching Gaelic Football for Champions*. This led to the organising and staging of the first national coaching course in Gaelic football in Gormanston College in 1964 and a second one in 1965.

Fully immersed in the needs of players requiring special coaching and fitness lessons, he produced a second book, *Fitness for Gaelic Football*, and quickly followed up with a video of the same title. This won the Irish Television award for non-broadcast training videos which fared commendably in the World Television Finals in New Orleans.

From 1976 to 1990, Joe spent considerable time and energy researching a method of presenting the playing rules of football with clarity. Having refereed at All-Ireland football final level, and having played at All-Ireland hurling final level, I was sharply reminded that my playing rules knowledge needed revision when I started. I also learned that over 50 per cent of players still do not know the rules, especially in football, and that goes for those officials in charge of teams also. Joe took on a gargantuan task when he started, as an individual, to draft and rewrite the entire playing rules. He must have been aware of the hazards involved in such a quest—as he was to find out. His research was initially discarded with contempt by officialdom. He more or less anticipated some opposition to change, but not to the extent it actually did. Undaunted, he gradually developed all the arguments for his format; more people started to listen. The huge undertaking took fourteen years to complete, and he rightly gives credit to the Meath County Board, the then chairman of the board Brian Smyth and secretary Liam Ó Craobhain, for their support. Motions appertaining to rule changes were passed at the Meath convention but were defeated at congress.

Joe's hard work was not in vain, however. Five years later, the motions were again passed at the Meath convention, and this time they got on to the congress agenda, which subsequently led to a special congress being held in December 1990. We now have a completely new format for presenting the rules of football and hurling, and defined terms are now part of the rules. The Down man is undoubtedly a Gaelic football enthusiast and has no time for those who seek to change the format which was laid down by the founders of the association. He believes our national games are important parts of our national identity and they should be treated with respect. I invited Joe on to my Sunday evening GAA radio programme during the close season in order to discuss with him the changing times of Gaelic football, and his opinions have never changed. He remains steadfast in most of his views.

I put the question to him: 'Have Gaelic games improved since his own playing days?' Naturally, Joe is a deep thinker and qualifies everything he speaks about in a very positive fashion. 'This is not as easy a question as may at first appear, for one should try to be objective, and this means dispensing with nostalgic memories of the 1950s and 60s era in which I played. Although the quality of the best football played by the best teams of any era may be taken as the standard by which to judge, I feel that the overall standards should be part of the consideration. One great team in an era of just one great team is not as impressive as one great team in an era where there are several great teams. One's view should reflect the overall standards of the time.'

Does one's experience and taste influence the decision? Joe responded: 'Clearly some people, usually the older fans, like the game where the ball is played most frequently with the foot, even though it can be shown that this was not the most efficient or successful game plan. Some people will argue that the frequency of high catches has declined, even though this assertion does not stand up to rigorous analysis— comparing the videos and counting the catches. It is very hard to dispel this nostalgic but mistaken view of the game.'

He makes a valid point when he states that the increase in the number of hand-passes now made by practically all inter-county teams is regarded by some as retrograde if not degrading our football game. This increase in hand-passing is the most significant change in our game since the turn of the century, and he feels it is here to stay. Hopefully, it will be refined by players and teams with the skill to retain possession and, importantly, advance the point of attack.

He then makes this point about the 'possession' game so successfully developed by Tyrone. 'Naturally the Tyrone style of possession football, which they have brought to a fine art, may be disliked by those who regard themselves as purists. There is no denying the fact that when team coaches accepted that possession should not be risked until a shooting opportunity developed, the short hand-passing game was here to stay.' Remaining with that point, Joe continued: 'Those who denigrate the game dominated by hand-passing and describe it as basketball overlook the fact that in all major games, including soccer, the hand is used to play the ball. In both forms of rugby football, the ratio of kicks to hand-passes is very small. Moreover, in American and Canadian football—offshoots of rugby—the ball is not kicked during play at all. Even in soccer, the hands are used to play the ball quite a lot.'

Joe takes none too kindly to the suggestion that the tackle, as in present-day football, is ruining the game and leading to a lot of stoppages and frees. He says that after the hand-pass, few other skills in any game have been hounded so much as the tackle. He says, despite what the rules of play state about it, some people appear not to accept that there is a tackle in our game. Unless they see a player grab an opponent around the body and pull him to the ground, they do not think they have seen a tackle.

Many times when we argue about the direction that Gaelic football is taking, Joe quickly reacts. He points the finger immediately at those who are articulating change in the playing rules. 'Those who wish to change Gaelic football into something closely resembling Australian Rules football know only too well, that if the Aussie rules-type tackle replaces our form of the skill, our games will be irrevocably changed. Gaelic football could survive even if the solo run and the number of successive hand-passes was restricted. These would be two more wounds like the loss of the ground kicks, but would be debilitating perhaps rather than terminal. The loss of our tackle would definitely be terminal,' he suggested.

Concluding this piece on the changing face of Gaelic football, Joe Lennon has the last few words: 'I do not think that our rules of play need anything more than minor amendments—cosmetic changes. We have very good sets of rules of play for both hurling and football. Those who say there is something seriously wrong with the football rules should realise that 95 per cent of rules of play for football are exactly the same as those for hurling. The game is its rules and the rules are the game. If we change the rules, we change the game.'

20

ANDY McCALLIN

The day of the dual player would appear to be coming to an end. Training has become so intense in recent years and over such lengthy periods that it has become more and more difficult for players to play at the top flight in both football and hurling. So, it looks unlikely that the coming years will see many additions to the ranks of dual players who enriched both games with their versatility and skills down through the years. Whether that is good or bad for the sports is a moot point, but what is beyond dispute is that the exploits of dual players have left a legacy of talking points.

That distinct group included an exciting talent from Co. Antrim, Andy McCallin, who not only displayed his skills to good effect in the top flight but also walked proudly into history in each code. He also commands a place apart in the annals of Antrim football as the county's solitary representative in the long history of the prestigious All Stars selections. McCallin helped to usher in the then new promotion as right full forward in the inaugural team of 1971. He was then in his early twenties and his selection was a tribute to his football ability when we consider that he shared the company of such stars as Donie O'Sullivan (Kerry), Pat Reynolds (Meath), Liam Sammon (Galway) and Seán O'Neill (Down). Although Antrim have not had cause to celebrate a major inter-county senior success in football for a lengthy spell, they have nevertheless consistently produced top-class players down through the years. That is why it is somewhat surprising that so far no other footballer from that county has since been honoured by the All Stars.

McCallin was a player of genuine ability, equally adept at football and hurling. He was a tireless worker, shrewd, creative, and a good finisher. He was also an influential figure in forging out some golden days for the saffrons in both codes.

The All-Ireland under-21 football championship was in its infancy when Antrim and Roscommon met at Croke Park in the final in 1969. The westerners had won their first final three years earlier, while the Ulster representatives were making their debut in the competition. McCallin, small of stature, had been to the fore with the Glens men on the way to the final and proved a very influential figure in the final at No. 13. He was also responsible for the decisive score of the day. Five minutes into the second half, wee Andy ran on to a punched pass from full forward Gerry Dillon and shot left footed for goal. His shot was deflected past the Roscommon goalkeeper by a defender—the only goal of the game. McCallin of the accurate left foot finished with 1-5, all but three points of his team's total, as the Ulster side squeezed through by the minimum margin. There then appeared to be bright days ahead for Antrim football, but the county has not won an Ulster senior title since or even contested another All-Ireland under-21 final.

McCallin, who won an Ulster junior medal in 1970, had stepped into the senior ranks with Antrim prior to that All-Ireland under-21 success. Indeed, he played in the Ulster senior final of 1970 and was their top marksman with 0-6 in an unsuccessful bid against Derry at Clones. A few months after that under-21 final win, McCallin was back at Croke Park, but in a different role, and also in winning and scoring form.

Antrim and Kildare lined out in the National Hurling League Division II final, with McCallin in the No. 13 jersey. The game had hardly started when the gifted young player had the ball in the Kildare net. They led all the way after that and, despite a sharpshooting performance from another dual player of that time, Paddy Dunney, who helped himself to 2-3 for the Lilywhites, Antrim took the title north for the first time by 2-13 to 3-8. McCallin followed up his early goal with a polished display of clever hurling to finish the star of the show. He was his team's top scorer with 1-5. That was the first leg of a great national double for Antrim and McCallin in hurling in 1970.

In August, the Glens men travelled to Ballinasloe to throw down the gauntlet to Galway in an All-Ireland intermediate championship quarter-final. The teams provided a keen encounter, with the sides level six times, but Antrim, with McCallin as their bright scoring star, finished ahead, 4-14 to 4-6. Not for the first time in a major game had Andy, at left full forward, headed his team's scoring returns with 1-4. That win earned the northerners a trip to Croke Park to take on Dublin for a place in the All-Ireland final. And what a thrilling encounter they provided before the Ulster champions, coached by former Cork ace Justin McCarthy, emerged winners by 3-15 to 2-11. Once again McCallin's speed, skill and finishing contributed richly to the success. Although he did not finish Antrim's top scorer that day (right full forward Brendan McGarry earned that rating with 2-2), he still finished with a splendid six points.

The story continued on an early October afternoon at Croke Park, and once again McCallin had a big say in ensuring that Antrim finished on the right note by seeing off Warwickshire. He scored four points as the Glens men powered to a resounding fifteen-point win—and a first All-Ireland intermediate hurling title. In the three games in the All-Ireland series McCallin scored 1-14.

Nor is that the end of the All-Ireland finals story. Eight long years later McCallin was back in search of a national award, but at club level. St John's, Belfast, showed good form in winning through to their first Ulster senior title and went on to reach the final against Thomond College, Limerick, who had earlier won their first Munster title. Thomond had a star-studded team that included Pat Spillane (Kerry), Brian Talty (Galway), Michael Heuston (Donegal) and Michael Kilcoyne (Westmeath). Team captain Pat Spillane gave them a good start with a goal after fifteen minutes and that really set Thomond College on the road to the title. However, the final provided much more entertaining fare than the final tally of 2-14 to 1-3 suggests. Not surprisingly, McCallin was the Belfast side's leading scorer with 1-1.

Andy was a regular with Antrim senior footballers for most of the seventies and year after year proved their leading scorer. He also made his mark as a dual player in the inter-provincial championship and got among the medals in the big ball game. In his early days in the senior grade he scored a fine goal as Ulster beat Connacht for the 1971 title— his only appearance in a football final winning team. Although he played hurling with Ulster, he did not reach a final, but still made his mark with the province.

This lively forward from Belfast St John's certainly had a huge impact on Gaelic games, even though an All-Ireland senior medal eluded him. And, one way or another, he saw more of the national championship action than many another from the North or further afield.

21

TEDDY McCARTHY

Who was the greatest dual player of all time? That is an impossible question to even try to answer, because many players have proved their class in both codes.

One also cannot overlook the fact that styles have changed down the years. The demands on players in terms of training and games schedules have greatly increased, especially in the modem era, and it is impossible to compare standards in one period with another.

Moreover, it would also be foolish to look exclusively to the men who won All-Ireland senior medals in both codes to try and select the greatest of them all. After all, down the years many starred with county teams in both codes and did not win even a provincial senior medal in either hurling or football.

So, it is really a pointless exercise to try and select one dual player for the supreme accolade. What can be said without dispute, however, is that Teddy McCarthy of Cork commands a unique ranking among the men who down the years displayed their skills to the best possible effect in both codes in top-flight competition.

Unique ranking? He alone won All-Ireland senior medals in hurling and football in the one year. Believe it or not, that record-making double in 1990 was his second time to inscribe his name in the ranks of dual All-Ireland medal winners.

McCarthy impressed at right half-forward in the Rebel county side that upset the odds when they beat firm favourites Galway in the 1986 Liam MacCarthy Cup tie. A remarkable feature of that success was that McCarthy played his first full senior hurling championship game in that particular match!

Three years later he became only the fifteenth player to win All-Ireland senior medals in both codes when he helped the footballers beat Mayo. That achievement on its own would have ensured him a proud place in the annals of Gaelic games. However, the Leesider went right to the top of the rankings of dual medallists by becoming the first—and so far the only one—to win the two premier awards in the games in the same month.

The Glanmire club hurler-cum-footballer's amazing double stands out as a tremendous achievement by any standard. Then as now, competition was very keen and the demands on players in terms of preparation and training very time consuming. And, just as is the case nowadays, it is a feat in its own right to capture an All-Ireland senior medal in any year, but to win hurling and football in the same month is *Boys' Own* story book material.

The double was a tribute not only to McCarthy's skills in both games, but to his dedication and enthusiasm. He made four appearances in hurling and two in football, missing Munster finals in both codes with an ankle injury. The fact that he fought back bravely from that set-back to regain his place in the Cork teams enhanced his feat even more.

A former county minor, his football talents were very much in evidence in the under-21 grade. He played important roles as a midfielder and as a forward in a golden era for Cork in that grade, winning three All-Ireland medals in succession (1984 to 1986).

The quality of his play was such that soon after winning his first All-Ireland senior hurling medal, he was chosen by Ireland for the 1986 International Series against Australia in Australia. He also got among the scores down under.

McCarthy lost no time in finding the target on his second appearance in the All-Ireland senior football final in 1988. A hard-working midfielder in the team that lost to Meath in the 1987 final, he was in the same position when the sides renewed rivalry the following year. That game was only three minutes old when he gave the Rebel county the best possible start by stealing in behind the defence to collect a pass from right full forward Denis Allen and found the net. That was the only goal of the game. The midfielder's score was followed by much wayward shooting by Cork—they had fourteen wides—and the game ended in a draw. Meath won the replay by a point. Cork, though disappointed, returned to final action the following year against Mayo.

That game is entitled to rank as the 'friendly final'. It was a memorable encounter, brightened by skilled play, good individual displays and fine sportsmanship. Cork led at the interval by two points, but three minutes after the change of ends Mayo went ahead with the only goal of the match. Cork bounced back from that set-back, and with McCarthy in fine form at midfield, went on to win by three points. Indeed, the brilliant dual star scaled the heights in the second half as he marched in spectacular style into the ranks of dual All-Ireland senior hurling and football medal winners. He also chipped in with a brace of points for the 0-17 to 1-11 win.

It was a remarkable coincidence that when McCarthy won his second All-Ireland senior hurling medal in 1990, it was at the expense of Galway who, as in the case four years earlier, had started firm favourites. He had a fine game at midfield, scoring three points in what was an enthralling final as Cork regained the title by 5-15 to 2-21.

The Rebel county had by then also earned their place in the All-Ireland football final against then keen rivals Meath. Could Cork become the first county to complete the first All-Ireland senior hurling and football double in the same year since Tipperary back in 1990? Would Teddy McCarthy record another individual double and also become the first to win both trophies in the same month? These were some of the questions that gave an added edge to an eagerly awaited final. There was also the fact that Cork had still to make a successful defence of the All-Ireland football title.

Unfortunately, the final did not live up to expectations, and it was punctuated with sixty-nine frees. Nevertheless, it still held interest all the way through and provided many bright moments. One of the best was the high-powered football of Shea Fahy at midfield for Cork. His quality play did much to ensure that the Munster county triumphed despite the handicap of playing with fourteen men for thirty-nine minutes (a forward was dismissed by the referee four minutes before the interval).

McCarthy lined out at left half-forward and had a good game, playing his part in a rare double for the county and a famous first for himself. That was his last All-Ireland senior medal in either code, but there could not have been a better way to end that chapter than on that historic note.

He won his only All Stars in football at right midfield in 1989 but failed to find favour in hurling. However, that takes nothing away from his outstanding contribution to the ancient game.

Was Teddy McCarthy, then, the greatest dual player of all time? That's a good question for debate, but one thing looks certain. It is likely to be a very long time—if ever—before his two All-Ireland medal wins in one year will be equalled.

22

JIM McDONNELL

Jim McDonnell could easily be described as one of the GAA's greatest sporting ambassadors, apart altogether from a lifetime involved in the promotion of Gaelic games, a brilliant player, administrator, GAA trustee and Compromise Rules tour manager. Following his retirement from playing, he took up fly-fishing and won an inter-provincial fishing medal with Ulster and was a former chairman of the Northern Fisheries Board. I always rated Jim McDonnell as one of the finest exponents of football, able to adapt to any position on the field of play. One of his great regrets was failing to win an All-Ireland medal in either senior or minor.

I had the pleasure of watching him in action when I refereed the 1952 All-Ireland minor final between Cavan and Galway, which the Connacht champions won deservedly on the day. Jim was a native of Drung and a former secondary school teacher and vice-principal in St Patrick's College, Cavan. He began his football career at college level and played with St Patrick's College, gaining selection for the Ulster Colleges inter-provincial team in 1953. He gained his place on the Cavan senior football team in the 1954 National League campaign right through until 1966, when he retired after twelve years of excellent service. He won three Ulster senior championship medals in 1955, 62 and 64 and captained the 1962 and 64 teams. While studying for his BA degree at UCD he won three Sigerson Cup medals in 1955, 56 and 57, captaining the team in 56. He also played for the Combined Universities and Ireland selections in those same years.

Jim's club career took off when he got his place on the Drung team in the 1950s, but he later joined Cavan Gaels and led the town team to their first senior championship title in 1965 when they defeated Bailieborough Shamrocks in the final. Cavan Gaels had been formed out of an amalgamation of Cavan Slashers and Cavan Harps and came into existence in 1957. As I mentioned earlier, McDonnell and great players like Tom Maguire, Charlie Gallagher and Gabriel Kelly operated on county teams who were very unlucky not to have won All-Ireland senior honours. Cavan's last All-Ireland title success was in 1952 under the captaincy of Mick Higgins. Indeed, for such a proud county, they have only five All-Ireland titles to their credit.

McDonnell's performance at wing back on the Cavan team in the All-Ireland semi-final against Kerry in August 1955 was masterful, especially since he was marking that elusive and very dangerous Kerry marksman, the late Paudie Sheehy. The game ended in a draw and the replay took place on 11 September. Kerry, who were noted as replay specialists, routed the Breffni men by 4-7 to 0-5.

The main talking point after the replay centred on the personal performance of McDonnell who was marking noted Kerry wing forward Tadghie Lyne and did a splendid job curbing the Kerry star. Cavan were not winning the midfield duels where Kerry's John Dowling was doing most of the damage. McDonnell was switched out to the area and immediately brought about a marked change. However, the Munster champions had already built up a sizeable lead, leaving Cavan with a mountain to climb. McDonnell's display both at wing back and midfield left an indelible imprint on the exchanges. Pádraig Puirseal, in his match report in the *Irish Press* the following day, singled out McDonnell for special mention. 'While Cavan were unable to rise to the same heights as that which marked their semi-final drawn game display, they had one of the best performers of the day in Jim McDonnell. Having curbed Kerry's Tadghie Lyne he was then moved to midfield where he very much curtailed the rampant John Dowling. It was McDonnell's best ever display at Croke Park.'

Following the rise of Down as Ulster kingpins when they won the Ulster title in 1959, 60 and 61, the last two years as All-Ireland champions, Cavan were going through a very lean spell. Down had taken over as the top county not alone in the province but also in the country. Cavan briefly halted the Down landslide by winning the Ulster title in 1962 and 64. The 1962 victory in Casement Park, Belfast, was played before an attendance of 40,000, and Cavan won the day 3-6 to 0-5. That made up for defeats by Down at a similar stage in the 1959 and 60 deciders.

The Breffni men played Roscommon in the All-Ireland semi-final in

1962. The Connacht champions, who were led by their captain Gerry O'Malley, came out winners by 1-8 to 1-6. Jim tried to inspire his side when he went into goal, after the Cavan goalkeeper was injured, and saved a penalty. But his efforts to reach the final were in vain. There was also disappointment in the 1964 All-Ireland semi-final when Cavan went under to Kerry. On the credit side, Jim won four Railway Cup medals with Ulster, beating Munster in the finals of 1950 and 60 and Leinster in the deciders of 1963 and 64. But the great Jim McDonnell sadly joined the ranks of those other magnificent players who were denied the coveted All-Ireland crown.

McDonnell's career as an administrator began before his playing days were over. In 1966 he was appointed a delegate to the Ulster Council and in 1970 he became chairman of the Cavan County Board, where he served a three-year term. He later became Central Council representative and was elected to the powerful management committee for a three-year period. In 1988 he was conferred with a major honour when he was appointed one of the GAA trustees at the Annual Congress held in Bundoran. He continued to serve the GAA in other capacities and was put forward for the GAA presidency in 1990 but came up against a strong opponent in fellow Ulsterman Peter Quinn, and the Teemore man was elected.

It was an unusual situation to find two Ulstermen in the field, but Quinn was a strong candidate and took his share of the votes from around the country and from the delegates abroad, particularly in the United States.

One of Jim's most precious possessions is a Cavan senior championship medal won with Cavan Gaels in the 1963 county final against Bailieborough Shamrocks. As captain he was hoping to bring the cup back to Cavan town for the first time since 1941 when Cavan Slashers had achieved that honour. Cavan Gaels won by a point, 3-5 to 1-10, and it was McDonnell's two goals that boosted his side to victory. He scored 2-2 over the sixty minutes.

Jim forged many lasting friendships, especially on the Gaels side, in particular, John 'Foley' O'Rourke, and the popular full forward in the team at that time, local 'hackney' man, Paddy Maguire. Incidentally, members of the Bailieborough team that day included Gabriel Kelly, who was Cavan team manager in the sixties and who also later lined out with Cavan Gaels as a player and later as team manager with Éamon

Curley, who was on the Roscommon team that had beaten Cavan in the 1962 All-Ireland semi-final.

Jim's wife is a Clare woman, Eileen Power from New Quay in the Kinvara area, and they have two sons and four daughters.

It is coincidental that when he was interviewed prior to the congress in 1990 about how he saw the GAA in the 90s and beyond, he said: 'My priorities, if elected, are to bring football and hurling back to the strength they enjoyed in the heydays of the 40s and 50s. With the finals of the World Cup in June in the same year as the election, I feel the GAA are going to be up against it endeavouring to attract the crowds, especially with Ireland's games live on television. The GAA will have to fight its corner as it is competing in the same market for the youth.'

Asked whether the GAA provincial councils should arrange games not to clash with the World Cup, Jim said: 'They shouldn't. They should go ahead with their games as normal and ignore what is happening elsewhere. The World Cup will be over but the GAA will be continuing to organise games without interruption into the following year. I think the World Cup has been hyped up far too much by the media.'

His opponent in the contest, Peter Quinn, had a much more radical and far-seeing view of the GAA and preached to the converted and others regarding the renovations at Croke Park in which he was the prime mover. He stated many times, that he hoped the stadium would be open to other sports in which the GAA would benefit from such events from a financial and public relations viewpoint.

How ironic that Croke Park is now the venue for World Cup soccer and rugby internationals in 2007 while Lansdowne Road is being re-developed. The use of Croke Park for soccer and rugby was approved at congress last year (2006).

| PACKIE McGARTY

The GAA All Stars awards scheme came far too late for Packie McGarty. At their inception in 1971 he was in the twilight of his career—not surprising, seeing as he first donned the Leitrim senior jersey as a 16-year old back in 1949. So his inter-county involvement had spanned four decades, the 1940s, 50s, 60s and 70s. And not a word about burn-out!

Packie was reared on football. His father Dan, a former Mohill star, was the club chairman and most of the meetings were held in the McGarty kitchen. Mrs McGarty, before the days of the automatic washer and the spin dryer, had scrubbed the Mohill jerseys and the well-worn togs and socks used by Packie and his older brothers Eddie and Willie. There were other influences too, not least the local national teacher, Mark Keegan, who nurtured a love of the GAA among his pupils.

There were to be many disappointments on the playing fields, but one that is indelibly etched in his memory was as a schoolboy in a 7-a-side tournament at the Mohill Show. Packie's team won and he eagerly awaited the presentation of his first ever football medal. To his horror, team captain Eddie Rowley was presented with an envelope containing seven half-crowns. At the time this was big money (maybe the fore-runner of 'pay for play'), but Packie cried all the way home. He would rather have got a sixpenny medal. He had no value on the half-crown; nor has he any value on a 1951 minor medal won with Fenagh because they were declared champions by default. The other finalists were disqualified for fielding what would be referred to as a few 'hairy minors'.

Packie treasured his 1950 minor medal because it was won on the field of play with a team that included Cathal Flynn, who was later to form a 'terrible twins' combination with McGarty on Leitrim and Connacht teams. An earlier under-14 medal won with Mohill in 1943 is also an important keepsake. In the Leitrim final, the 10-year-old Packie was the star of the show. Eddie Rowley captained that team too and he and Packie were to be team mates for many years for club and county, including the 1952 All-Ireland junior final, when Leitrim lost to a strong Meath team in Breffni Park.

Not alone did Packie's best days precede the All Stars, but also many of the phenomena of modern day football, including team managers, psychologists, hamstrings, dieticians, statisticians, physios, iced baths, gyms, training tops, bladed boots, 'warm-down' or training camps in La Manga. Half a century ago Packie McGarty and the others of his era required no gym work—manual labour did the trick. Packie's muscles were well toned hoisting ESB poles around the Donegal mountains, later on the building sites of London and labouring with Roadstone in Clondalkin, the Dublin suburb in which he was eventually to enter the supermarket business.

While in London, Packie would work a half-day on Saturday, catch one of the few evening flights to Dublin, line out with Leitrim in the championship or league and be back in time for an early Monday morning start in Cricklewood or Kilburn. He had the disappointment of losing a London county final with Tara's just as he had with his home club in Mohill in a Leitrim final and also in three Dublin county finals—two with Seán McDermotts and one with Round Towers of Clondalkin. Seán McDermotts had a team of inter-county stars, including the Leitrim contingent of Packie, Cathal Flynn, Frank Quinn and Jim Lynch, but they met an even more formidable force in St Vincent's, the famed Dublin club that had thirteen of their team on the county side.

The hard luck stories for McGarty were replicated in the inter-county championship in the 1950s when Leitrim lost four Connacht titles in a row to arch rivals Galway. So, was Packie McGarty a born loser? Far from it. Any regrets at not winning finals or titles were not for personal reasons, rather from a genuine disappointment that he could not give the club and county supporters something to celebrate. But he did give every Leitrim heart reason to rejoice by sharing with them all his undoubted footballing skills and, above all, his burning pride in the green and gold jersey and by representing his county with distinction on the wider stage.

Packie could field a ball like Willie Joe Padden, solo run like Iggy Jones, terrorise a back line like Kieran Donaghy, pick off points like

Gooch Cooper, kick frees like Jimmy Keaveny and motivate a team like Peter Canavan. As a mere 19-year old he was selected on a Connacht team that included such names as Seán Purcell, Pádraig Carney, Seán Flanagan and Gerry O'Malley, and he ran rings around Jas Murphy of Kerry, scoring 1-4 before 20,000 spectators in Tralee. GAA scribes Paddy Downey, Pádraig Purcell and John D. Hickey made notes of this will-o'-the-wisp from Leitrim and were to devote many column inches to him for many years to come.

McGarty was to give many an outstanding display, irrespective of the grade, the occasion or the opposition. Small in stature, he was big in performance as was evidenced when he helped Connacht to three Railway Cups, starring for Ireland for three consecutive years against the Combined Universities, delighting our exiles at the Cardinal Cushing Games in New York, but particularly with his Herculean displays for Leitrim. His name and fame spread far and wide, and even yet GAA people delight in recalling their own McGarty moment. His greatest hour is often acknowledged as the 1958 Connacht final against Galway in St Coman's Park, Roscommon. Little wonder that his marker, Jack Mahon, like many other great defenders, failed to put the shackles on this great forward at the highest level of the game.

Leitrim came so close to provincial success in the 1950s, despite it being a golden era for Galway, a side which included the lethal Purcell-Stockwell combination. Many of the junior side in 1952 had developed into senior players and were bolstered by Josie Murray, Paddy Dolan and Jimmy O'Donnell from the minor team that reached the 1956 All-Ireland final. Glory days would surely have come in 1958 had Eddie Rowley not emigrated and had Joe Bohan, Paddy McTague and Mike Dillon—the star half-back line of the Leitrim club in New York—not left for the Big Apple a few years previously.

Mike Dillon was to achieve national honours the following year when he captained New York in the National League semi-final, but they came up against a strong Derry team led by Seán O'Connell. This appearance by Leitrim at headquarters was to be the last until the county won its second Connacht title in 1994 and faced the Dubs on their home patch. A proud Leitrim supporter in the new Croke Park that day was one Packie McGarty.

Packie feels it is hard for the so-called weaker counties to break the stranglehold of the strong, not from lack of ability or effort, but more so because of lack of belief in themselves. There can be a tendency to be content just to put on a good show and he feels this mind-set had a bad effect on the Leitrim team of his era.

Medals and titles may be few in Packie McGarty's collection, but he has no regrets as he looks back on his playing days, from the impromptu three goals in his bare feet in the Hollow Banks Bog in Mohill to lining out with Ireland in Croke Park. He was always proud to be chosen to wear a team jersey, especially the green and gold of Leitrim. He is shy to the point of embarrassment at the many honours bestowed on him in recent years by his club, Mohill, by Leitrim GAA and by countless clubs, community organisations, cultural committees and award schemes, all of whom are anxious to pay due recognition to a sportsman and a real gentleman who lifted the minds and aspirations of his people.

A happy memory for Packie from 2006 was Mohill's success in the Leitrim senior championship after a gap of thirty-five years. But he has a treasury of other memories and he can vividly recall practically every game, every score, every opponent. And if you engage him in a discussion on Gaelic football, he'd talk for Ireland. Little wonder that this man was an automatic choice on the Connacht Railway Cup Football Team of the Century, and that every single one of the thousands of nominations for the Leitrim Team of the Millennium had the same name for the centre half-forward position—the youngster who wanted a medal instead of a half-crown—the name of Packie McGarty.

24

PETER McGINNITY

Although Fermanagh is the only Ulster county still to win the provincial senior football title, it has still made a rich contribution down the years to the annals of the northern championships in all grades. Though they contested their first Ulster senior final as far back as 1914, the fact that the title has proven a most elusive jackpot has not dulled their enthusiasm or support for the games.

In recent years Fermanagh have scaled new heights. They have given some impressive displays in the Allianz League, and there were those heady days in 2004 when the county made the country sit up and take notice. An All-Ireland senior semi-final outing was earned for the first time, and Fermanagh celebrated with a deserved draw with Mayo before bowing out by just two points in the replay.

Down the years, too, the county has produced some outstanding footballers. One who immediately springs to mind is Peter McGinnity, a man who had that elusive extra special quality that distinguishes the great performer in any sport. Regretfully, he ranks among the giants of the game who ended their senior inter-county careers without winning an All-Ireland senior medal, or even a provincial senior souvenir.

McGinnity, who is over six foot tall, lost little time making his mark on the inter-county scene. He was a budding starlet of around 16 when he helped Fermanagh in attack to blaze a new trail by capturing their first Ulster under-21 title in 1970. A youngster has to have ability well above the ordinary to make an impact like that at such an early stage in inter-county competitions, even at minor, never mind a higher grade. Little wonder, then, that he went on to climb the ladder of football greatness.

Fermanagh reached the All-Ireland under-21 championship final in 1970, but went down to Cork at Croke Park. However, the young

Fermanagh man who lined out at left full forward still had a good game and got on the score sheet with a point.

Hopes of a first All-Ireland title since the junior title was won in London in 1959 looked bright as the county, with McGinnity again to the fore up front, reached the 1971 under-21 national final. Once more, however, Cork foiled the glory bid. McGinnity scored a point. But there was plenty of evidence in those campaigns to suggest that Peter was a young footballer with the ability to capture plenty of headlines in the future at senior level.

He was back experiencing the tensions of an All-Ireland final in 1978 as a forward in the St John's, Belfast, squad that lost to the Pat Spillane-led Thomond College in the club decider.

Fermanagh found the Ulster title a bridge too far during Peter's inter-county senior career. The nearest brush he had with the famed Anglo Celt Cup, the trophy awarded to the winners of the northern championship, was in 1982 when the Erne county reached the final for the first time in thirty-seven years.

As Fermanagh lined out against Armagh before an attendance of some 18,000 in the sunshine at Clones for the first final meeting of the counties, hopes were high following unlikely but deserved wins earlier in the championship over the fancied Derry and Tyrone sides. However, Fermanagh took a long time to find their best form. They played second fiddle for around twenty minutes but then stepped up a gear and scored three points to leave them well in the hunt at the interval when the Orchard county had just a two-point advantage (0-5 to 0-3).

Armagh had the better of the exchanges in the opening quarter of the second half. Then, in the sixteenth minute midfielder McGinnity stepped into the picture. He took a well-delivered pass from his partner Philip Courtney near the fifty yard line and went off on a pulse-raising run before sending to the net from about twenty-five yards for one of the goals of the championship.

That brought Fermanagh level, 1-3 to 0-6, and three minutes later McGinnity was back with a point from a free to put his side ahead. That long hoped for first title beckoned, but, amazingly, with morale at a high peak just then, Fermanagh failed to score again. Armagh finished the stronger to regain the crown after two years on a 0-10 to 1-4 score-line. McGinnity was his team's top scorer with 1-2.

Nevertheless, the Roslea club man, who was an excellent high fielder and adept at creating chances, still had a good year and finished joint top scorer for the northern championship season overall with 1-9.

Later that year Peter was chosen at right full forward and walked into history as Fermanagh's first-ever All Star. He was to hold that distinction until 2004 when two Fermanagh players joined the ranks. On the playing fields, too, there were some golden moments for McGinnity in a lengthy senior inter-county career.

He stepped up to the inter-provincial ranks in 1973 to start a lengthy spell in the provincial colours that lasted until 1978 when Ulster lost their semi-final. The clever and polished Fermanagh man experienced the disappointments of playing in losing finals in 1975 and 78, but what a dramatic change in fortune came his way in 1980! Not only did he win a Railway Cup medal, but he also became the first Fermanagh county player to captain an inter-provincial title winning side. He led the province really well in their wins over Connacht and Munster to become only the second Fermanagh county player to appear in a Railway Cup winning team. In the final he was one of the North's best players and he also hit two points.

In an era when Ulster were a real power in the sport and competition for places in the team was particularly keen, McGinnity continued to prove one of the stalwarts of the inter-provincials and won further medals in 1983 and 84, both at right half-forward. He continued to play with Ulster up to 1987, but the province did not reach the final during his concluding season in the side.

A milestone on the inter-county front was passed in 1977 in the Dr McKenna Cup (an all-Ulster senior knock-out competition) final at Omagh against Donegal. Fermanagh were bidding for their first triumph in forty-four years. With McGinnity at midfield they made it by a single point, 1-8 to 1-7.

McGinnity played college football with St Michael's, Enniskillen, before graduating to the premier inter-county grade. And what wonderful service he gave to Fermanagh over a nineteen-year career that ended in 1988. Towards the end of his time with the side, he also filled the role of player-manager for a couple of seasons. That record says much for his dedication and enthusiasm, all the more so as there were no provincial title wins along the way to provide those vital added incentives and boost morale.

Billy Goodison, long serving Wexford half-back and All-Ireland football referee in 1955.

Pat 'Red' Collier, *extreme left*, in the 1967 All-Ireland football final against Cork.

Tony Hanahoe (Dublin) scores a point against Galway in the 1974 All-Ireland final.

September 1975. Dublin's Tony Hanahoe (*left*) in action during the All-Ireland football semi-final, Kerry v Dublin, Croke Park. (*Sportsfile*)

Kevin Heffernan (*left*) at a squad training session at Parnell Park before the 1983 All-Ireland football final. (*RTÉ Stills Library*)

November 1981: Kevin Heffernan greets Mick O'Dwyer before the Dublin-Kerry National Football League game at Croke Park.

UCG's 1933 Sigerson Cup winning team, captained by Mick Higgins, seen here holding the ball and cup.

23 May 2005: Then surviving members of the 1947 All-Ireland football final played between Cavan and Kerry in the Polo Grounds, New York. (*From left*): Mick Higgins (Cavan), John Wilson (Cavan), Teddy Sullivan (Kerry), Mick Finnucane (Kerry), Simon Deignan (Cavan), Tony Tighe (Cavan) and Gus Cremin (Kerry). (*Sportsfile*)

Seamus Hoare, legendary
Donegal goalkeeper.

Eugene Hughes in a typical attacking pose. (*Inpho*)

Iggy Jones, a bright star of colleges and inter-county football.

Sligo's Mickey Kearins (14), seen here tussling with Mayo's Ger Feeney in a Connacht championship game.

Joe Lennon raises the Sam Maguire Cup after Down's victory over Kerry in 1968.

Andy McCallin (Antrim), All-Ireland under 21 football medallist and great dual player (inter-county and club). (*Sportsfile*)

16 September 1990: Teddy McCarthy (Cork) in action against Brian Stafford (*above right*) and P.J. Gillic. All-Ireland football final 1990, Croke Park. (*Sportsfile*)

Jim McDonnell, one of Cavan's most consistent and celebrated half-backs.

Packy McGarty (Leitrim), one of football's most exciting forwards of all time.

Bloodied but unbowed! Roslea captain Peter McGinnity being interviewed after the 1982 senior championship final.

John 'Jobber' McGrath (Westmeath), an outstanding hurler for county and province.

Martin McHugh (Donegal) tries to evade the clutches of Derry's Henry Downey in the 1993 Ulster football final. (*Inpho*)

Jim McKeever was the first winner in 1980 of the Derry County Board's An Curadir Mir (The Champion's Portion) award. He is pictured here at the presentation of the award by His Eminence Cardinal Tomás Ó Fiaich.

The Meally Clan of the Railyard club in Kilkenny. *From left*: Michael Meally (Senior), chairman of the Kilkenny Football Board 1952–63 and 1970–74, Michael (Junior), Martin and Kieran, with some of their trophies and medals.

Paddy Moriarty, a star in defence or attack with Armagh. (*Sportsfile*)

Sean Walsh of Kerry and Brian Mullins of Dublin, rise for the ball.

Jimmy Barry Murphy (Cork) (*left*), racing past Ulster defender Peter Mulgrew, scoring the first of his four goals for Munster in the 1975 Railway Cup final. (*Cork Examiner*)

1935 Railway Cup football champions, Leinster. *Back row, second from left in jersey:* Tommy Murphy.

Jimmy Murray, Roscommon's victorious All-Ireland captain in 1943 and 1944.

Johnny Nevin, Carlow's long-serving dual player, in football action against Longford's Michael Kelly in a 2004 Leinster football championship tie. (*Inpho*)

Dermot O'Brien, Louth's 1957 All-Ireland senior football title-winning captain, v Cork. (*Cork Examiner*)

Kevin O'Brien, who starred with Wicklow and Leinster, and won an All-Ireland club medal with Baltinglass in 1990.

Mick O'Connell (Kerry) in pensive mood. (*RTÉ Stills Library*)

Mick O'Connell's (Kerry) high-fielding qualities in evidence against Down in the 1968 All-Ireland football final. Also pictured: Sean O'Neill *left*, and John Purdy (Down). (*Sportsfile*)

When his studies took him to Belfast, he joined the St John's club in the city and helped them to three county senior titles and the Ulster crown on the way to that All-Ireland final outing in 1977.

McGinnity returned to St Michael's as a teacher and has been involved in coaching at the college.

All in all, he has served the game really well both as a player and in later times as a coach.

25

JOHN 'JOBBER' McGRATH

'How oft we watched him from the hill, below in Cusack Park,
In the green and white of Rickardstown, how oft' he made
his mark.
The famed maroon he also wore and loudly did we cheer
In Páirc an Chrochaigh and venues far and near.
For Leinster too he played his part and hurled in Ireland's
green,
No mean his feat amid the elite and sporting was his mien.
Oh well may Westmeath praise him and have a special grath
For this man, our own famed man, the peerless John McGrath.

If ever in the realms of sport a hall of fame is established in Westmeath, then there will be little difficulty in deciding which hurler should be the first to have his name inscribed on the roll of honour. For services to club, county, province and country, John Jobber McGrath would certainly qualify. And there would have to be much more than that in his citation because by his artistry and sportsmanship he deserves a chapter in the annals of the great in the GAA.

North Westmeath has always been a hurling stronghold in the Lake county, and part of that traditional hurling area was the Rickardstown club and the birthplace of Jobber McGrath. The club, though now extinct, still holds a special place in the folklore of the Westmeath hurling fraternity. The year 1947 marked the first appearance of Rickardstown in a senior county decider and although defeat was their lot, it took just five years more to achieve their reward. The breakthrough came in 1954 when they captured their first major honour with a 3-3 to 2-7 win over neighbouring Collinstown in a replay. Jobber was his side's top scorer in both games, 0-8 in the first and 1-4 in the replay.

In 1956 Castletown-Geoghegan, after a lapse of thirty-three years, took the title at the expense of Rickardstown, who had their revenge three years later when they triumphed 6-7 to 1-3 over a Castletown side who were the reigning champions. Victory that day was masterminded by Jobber. The club went on to win one more title before disbanding and amalgamating with neighbours Collinstown and Glenidan to form the very successful Lough Lene Gaels, a top club in Westmeath today. It was, rather surprisingly, as a goalkeeper that Jobber first wore the maroon and white of Westmeath in a National League game against Meath in 1847, but it was outfield and mainly as a midfielder that he was to establish himself in the minds of hurling followers throughout the country. He was comfortable in top-class company and his genial personality ensured his popularity among his peers.

In 1955 Westmeath made commendable progress in both codes in Leinster. The hurlers reached the Leinster semi-final where they came up against a Wexford team on their way to All-Ireland honours and were beaten 5-9 to 3-4. In that game Jobber was pitted against players like the Rackard brothers, Ned Wheeler, Tim Flood, Nick O'Donnell and Jim English, but the tall, blonde Rickardstown man was quite at home in their company. Jobber was later to pay tribute to Bobby Rackard: 'The greatest hurler I ever saw; he was an amazing man with a hurley . . . I played against him a few times and I always enjoyed his skill and sportsmanship.' Jobber won the first of three inter-county trophies when he helped Westmeath to win Division Two of the 1947–48 National Hurling League.

There is an interesting anecdote concerning that particular league when the midlanders journeyed to Casement Park, Belfast, to play Antrim. Some time previously the Antrim footballers, then a force to be reckoned with, came to Croke Park and won a tournament. A few days before Westmeath were to travel northwards, county officials were contacted and asked if they would oblige by bringing the trophies to the Antrim footballers. Assuming the trophies to be the usual set of medals, a Westmeath official readily agreed. Too late it was realised why the Antrim footballers did not take home their own 'trophies', because they turned out to be an expensive set of overcoats, presented by a prominent Dublin drapery. Excise regulations had prevented the Glens men from bringing their prizes back with them. Nothing daunted, however, the Westmeath officials overcame the difficulty, and when the hurlers crossed the border, each player sported a brand new overcoat.

Sunday, 24 August 1952, marked Jobber's first appearance in Croke Park and the attainment of his second inter-county medal when Westmeath beat Kerry in the 'Mean Corn Iomaine final'. Division Two league honours were won again in 1967 when Jobber helped Westmeath to a 3-9 to 3-7 defeat of Laois. Later that year he played in the Leinster championship against Offaly, with Westmeath winning 5-10 to 4-8.

The *Westmeath Examiner* report on the game stated: 'Whenever the complete history of the GAA in the county is written, there is no doubt about Rickardstown's "Jobber" McGrath having a special place in it. His display in O'Connor Park on Sunday certainly earned him the title "Father of Westmeath Hurling".' Outside the confines of his native county, Jobber has justifiably earned the respect and indeed admiration of players and followers throughout the land.

In the 1950s his ability was recognised by the Leinster selectors, and in 1956 he partnered Wexford's Jim Morrissey at midfield on the team that hammered Munster 5-11 to 1-7 in the Railway Cup final, a win that compensated, in part, for a disappointing loss in 1954. Also in 1956 Jobber was chosen on the Ireland team to play the Combined Universities, a crowning achievement for his dedication to the game of hurling.

In 1984 Jobber was chosen at midfield on the Centenary Year team, 'a great player that never won an All-Ireland medal'. He was chosen at midfield along with Joe Sammon of Galway. Many of the counties among the hurling elite would have been delighted to hand Jobber a jersey, but he chose to remain loyal to his native county.

John Jobber McGrath passed away suddenly in 1980 at the age of 56, and hurling lost one of its favourite disciples, a true gentleman and a wonderful person. A thorough sportsman both on and off the field, he will always be remembered fondly by hurling followers everywhere.

26

MARTIN McHUGH

It was the day that a long-held dream of Donegal enthusiasts became a reality. That was the September afternoon in 1992 when north-west county upset the odds by marking their All-Ireland senior football final debut with a memorable win over the firm favourites Dublin. There had been many false dawns, many heart-breaks and dis-appointments for the county prior to earning that historic appearance with a semi-final win over Mayo. Indeed, many outside the county were convinced that this Croke Park visit would end up as another disappointment.

Dublin went into the final with a strong pedigree. Apart from the fact that their side included two All-Ireland senior medallists, goal-keeper John O'Leary and full back Gerry Hargan, three others had played in losing finals. The Dubs, with twenty-one titles, were rich in championship experience and had arrived at the final after an impressive march during which they had scored seven goals.

But Donegal made light of their outsiders' ranking. They turned in a power-packed display, one in which every one of the sixteen men who appeared during the game played his part impressively in writing a bright new chapter in the annals of the championship. And this, despite the fact that fate delivered a crippling blow on the morning of the final when left half-back Martin Shovlin, one of the best players on the team, had to withdraw because of injury.

A real test of character then for the Donegal men, even before the ball was thrown in. But they rose to the challenge in fine style, with John Joe Doherty replacing Shovlin and making light of his late, dramatic call-up with an excellent performance.

Donegal's first score after seven minutes might well have been a goal. Dublin were two points ahead when James McHugh eluded the defensive screen and sent a great shot goalwards, only to see the ball come back off the crossbar. His brother, Martin, collected the rebound and Donegal had to settle for a point.

Centre half-forward Martin McHugh went on to stamp his personality on the game in exciting fashion. His football was at times breathtaking. Every time he ran with the ball, the Dublin defence appeared vulnerable. He was a constant thorn in the metropolitan rearguard, scored three points, and all in all proved a bright architect in forging out the well-merited 0-18 to 0-14 win.

Donegal conceded a penalty after nine minutes, but received a real boost when the ball was driven wide. The northerners really got their game together after that, and playing cool, confident and controlled football, took the lead for the first time with a Declan Bonner point after twenty-two minutes. They went on to finish ahead at the interval, 0-10 to 0-7.

It was not an intimidating deficit for a team of the craft and skill of Dublin to face at the restart. Indeed, there were many who believed they could up their performance and overtake Donegal in the second half to justify their favouritism.

However, Donegal, far from showing any signs of losing their momentum, continued to play with an authority not seen in the past from the county team. They went six points clear after twenty-three minutes. Dublin pulled their deficit back to three points, but Donegal refused to panic. Manus Boyle steadied the northern ship with a point from a free, and in the closing period goalkeeper Gary Walsh brought off a superb save from full forward Vinny Murphy.

Right full forward Declan Bonner provided the final stamp of authority with a classic point with his left foot from the right wing to ensure that Donegal deservedly became the first county since Down in 1960 to make a winning Sam Maguire Cup debut.

The Donegal men played with great verve and skill all through. Manus Boyle was their ace marksman with nine points (five from frees). James McHugh, so lively and efficient up front, and Martin Gavigan, a tower of strength at centre half-back, were others whose contributions were just a little special.

As for Martin McHugh, one of the smallest players on the field but with a real hunger for victory, he coloured the occasion with a splendid exhibition of his gifts. He was alert, tireless in his efforts, and used the ball well as he took the game to the opposition and created openings for his co-forwards. Then there were those three very valuable and well-taken points.

It is a measure of the quality of Martin's play not only in that game but all through the season that he was later in the year honoured by the All Stars at centre half-forward and also chosen as the Texaco Sportstar Award winner in Gaelic football. He remains to this day the only Donegal man to gain the latter award. Even though that was his All-Ireland senior final debut, the Kilcar club man still brought plenty of experience to that outing.

Martin was one of a talented group of footballers who achieved a memorable breakthrough for Donegal in 1982 by beating Roscommon in an under-21 final at Carrick-on-Shannon to capture the county's first All-Ireland crown in any grade of football. He lined out at right half-forward in that game. The final was only two minutes old when he opened the scoring from thirty yards out with a point.

Martin went on to turn in a five-star performance, and two minutes from the end he was a central figure in a dramatic ending to the game. Donegal, who held Roscommon scoreless in the second half, were three points clear when they were awarded a free from fifty yards out. McHugh stepped up to take the kick. His aim was true and the ball found the net. The Donegal followers were delirious and it was some moments before they realised the goal was disallowed because of an infringement. Nevertheless, the north-west men held on for a well-merited 0-8 to 0-5 win, and McHugh finished top scorer with five points (two from frees).

A new era in Donegal football history was begun in more ways than one with that success. Five years later the county regained the All-Ireland under-21 title, and players from those two successful teams provided a solid framework for the senior side that were to achieve that memorable breakthrough in 1992.

Martin made his senior championship debut in 1981 against Armagh in an unsuccessful Ulster tie at Armagh. That came after he celebrated his call-up to the county senior team the previous October against Tipperary in a league game and signalled his arrival with four grand points.

That was the start of a splendid fourteen seasons in the county colours, during which Meartain Beag established himself not only as one of Donegal's greatest ever players, but one of the outstanding exponents of forward play nationally in any era.

He won his first Ulster senior championship medal in 1983 when Donegal beat Cavan. Despite losing the All-Ireland semi-final to Galway, he was later that year honoured for the first time in an All Stars team at right full forward.

When Donegal regained the title in 1990, he was joined in the team by his brother James. Then came that glory year of 1992 when Martin won his third provincial title on the way to that coveted All-Ireland souvenir.

His ability to find his way through to the scoring target is also illustrated by the fact that in his very early years in the premier county side he became in 1984 the first from the north-west county to score more than 100 points in a season. That year he chalked up 4-95 (107 points).

Ulster scaled impressive heights in the Railway Cup during McHugh's inter-county career. Not surprisingly, he made a major contribution to the success story with his cultured play by helping the province to capture five titles between 1983 and 1993. His medals total is a record for a Donegal footballer.

McHugh also created quite a stir on the local front. At only 19 he proved a very influential figure for Kilcar in their 1980 final win over Ardara for the club's first county senior final win in fifty-five years. Martin scored ten superb points, some from almost impossible positions. He went on to win three more county medals for his collection. Weigh in Dr McKenna Cup (an all-Ulster senior football competition) medals for 1985 and 1991 and it adds up to an impressive total.

When he retired from inter-county football, Martin continued to play a prominent role in Gaelic games. He took over the manager's job with Cavan and had not long to wait in that role for success. In 1997, under his guidance, the Breffni county ended a thirteen-year famine in the North by beating Down in the Ulster final.

JIM McKEEVER

Jim McKeever of Derry did not win an All-Ireland senior football medal during his career, but that still cannot cloud the fact that he well and truly established himself as one of the true greats of the game. Not only that, he also charted his way into historic territory in more ways than one.

McKeever must rank as one of the greatest midfielders in any era in the history of the game. True, he also proved his worth in attack, but it is his high-grade football in the middle of the park for which he was most noted.

In 1958 he led Derry to their first All-Ireland senior final appearance. Later that year he was chosen as the Gaelic football award winner in the first Caltex, now Texaco, Sportstars of the Year awards. He was to remain the only non All-Ireland medal winner in the code in each year to hold that position until Kevin Heffernan was honoured in 1974, the year Kevin managed Dublin to win the Sam Maguire Cup. That was somewhat ironic in view of the fact that Heffernan led Dublin to victory over Derry in the 1958 All-Ireland decider.

The All-Ireland senior football semi-final between Derry and Kerry in 1958 had all the appearances of a David and Goliath affair. The Oak Leaf county had won only their first-ever Ulster senior title a few weeks earlier, while the Kingdom went into that game the proud holders of eighteen All-Ireland senior crowns and with a framework of footballers who had helped to fashion the last of those titles in 1955. But one of the best features of sport is that unexpected results can happen to enliven the scene and provide exciting new talking points. That is exactly what happened at that meeting of the minnows from the Foyleside and the crafty men from the deep south.

A few weeks earlier at Clones, McKeever illuminated the Ulster final with his brilliant performance at midfield as he skippered his side to success against Down for that initial senior provincial title triumph. He and then teenager Seán O'Connell followed on by proving two of the key men in bringing about one of the major upsets in the annals of the All-Ireland senior championship with that against-the-odds win over Kerry.

McKeever did much to settle the Croke Park newcomers in the unnerving opening quarter with his purposeful play and leadership. Then, in the second quarter, the Ballymaguigan club man's intelligent promptings and power-packed play helped the new Ulster champions to collect 1-3 in that period—a return that had a major influence in finally earning Derry their ticket to the final.

Nevertheless, the issue was still finely balanced as the semi-final had two minutes to run in the rain at headquarters when O'Connell stepped into the picture in a big way. He took a pass from Peter Smith, who lined out at left half-back, and superbly sent the ball to the Hill 16 end net for a dramatic score that clinched the day for Derry, who finished with a point to spare.

Derry's bid to bring the Sam Maguire Cup across the border for the first time failed to materialise in the final show-down with Dublin. However, they made a more spirited bid than the 2-12 to 1-9 scoreline would suggest.

The outlook appeared bright enough for the Ulster champions at the interval when they trailed by just 0-8 to 0-4 after playing against the wind and into the Canal goal. Points by McKeever and O'Connell boosted northern morale, and after ten minutes the Ulster men were right in the title chase when full forward Owen Gribben goaled to level the scores at 1-6 to 0-9.

Dublin sent Liam 'Lar' Foley from right full back to midfield in a bid to counter the brilliant McKeever. They moved with more purpose after that, and a somewhat fortunate goal sent them on their way. A harmless centre by left half-forward Des Ferguson bounced about twenty-five yards from the Derry goal. Right half-forward Paddy Farnan and left full back Tommy Doherty moved to the ball. The Derry defender slipped and was rounded by Farnan, who finished to the net to give his side a 1-9 to 1-6 advantage.

Despite the defeat the final was still a game in which the lithe McKeever franked his right to rank as one of the greatest midfielders of all time. He had a superb game. In the second half, in particular, the Derry man scaled the heights as he gained midfield mastery, and his football over the hour was of a class that stamped him in the view of many as the outstanding player of the year.

That view was reinforced with his selection later in the year as the first ever Caltex Footballer of the Year. The history-making award was all the more noteworthy because he had finished on the losing side in the All-Ireland.

Jim McKeever's inter-county career began in 1948, and over the following fourteen seasons in the top flight he played some great games for Derry, Ulster and Ireland. He played in his first major national decider in 1956 when helping Ulster from midfield to capture the Railway Cup for the first time in six years. The Derry man collected his second inter-provincial medal in 1960 when he lined out in attack against Munster but was later switched to the centre of the field and produced a stellar show that sparked the North to a one-point win.

McKeever's inter-county senior career coincided with an annual representative fixture. In 1950 a new series was ushered in for the Dr Ryan Cup between Ireland and the Combined Universities in football. That was played each year, usually in March, at Croke Park, until 1959 when there was a break because of reconstruction work at headquarters. The series resumed in 1960 but came to an end in 1962.

It says much for the consistently high standard of play McKeever produced during his career that he was honoured four times by the Ireland selectors—1956, 57, 58 and 60. Nor does that tell the full story, as he was one of only five players to head the honours list with four jerseys each. He was also the only Ulster man in that select company of football giants.

McKeever also helped to usher in a new era overseas for Gaelic games. In 1958 football and hurling inter-county games were played at Wembley Stadium in London for the first time. The initial programme featured Galway and Derry in football, and Kilkenny and Clare in hurling, and attracted an attendance of 33,240. Galway won the football game 3-9 to 2-5 in which McKeever lined out at midfield.

Jim McKeever was a supreme stylist who had few equals as a high and reliable fielder. He was fast, clever, quick to size up a situation and exploit it to the best possible advantage. His distribution was first class at all times and he set the seal on his many fine qualities with his non-stop and progressive work in every match. He was also an inspiring leader.

The inter-provincial medals, the Ulster senior souvenir (his only one) and those Ireland appearances rank as Jim's top awards in a wonderful inter-county career. He also featured in many club games with his sheer brilliance, winning two county championship medals with Newbridge and one with Ballymaguigan.

28

MARTIN MEALLY

Even though Kilkenny has not contested a Leinster senior football final since 1922, the county has still managed to produce a good number of outstanding footballers over the years. Many, had they been playing with other counties, would probably have become household names, but with Kilkenny's lack of success with the big ball, that was not to be.

Martin Meally, who was born in Massford, Moneenroe, in north Kilkenny beside the Laois-Carlow border, would have to be included among Kilkenny's finest footballers over the years. Between 1953 and 1973 he won a record number of fifteen Kilkenny county senior football medals with the Railyard club. For most of that time he also played senior football with Kilkenny and also figured with the county senior hurlers for a while. Indeed, he represented the county at minor, junior and senior level in both codes.

Martin has been involved with football and hurling all his life. When he was growing up in the forties there were 'no cars, no television and no electricity, and radios were few and far between,' he said. 'However, we had our football. To me and many others, the Railyard Football Club was the most important focal point in the parish and playing football was our main pastime. All we wanted to do was to get on the Railyard football team when we grew up.'

The school children of his generation were lucky to have had a couple of great teachers who were also keen football men in the little village of Moneenroe. Francis McCann, the headmaster, a native of Crossmaglen in Armagh, was very strong on the basic skills, including fielding and kicking the ball reasonably well with both feet.

Meally fondly recalls little games in the schoolyard during the lunch break when McCann stood in one goal and another teacher, a Mr

O'Dwyer from Cork, stood in the other. 'If the match was good, then the lunch break was extended. On returning to the classroom, the headmaster led a discussion on the football and how we could improve the next day. That was how we learned our football during our school days,' said Meally.

Martin bemoans the fact that the standard of football has sunk so low in Kilkenny. The county teams regularly receive hefty defeats nowadays. 'That was not the case thirty or forty years ago when Kilkenny were able to hold their own against neighbouring counties,' he said.

Martin remembers, in particular, a first-round Leinster senior championship game with Carlow when Kilkenny made their opponents work hard for victory. A week earlier Carlow lost by just two points to Down, then at the height of their power in the National League. He also believes that his club, Railyard, was as good as the best in Carlow, Laois and Kildare around that time.

He won the first of his staggering fifteen county senior medals in 1953 when he was still a minor. He represented Kilkenny at minor level in both hurling and football in the same year.

Meally was also a good senior hurler and won a Walsh Cup medal with Kilkenny in 1959. A year earlier he was a member of the Erin's Own, Castlecomer, side that won the county junior hurling title. He also played with the Rest of Leinster against Offaly in 1962.

Martin also made a big name for himself as a knight of the whistle. He refereed numerous colleges' finals and three All-Ireland finals in football—junior in 1972, minor in 1976 and under-21 in 1977.

His late brother Kieran was also a fine footballer and won fourteen county senior medals. The youngest of the clan, Michael, was a member of eleven Kilkenny final successes with Railyard.

29

PADDY MORIARTY

Energy, persistence, eagerness, spirit and versatility—outstanding qualities in the make-up of any player and ones that Paddy Moriarty exhibited to a superb degree throughout a successful senior inter-county career.

Moriarty made his senior inter-county debut in 1970 with Armagh and went on to make a major impact both as a forward and as a half-back during a lengthy career that extended into the early eighties. He also helped to make football history not once but twice. It is also a measure of his cultured and efficient play that he won All Stars awards both as a forward and as a back, and provincial medals in both roles as well.

Moriarty experienced the glamour and tensions of an All-Ireland senior football final for the only time in 1977. That outing was against a very experienced Dublin side that had, a year earlier, regained the All-Ireland title after an interval of two seasons. Armagh, in sharp contrast, were appearing in their first Sam Maguire Cup tie in twenty-four years. They brought colour and excitement to that decider, and after an impressive march to the concluding round including a semi-final win over Roscommon, hopes were high of recording a long wished for first-ever title.

The all-ticket event drew an attendance of 64,502 and Armagh got off to a demoralising start as Dublin ended their first attack with a goal. The Ulster champions did not wilt, and five minutes later were awarded a penalty. A good movement was ended when left full forward Peter Loughran was fouled inside the square. Centre half-back Paddy Moriarty made the long trip from defence to take the kick. He made no mistake, sending a hard shot past Paddy Cullen to the Dublin net. However, the wily Dubliners took charge after that and went on to record a comfortable win in a disappointing final.

There was a touch of drama almost on the final whistle. Armagh were awarded a second penalty and once more Moriarty, who had a good game, came up to take the kick. This time Cullen made a fine save at the expense of the only 50 of the game. Dublin finished comfortable winners, 5-12 to 3-6.

Paddy's versatility and class with a football were replicated just as successfully with a sliotar. As in football, he played in all grades with the county in hurling.

Long before the All-Ireland senior final outing, Moriarty's talents were recognised by the All Stars selectors in the very early days of those awards. Indeed, he had not long to wait for such an honour. Just over a year after joining the county senior side, he was named at left full forward in the 1972 All Stars team—only the second in the history of this prestigious promotion—and the first Armagh man to gain such an honour. Then, despite the All-Ireland final defeat and his short spell at centre half, he collected a second All Stars trophy in 1977, that one at centre half-back. He is one of only six players to have been honoured both as a forward and as a defender. Paddy later joined a select company of players who won Railway Cup medals with two different selections.

In the early 1970s the Combined Universities competed for three years in the Railway Cup (now the M. D. Donnelly inter-provincial). The students beat Connacht in a final replay at Athlone in 1973 to capture the title for the only time. Moriarty, then a student at Queen's University, had a very good game at right full forward.

A whole-hearted and accomplished footballer who gave 100 per cent in every match, the Wolfe Tones club man had a lengthy wait for his first Ulster senior medal. That arrived in 1977.

That year's provincial show-piece game against Derry at Clones marked the Orchard county's first appearance in the concluding round since 1961, and they were also striving for a first title in twenty-four years. Two goals in two minutes coming up to half-time sent them firmly on the road to a convincing 3-10 to 1-5 win.

Right half-forward Larry Kearns and midfielder Colm McKinstry combined to pave the way for right full forward Moriarty to expertly steer home the first goal. He finished Armagh's second highest scorer on the day with 1-1.

Moriarty was at full forward for the All-Ireland semi-final against

Roscommon and added another fine goal to his record as the teams played a spirited draw. However, in that game he also demonstrated his ability as a centre half-back. After fifty-four minutes centre half-back Tom McCreesh retired and the selectors brought Moriarty back from the attack to the pivotal role. He did well during his limited spell in the position. The selectors were evidently impressed as he was chosen at centre half-back for the replay, with McCreesh at full back.

And how he rewarded the selectors' confidence! He was superbly on his game from the throw-in and foiled Roscommon attacks time and again. The ace forward-turned-defender also covered much ground during the match as he roamed here and there in a tireless display without, at the same time, neglecting his duties as a defender.

His contribution to the 0-15 to 0-14 win in a thrilling encounter was immense. And, after having appeared earlier in an attacking role, he won his second All Stars award later in 1977, not surprisingly, at centre half-back.

The versatile Moriarty joined the ranks of Ulster title winning captains in 1980. He lined out at right half-back against Tyrone in the final at Clones but later moved to centre half and had a big say in engineering a hard-earned win in a goal feast. Armagh qualified for the All-Ireland semi-final by 4-10 to 4-7, and then came another transfer for Moriarty for the renewal of rivalry with Roscommon at Croke Park. He returned to his earlier role as a seeker of scores at right half-forward and had a fine game, but the Connacht champions still got revenge for their 1977 semi-final replay defeat, winning by six points.

Five years after helping to write a new chapter in the Railway Cup with the universities, Moriarty returned to Railway Cup final action with Ulster as right half-back, but their hopes were ended by Munster. However, he had better luck a year later at centre half when Ulster regained the title. He was back as the pivot in the successful defence of the Railway Cup a year later.

Moriarty's consistency at the time in the top flight was confirmed by the fact that when Ulster won their next title in 1983, he was still a key figure at centre half-back.

Although some will not associate the Orchard county with hurling, the game has a strong following there. Moriarty played many times for Armagh in the code. He also won an Ulster junior hurling medal.

The Armagh man also put his talents on parade in the Sigerson Cup (Universities' championship) and played with Queen's in attack in their unsuccessful final bid against UCD in the 1974–75 final.

A player who gave tremendous service to the county senior side in both hurling and football, Paddy Moriarty won his last Ulster senior medal in 1982.

30

BRIAN MULLINS

In an earlier book of mine I unhesitatingly selected Brian Mullins as one of the best midfield players that I had seen and I make no apology for stating that fact. Big in heart, big in mind and big in body, Kevin Heffernan admired him for his greatness in the white heat of championship tests. Said Heffo: 'The greatest performance that I ever saw on a football field was given by Brian Mullins in a National Football League game in Cork at the Mardyke in 1975. It was an important game for us. He took on Cork on his own and we won.' It was to be some years later that the full measure of Brian's greatness was to manifest itself in the Dublin colours.

He began his football career at under-age level with his native Clontarf. Following in his brother's footsteps, he transferred to the powerful St Vincent's as a 16-year old. He was selected on the Dublin minor football team in 1971 and 72, and a year later he made his first appearance in a major final in Thurles when St Vincent's went under to Nemo Rangers in the All-Ireland club final replay. He figured on the under-21 football side in 1974, and the following year he was on the under-21 team which lost to Kerry in the All-Ireland final at Tipperary town.

After more than a decade in the inter-county wilderness, Dublin went into the 1974 championship with Kevin Heffernan in charge of a team which included the youthful Brian Mullins. The Leinster campaign was to prove a learning process for the young lion who relished the midfield action. Dublin opened with a win over Wexford. Jimmy Keaveney was later called out of retirement; Heffernan needed a solid free-taker. Wins followed against Louth, Offaly, Kildare and against Meath in the Leinster final, their first victory since 1965 with Keaveney their only link from that side.

The 1974 All-Ireland success against Galway has been well chronicled, being the first All-Ireland win for Dublin since the 1963 final, also against Galway. But the result held a special significance for Brian. He emulated the feat of his grand uncle, the 6 foot 6 Paddy Casey from Kerry, who played on the Dublin winning team of 1906 against Cork. While Brian revelled in the glory of the 1974 success, he had a great partner in Steve Rooney from O'Dwyer's, Balbriggan. They dovetailed beautifully, having built up a good understanding from their run through Leinster.

Mullins held team manager Heffernan in very high esteem and was impressed with the training methods employed by Lorcan Redmond and Donal Colfer. 'During the arduous team training, I was carried away by the things I found. Training was so thorough, so professional. After going through it, it was harder for me to accept mediocrity. In my view, players are either in or they're out. The guys I played with never funked it,' he said.

Mullins was a student in Thomond College at the time and there was great banter between the players, especially after training sessions. Mullins was always one of the first to arrive. When Keaveney complained about students having nothing to do except train for football, Mullins gave him a very short answer. After graduating from Thomond College, Mullins began teaching in Greendale Community School in Kilbarrack on Dublin's northside. He took eighteen months' leave of absence in 1980 to do an MA in athletics administration at New York University.

He was always a very committed player. The year 1976 was special for Dublin with the winning of the All-Ireland championship and the National League. In the latter decider Dublin defeated Derry, in which Mullins reached stellar heights in a partnership with Kevin Moran at midfield. The match was a cracking contest with Dublin edging the verdict 2-10 to 0-15. The All-Ireland final began with Kevin Moran's electrifying upfield surge, just missing what would have been the most glorious goal in the history of the game. The basis for victory was more assuredly the dominance of Mullins and Bernard Brogan at midfield. Mullins was moved to centre forward with twelve minutes left. He took a pass from Anton O'Toole and despite being under pressure from the Kerry backs, crashed the ball to the Kingdom net. There was further glory for the St Vincent's contingent on the county team when the club travelled to Portlaoise to play Roscommon Gaels. The Dublin men carried off the title with Brian Mullins and Fran Ryder linking attack and defence with great proficiency.

There were highs and lows in Brian Mullins's career. When Kerry defeated Dublin in the 1977 National League final, which brought revenge for their 1976 All-Ireland defeat, Dublin fielded without Brian Mullins at midfield. He was well and truly grounded with a bad dose of the flu. His absence was very evident because Dublin lacked his industry and work rate in the middle of the field. In April that year Dublin travelled to America, and in an interview in the *Dublin Year Book* with Tommy McQuaid, Mullins described the game against the All Stars in Los Angeles as one of the greatest he was ever involved in from a competitive viewpoint. GAA followers readily agree that the 1947 All-Ireland hurling final between Cork and Kilkenny was the greatest in the history of that game. This also applies, where quality is concerned, to the All-Ireland football semi-final between Dublin and Kerry, which Dublin won.

Kerry, who had played superbly, led 1-6 to 0-6 at half-time. On the resumption some brilliant forward combination work resulted in a Dublin goal. Bernard Brogan was introduced at midfield in place of Fran Ryder, who was injured. Immediately the great partnership of Mullins and Brogan sparked into action and Dublin regained the initiative. The pace of the match was staggering as both teams matched each other in the battle for the high ground. The game ebbed and flowed, and with seven minutes remaining Kerry were hanging on grimly to a two-point lead.

The Hill was in full cry and the Dublin players responded. Dave Hickey got possession, broke through the Kerry defensive wall and cracked the ball to the net. The Hill went wild again when Bernard Brogan, on a last-minute flying solo run, burst through to hit a thundering shot to the Kerry net. Dublin had achieved what appeared to be the impossible, on a 3-12 to 1-13 scoreline.

The 1978 All-Ireland final was again between the great rivals, Dublin and Kerry. It was remembered mostly in Dublin for Mikey Sheehy's opportunistic goal to an empty net. Dublin keeper Paddy Cullen was outfield protesting over a decision by referee Séamus Aldridge to award Kerry a free.

After the Sheehy goal, everything went wrong for Dublin. Key players Brian Mullins and Kevin Moran carried injuries into that final, easily won by Kerry. In 1980 Brian again made the newspaper headlines, but not in the way he intended. He hated the media attention he normally received for his brilliance in the game he loved. He brushed aside efforts from match reporters for after-match comments. He slated some reporters for the comments they did print, even though he had refused them earlier in the dressing room. He told one well-known reporter that 'he had no comment to make' and could 'not be quoted on that', with a glint in his eye.

I had great respect for the big man with the big heart and I was one of the fortunate ones who did get a few quotes for my match reports in the *Evening Press*. Heffo was a different kettle of fish. As near neighbours, he would normally drop down to my house late at night and consume a packet of cigarettes. However, after matches he would pass me on to co-selectors Donal Colfer and Lorcan Redmond for the after-match comments. They always obliged. When my match report would appear the following day in the *Evening Press*, it would contain liberal quotes from Kevin Heffernan that I had apportioned him, though he had never made them. That used to rattle him.

Late on Friday night, 27 June 1980, Brian Mullins crashed his car, travelling at high speed, when it went out of control and hit a lamp post. A sportswriter friend of mine, David Walsh, described in his article in *Magill* magazine the thoughts that flashed into Brian's head at the time. Brian explained: 'I could see that the car was going to hit the post and I knew that I was going to die. It was a surprisingly relaxed feeling. Two thoughts struck me. "Thanks" and "Look after Helen" [his wife]. I lost consciousness and when I woke up, I thought I was dead. For a while it was completely dark and I could not hear a sound. Eventually there was this sound of a motorbike and I said, "Brian, wherever you are, this life or next, they have motorbikes." I tried to move but could not. I reached down and could feel the bone coming through the skin of my right leg. I had a lot of damage to my jaws and had lost eight teeth. The thing that kept going through my mind was, as I sat in the car having survived the crash, that the car was about to go up in flames and I was going to die that way. I think I may have passed out again because the next moment there was a fireman at my side and I will never forget how skilful he was in removing me from the car.' Brian was 25 when the crash occurred. It took him two years before he was fit to play serious football again.

During his intensive work in the physiotherapy room he was noticed by a young lady who recognised him as Brian Mullins. She knew he had been in a bad accident. She was there in the Mater Hospital to begin a course of physiotherapy on an ankle which had been broken two months earlier. She was asked to do certain exercises which she found impossible. She was told to take a rest. Lying back on the pillow behind her, she watched Brian doing his exercises. She said: 'He was clearly in great agony, lifting himself up, counting one second and then lowering himself back down. Then up again, counting up to two seconds before going back down again. Up and down and always in agony. I could see that he was forcing his body to do things that it did not want to do. Watching him do that sorted out an awful lot for me. I decided that I would do my exercises, no matter what the cost.' The young lady who was inspired by the courage and sheer guts and determination of the Dublin star was successful too in her recovery to full health.

Mullins's great persistence and will to recover in order to play again was one of the major talking points for years after his recuperation from the crash. However, the weights and gym work which he was forced to do lessened his mobility and flexibility. Defying all the odds and somewhat heavier than in previous finals, Mullins donned the sky blue of Dublin again in the 1983 All-Ireland semi-final replay against Cork on 28 August that year in Cork. Páirc Uí Chaoimh was packed to capacity. Dublin's support was unbelievable and it helped in no small way towards turning the outcome Dublin's way. But once again the powerful and inspirational midfield display from the indestructible Mullins laid the foundation of Dublin's 4-15 to 3-10 win. Brian's goal from a first half penalty rocked Cork on their heels. The other three goals came from Ciaran Duff, Barney Rock and Joe McNally.

Ironically, Barney Rock was having a torrid time from the roaming Jimmy Kerrigan. In the second half, he was on the brink of being substituted, but his brilliant goal quickly changed the whole picture and the entire trend of the game. Barney never looked back for the remainder of the contest.

It was Galway again in the 1983 All-Ireland final. Anton O'Toole said afterwards, that while it was one of the worst All-Ireland senior finals of all time, it saw Dublin score their greatest victory from the point of view of an undying determination and will to win through a supercharged second half. Dublin came out on top with only twelve players on the field at the final whistle.

Brian Mullins was sent off before half-time following a clash with Galway's Brian Talty. The exchanges heated up after the resumption and, in what looked a harmless incident, Ray Hazely (Dublin) and Tomás Tierney (Galway) were sidelined by referee John Goff (Antrim), though I did think at the time that both were victims of the prevailing atmosphere. Ciaran Duff was sent off some time later. This left Galway with fourteen men against Dublin's twelve and the Connacht men had the benefit of a very strong breeze.

Galway at that point looked out and out favourites to win. However, in an amazing display of raw courage too impossible to contemplate, the 'defiant twelve' held the might of the fourteen Galway men to carry off the spoils. Dublin, led by their captain Tommy Drumm, lone mid-fielder John Caffrey, Mick Holden and a heart-stopping display by Pat Canavan in the Dublin defence, carved a niche for themselves in the history of Dublin football.

Brian Mullins figured against Kerry in the All-Ireland finals of 1984 and 85 but failed to add to his four All-Ireland senior medals, one National Football League medal and two All Stars awards in 1976 and 77. He moved to Donegal as a school principal and took over the management of the Derry team which beat Meath in the National League final in 2000. He is now Director of Sport in UCD.

Brian's inter-county career came to an end after the 1985 defeat at the hands of Kerry. He was at that time in his thirties. He had fulfilled a number of pledges he made at an earlier stage in his playing career. He delighted in winning his four All-Ireland senior championship medals which he shared with his family. As a teenager, he promised his mother that if ever he won an All-Ireland, he would give the medal to her. Her brother Bill Casey had won five playing for Kerry. But it was Brian's wish that she would have a medal won by her own son.

His most cherished medal went to his wife Helen, simply because she had to shoulder the bulk of the family responsibilities when Brian suffered that horrific car crash in 1980. Confined to hospital for a long time, he can never forget the care and attention Helen lavished on him in that hard, trying and demanding recuperation period when she was left to bring up their young family. They have always been a very close-knit couple.

He gave Helen's mam his third medal and he gave the fourth to the Live Aid auction which raised £2,500. His All-Ireland club medal went to his sister.

Brian Mullins, big in heart, big in mind and big in body, has endured many great battles and still lives to tell the tale.

31

JIMMY BARRY MURPHY

I must confess to being a great fan of Cork's Jimmy Barry Murphy. He belongs to an elite and accomplished band of dual players who have graced the playing fields at All-Ireland level with distinction. I have always admired him as a versatile and talented player and, more importantly, a thoroughly sporting legend. He was a gifted footballer and combined those skills with the natural grace and elegance he demonstrated on the hurling fields. A product of Coláiste Spioráid Naomh, Cork, he was to leave an indelible imprint on the sporting pages in the games in which he excelled. His fame alone made him an inspirational figure-head for the youth of Cork, who looked on him as a gifted idol and one to be followed and emulated.

He learned his hurling skills on the streets of Cork and then moved on to stellar heights winning all-Ireland club hurling and football honours, minor hurling and football crowns, all-Ireland senior hurling and football titles and provincial honours. His only regret, I'm sure, was not captaining the Cork hurling team to victory on All-Ireland day. The fact that Jimmy Barry Murphy was a dual player posed problems for him at times with the demands imposed by the county hurling and football selectors, apart from club duty with St Finbarr's. He was only 19 years of age when he won an All-Ireland senior football championship in 1973 when Cork defeated Galway before an attendance of 73,309. The match reports on the following day lauded the individual display served up by the young Barry Murphy in his side's 3-17 to 2-13 victory.

Jimmy scored 2-1 on that occasion, and the magnitude of his performance was reflected in the opportunism he displayed in quest of those important scores. The records show that the previous year he scored 2-1 also when helping the Cork minors defeat Tyrone in the

All-Ireland minor final, a magnificent feat in itself. In the Munster senior final in 1973 Cork swamped Kerry by 5-12 to 1-15 and toppled Tyrone 5-10 to 2-4 in the All-Ireland semi-final. Galway provided the opposition in the All-Ireland final, and when the Leesiders led 1-9 to 0-3 after twenty minutes, another rout looked on the cards. But Galway had other ideas. They fought back gallantly through the efforts of Liam Sammon, Liam O'Neill, Tommy Joe Gilmore and Billy Joyce. But there was no stopping Cork that day. The lion-hearted Frank Cogan, Kevin Ger O'Sullivan, Denis Coughlan and the versatile Brian Murphy covered all options, and with Jimmy Barry Murphy leading a prolific attack, the honours went to the lethal Cork brigade.

It was a significant Cork success and more so for team captain Billy Morgan. He had the great satisfaction of bringing back the Sam Maguire trophy to the Leeside after a lapse of twenty-eight years. Undoubtedly, the work of team coach Donie O'Donovan was a particular factor in achieving success for Cork. Donie was a very modest individual, always emphasising the great qualities of the team. He dismissed his own contribution to that momentous win and he had a sympathetic word for the losers too.

Unquestionably, the players swore by him, and those I quoted in the after-match comments left me in no doubt that without Donie O'Donovan's guidance there would have been little to shout about in 1973. Jimmy Barry Murphy said: 'He was a team's man. He wasn't one to rant and rave. He spoke quietly but effectively. He saw where we could improve areas of the play, where we needed to tighten our game. He knew that Cork needed a victory badly after all the set-backs we had suffered for years. That was why we would have died for him out there today.' The young St Finbarr's star caught the eye of gifted sportswriter Raymond Smith who, in one of his popular publications said of Murphy: 'He had an uncanny ability to see an opening, an uncanny knack also to position himself to be there for a telling strike and a killer goal. I see him now as I saw Denis Law beside George Best and Bobby Charlton. I saw him playing off Ray Cummins at full forward and at times too off the charismatic Declan Barron, and this trio together could be destroyers because they had gifted qualities.'

Jimmy Barry Murphy's brilliance as a forward made him a prime target for the 'thou shalt not pass' defenders who feared him. He enjoyed playing all sports but hated the constant 'pulling and dragging' that is still destroying present-day football. Gifted players like Jimmy provided class entertainment for football followers, but he was one of many skilful players who failed to get proper protection from referees who ignored the fouling tackle that is still marring our games. It was not surprising that Jimmy turned his back on Gaelic football and opted instead for soccer when he joined Wilton United, a local team. He quickly progressed and played for Cork Celtic for a season. Noted soccer writer Billy George told me that Jimmy Barry would have easily made the top echelons of the sport had he persisted with it.

Jimmy still loved the big atmosphere and the big occasion. In 1974 he was on the Cork football panel which began the defence of their All-Ireland crown. Kerry were still the prime danger in Munster and Cork knew it. Donie O'Donovan was still the team coach and manager and he never stopped motivating his charges. He told them that another All-Ireland title was there for the taking if they put their minds to it. Donie was right. Cork beat their old rivals Kerry in the Munster final by 1-11 to 0-7.

The standard of football in Leinster at that time was very mediocre and it was inevitable that old rivals Dublin and Meath would be the main contenders for provincial honours. Dublin prospects did not look great as they made heavy weather of defeating Wexford and Louth. They were marginal favourites to beat Meath in the Leinster final, but the Heffernan, Colfer, Redmond selectorial panel knew if Meath were to be beaten, there would have to be a marked improvement in Dublin's attitude. In the weeks before the final the Dublin players upped their preparations and that was sufficient to get them over the Meath challenge on a 1-14 to 1-9 scoreline.

Cork were favourites going into the All-Ireland semi-final and rightly so. They had put paid to old rivals Kerry in the Munster final and were thinking more of a possible All-Ireland tilt against Galway. Dublin's threat was viewed as minimal in the pre-match write-up by the sports-writers, despite the fact that Croke Park was always viewed as a home venue for the Dubs. The history books record that Cork never played up to form against Dublin in the 1974 All-Ireland semi-final and the reigning All-Ireland title-holders went down by 2-11 to 1-8.

In his match comments the following day in the *Irish Independent*, John D. Hickey wrote: 'Dublin have progressed quite beyond recognition from the team I saw earlier this season.' Few could quibble at the time at that comment. Dublin played out of their skins against Cork. Dublin's trump card was the sterling display given by the midfield partnership of Brian Mullins and Steve Rooney, whose superiority in that area was fundamental in giving the home side the necessary power and strength to take command of the game.

The Cork attack came up against one of the toughest defences they had met for some years. Jimmy Barry Murphy fired home from the penalty spot and added two more points to his tally. But the rest of the Cork forwards failed to make any great progress in quest of scores. Viewed from a Dublin perspective, Anton O'Toole said: 'In a way it was the sweetest of all our victories in the decade as we came from literally nowhere to win the title subsequently. We were by far a more mature and confident team in 1976 and 77. For Dublin to dethrone champions Cork in the 1974 semi-final looked an impossible task beforehand to most pundits, but we did it and no one could deny the merit of our success.' Jimmy Barry Murphy conceded that the 1974 semi-final defeat may well have been on the cards, but Cork hopes of winning back-to-back All-Ireland titles was still very strong in the Cork camp at the time. He felt that the prime factor in Dublin's win was that Dublin were a coming team who had yet to reach their peak but that the indications were already there that season that they were going to be something different.

Cork had to wait until 1983 to reach their next All-Ireland senior semi-final, only to fall again to Dublin, the ultimate winners, who beat Galway in the final in which Dublin finished with twelve players. Six years later the Leesiders made amends when they brought the Sam Maguire Cup back to Cork, and they retained it the following year but have not figured since. A glance through Cork's All-Ireland senior championship appearances would suggest to me that the Leesiders were most unlucky to lose some of those contests. Indeed, Cork's tally of six All-Ireland football crowns does scant justice to the gallant and spirited displays served up by the county in quest of the coveted honours, still eluding them since their last triumph in 1990.

When Jimmy Barry Murphy opted out of football and later, hurling, he was the holder of one All-Ireland senior football title and five All-Ireland senior hurling crowns. He immediately started coaching the minor county hurling team to top honours. He was badly needed by the senior hurling team as coach when he took over in 1996 and ended a bad losing spell when he captured the Liam McCarthy Cup in 1999. Jimmy has won every honour in football and hurling and is the holder of three All Stars awards.

His only regret is that All-Ireland senior hurling losses occurred during the two years he captained the Cork team in 1982 and 83. He left an indelible imprint on the playing fields with his majestic hurling at all levels of the game, allied to the skills he displayed during his brief inter-county football career. He was an all rounder in sport and a true sporting legend.

32

TOMMY MURPHY

No book on the greats of Gaelic football would be complete without the inclusion of Tommy Murphy of Laois, whose name is still spoken of with reverence in any discussion on the best footballers of the past. Put simply, Tommy Murphy is one of the all time greats of Gaelic football.

To attain such a reputation in the game, a player is normally measured by the number of All-Ireland medals won or by his great scoring exploits, but Tommy Murphy, though he is included as one of the finest exponents of Gaelic football ever to grace the game, never even had the honour of playing in an All-Ireland final. He was, however, lucky enough to be on the scene in a golden era for Laois football when they won four Leinster titles in a ten-year period including three in a row, 1936 to 1938.

Laois had won their first Leinster title in 1889, but they were not to win one again until 1936 when a team backboned by six Delaneys from Stradbally ended the long barren period in a year that a young Tommy Murphy was a 15-year-old student at the famous Knockbeg College on the Laois-Carlow border. That year Tommy played on the Laois minor football team.

It was in Knockbeg that the young Murphy's talent was recognised and he was selected on the Leinster Colleges team that won the then inter-provincial championship with Tommy a star player in 1937 and 38. While Laois won the Leinster title of 1936, beating Kildare 3-3 to 0-8, they suffered a crushing defeat in the All-Ireland semi-final to Mayo by 4-11 to 1-5 and, amazingly, the sides did not meet again in championship football until 2006. A year later when Laois began the defence of their Leinster crown, 16-year-old Tommy Murphy was included in the panel and quickly made it on to the first fifteen. He immediately grabbed the imagination of the public.

Tommy made his championship debut against Offaly in Newbridge and his direct opponent was a Railway Cup star at the time, Bill Mulhall, a feared competitor for any seasoned player, let alone a teenager. Murphy did so well that he became a regular and there started an inter-county career that ended sixteen years later against Wexford. In all of that period he was known simply as the 'Boy Wonder', even when he had finished his inter-county career in 1953. Coincidentally, I played on a Dublin team that year against Laois at Croke Park in a National Football League game. The then GAA general secretary Pádraig Ó Caoimh wouldn't allow the game to start until the ground staff cleared ice off the steps of the small stand near the railway wall. An announcement was made declaring that the popular Laois star Tommy Murphy was retiring from inter-county football after that match. Tommy, a great favourite with Croke Park spectators, was the recipient of sustained applause following the announcement.

Laois went on to beat Louth in the Leinster final in 1937 and set up an All-Ireland semi-final clash with Kerry that still evokes bitter memories for old O'Moore supporters. They were unhappy that, firstly, the game and the replay were both played at Munster venues; and, secondly, they believed that Tommy Murphy was 'taken out' at a crucial period in the replay and had to leave the field of play injured. Tim O'Donnell, a great Kerry stalwart wing back who played that day, was very indignant when his name was mentioned in connection with Murphy's injury. He told me many times when we discussed the incident that he was not involved and was very much saddened when the Laois star had to leave the pitch following a very physical charge on Murphy by another Kerry player, whom he named.

The first game before 14,000 spectators in Cork ended all square, 2-3 to 1-6, after Murphy set up Danny Douglas for the equalising point. But the replay in Waterford is hotly debated to this very day. Kerry led at half-time, but shortly after the resumption Bill Delaney placed Murphy and the young lad scored a dynamic goal with a perfectly directed left footed pile driver. Laois went clear with points from Tom Keogh and Mick Haughney. With nineteen minutes remaining and with Laois dominating, Murphy, who was starring, was 'heavily grounded in a deliberate fashion', as Danny Douglas put them three points clear. But to the utter dismay of the Laois supporters, Murphy was forced to retire. Tim 'Roundy' Landers blazed home the levelling goal for Kerry, and just before the final whistle M. Lyne swung over the winning score.

Laois were heart-broken and believe to this day that they would have won, had Murphy been able to finish the game. Their frustration was compounded when Kerry went on to win the All-Ireland. There was to be a consoling sequel to that final. When the All-Ireland finalists were invited to play exhibition games in America, Kerry were unable to travel and they nominated Laois to make the trip. The 17-year-old Murphy looked so boyish that the officials at the Polo Grounds were reluctant to admit him as a player. But he took America by storm and gave such an exhibition out there that his reputation snowballed as a top footballer.

That year, 1937, he became the youngest ever player to be selected on the Leinster team in the Railway Cup and he went on to win four inter-provincial medals with and against some of the greats of that period. There were eight Laois men playing on the 1939 winning side.

Laois won the Leinster title for the third successive year in 1938, beating Kildare, and that set up another semi-final meeting with Kerry—but this time at Croke Park. Tommy Murphy's opponent was the famed Paddy Kennedy and it was fitting that both men were to be selected at midfield in 1961 on the Gael Linn Best Football Team of All Time.

Laois were hoping for revenge, but while the teams were level at half-time, Kerry shot 2-2 in the third quarter, only for Murphy's men to put in a storming finish and score two goals themselves. However, they lost out by just two points in the end, 2-8 to 2-6.

It was to be the end of that great Laois team of the 1930s, but not the end of Tommy Murphy. He continued to thrill audiences at grounds all over the country. He captained Laois to the Leinster final in 1940 when they were defeated by a goal by defending champions Meath. They also lost the 1943 final against Louth.

In 1946 Laois were back in the final against great rivals Kildare and prospects of a classic encounter drew a crowd of 23,353 to Croke Park with gate receipts of £2,136. Because the Laois team was ravaged by injuries in the lead-up to the game, a postponement was sought but refused, and the game was in doubt right up until the starting time. The great Bill Delaney took the field with heavy bandages on his cracked ribs and there was an air of despondency in the Laois camp. But

cometh the hour, cometh the man, and Tommy Murphy turned an
expected Lilywhite whitewash into a one-man show of strength. From
the centre half-back position he kicked eight points as Laois won by
0-11 to 1-6. It was one of Murphy's finest exhibitions, though Laois lost
the All-Ireland semi-final narrowly to Roscommon. He would lose two
more Leinster finals with Laois who, amazingly, were not to win another
for fifty-seven years until the arrival of Mick O'Dwyer in 2003.

One of Tommy's outstanding displays came in the Leinster jersey
when he played against a dominant Connacht side in the 1945 Railway
Cup final. He proceeded to transform the game and led the team to
victory with an inspirational performance, 2-5 to 0-6. Analysts and
spectators said at the time that Tommy Murphy 'had it all'. He could
fetch a ball from the clouds with both hands or take it down with one
hand and transfer it to the other. He could solo and kick accurately
with both feet, passing the ball with unerring accuracy.

An extract from a song called 'The Wonder Boy' sums him up.

For catching and fielding and jumping so high
With one hand outstretched he'd pull the ball from the sky.
They came in their thousands to see the supreme
Tommy Murphy from Graigue, the football machine.

Or from another called 'Tommy Murphy of Laois'

So here's to the gallant Tommy Murphy, boys,
A man who could outfield the best.
At the youthful age of sixteen
His skill was first put to the test.

He rarely played a poor game and it is said that even when he did, he
was better than most of the others. He was never known to have been
outplayed by an opponent. I remember Tommy Murphy for his brilliance
as a midfield player although he filled roles at centre back and centre
forward as well equally impressively. I would put him alongside Mick
O'Connell (Kerry), Cathal O'Leary (Dublin) and perhaps Willie Bryan
(Offaly) who had a unique gift of being able to outjump taller opponents.
It demands timing and superb anticipation which all three players
possessed. I could also add that sportsmanship was a priority with them.

Tommy Murphy won eight Laois senior football titles with his beloved Graiguecullen between 1938 and 1949 and, amazingly, they have won only one title since.

Tommy died at the young age of 64 after battling ill health for a number of years. While he was selected on the Greatest Team of All Time in 1961 and won an all-time Bank of Ireland All Stars in 1981, there was controversy when he was omitted from the Centenary team in 1984 although he was selected on the fifteen that 'never won an All-Ireland' that year.

Compensation was made, however, when in 2000 he was named alongside Mick O'Connell at midfield on the An Post Team of the Millennium. Tommy Murphy was a magnificent footballer whose superb style captivated spectators over three decades and who drew admiration from opposing players and their supporters in equal measure. He epitomised all that is good in Gaelic football and was a shining example and a hero when the world was in turmoil—and in an Ireland where the GAA played such an important and crucial role. Tommy Murphy, the boy wonder, was indeed one of the all-time greats and a very fitting inclusion in this collection.

33

JIMMY MURRAY

In 1944 Jimmy Murray from Knockcroghery, Co. Roscommon, joined a unique band of players who had successfully achieved the rare distinction of captaining back-to-back All-Ireland senior winning football teams. In an era where Kerry were easily the dominant force, the Roscommon achievement was all the more remarkable and widely acclaimed. The other back-to-back winning captains were John Joe O'Reilly of Cavan in 1947 and 48; Seán Flanagan of Mayo in 1950 and 51; Enda Colleran of Galway in 1965 and 66; and Dublin's Tony Hanahoe in 1976 and 77.

But Jimmy 'Jamsie' Murray of Roscommon stands alone in GAA history, having led his county team on five occasions around Croke Park in the All-Ireland pre-match parade. This happened twice in 1943 when Roscommon beat Cavan in a replay to bring the Sam Maguire Cup to the county for the first time, once in 1944, and twice again in 1946 after Kerry forced a replay by scoring two goals in the closing minutes. The Munster men went on to win the replay and deny the Roscommon captain of unbelievable and unmatched honour for himself and the county.

I can safely say that the Roscommon teams of that period were powerful sides and would compare favourably with any of the present-day squads. The real powerhouse centred on the half-back line of Brendan Lynch, Bill Carlos and Ownsie Hoare. The two midfielders were Éamon Boland and Liam Gilmartin, both of whom were brilliant fielders of the ball and long kickers who provided a great service to their attack. The half-forward line had Phelim Murray, Jamsie Murray and Donal Keenan, all three gifted, accurate score-takers.

What was probably unique at that time was the ability of some players to switch to other positions, as did Ownsie Hoare and Phelim Murray.

Hoare filled the left wing back berth in the 1943 final replay against Cavan with Phelim Murray at right half-forward. In the 1944 All-Ireland team which beat Kerry, Ownsie played in goal with Phelim Murray at left wing back. The changes never affected the performance of the team in any way.

Bill Carlos was the personification of greatness at centre back. He was a sturdy figure, but when he rose to contest a high ball, you had the feeling that it was his to command. Forwards were simply brushed aside and the ball was delivered with great authority. In the 1944 final the combined work of Boland and Gilmartin clearly outmatched the best efforts of the formidable Paddy Kennedy and Seán Brosnan—a feat in itself. Jamsie was the skilful leader in attack. His timing was excellent. He was medium size but he competed successfully against taller opponents, displaying a resolve that always gave him an edge in the battle for possession.

Jamsie was one of five great players who were past pupils of Roscommon CBS, where they honed their football skills for the major breakthrough at All-Ireland level in 1943 and again in 1944 with Brendan Lynch, Bill Carlos and Phelim Murray in the half-back line, a line of defence that was to prove awesome in subsequent games. The high fielding Liam Gilmartin, who partnered Boland at midfield, was also a CBS Roscommon product, as was Jack McQuillan at full forward. A lot of credit went to Brother Moloney and Brother Kennedy for their part in coaching many of their Connacht Colleges successes.

Between 1942 and 49, Jimmy Murray won six senior county football championship titles with St Patrick's, Knockcroghery and a senior hurling medal with Roscommon Gaels in 1945. In his long career his style never varied as a skilful forward, whether in the centre or operating from a corner berth. He was undoubtedly a figure-head captain during Roscommon's glory period at All-Ireland level. It is unbelievable to note that Roscommon were actually graded junior in 1938, but showing true grit and resolve they became one of the most successful teams five years later when they carried off the All-Ireland crown in 1943.

Jimmy Murray felt that the basis for that win was fashioned when they beat Galway in the Connacht final, having tasted defeat the previous two years at the hands of the Tribesmen. In the Connacht Senior Football League final in 1942, Roscommon, who had defeated Leitrim, Mayo and Galway but had lost unexpectedly to Sligo, met Galway in a

play-off at Roscommon. The game which attracted a large crowd was a
thriller, especially the last twenty minutes in which the teams were level
on two occasions. Galway's fate was sealed when Jamsie placed Donal
Keenan, who flashed over a cracking point for victory. After the match,
corner back Harry Connor said we had 'won something senior at last'.

But the euphoria of winning that 1942 League final proved to be a
false dawn when the two counties met later that year in the Connacht
final at Ballinasloe. 'We were confident enough after our league
win,' said Jamsie, 'but as the game wore on I did feel that we were not
imposing ourselves in the exchanges and the luck factor was not
helping us either.' The game was very exciting with the lead changing
hands on several occasions. Phelim Murray, Jamsie's brother, gave the
team a major boost when he scored a brilliant point from a very acute
angle, and minutes later Hugh Gibbons got possession and released the
ball to Jamsie who rounded two defenders and cracked the ball to the
Galway net. At half-time the score stood Roscommon 1-1, Galway 0-4.

The second half produced typical championship fare, the scoring
was close, but Galway had a slight edge and that was reflected in the
opening stages when Galway applied the pressure with points from
substitute Pierce Thornton and Charlie Connolly. The Roscommon
forwards did have a number of good chances, but they failed to make
them pay off. Galway were hanging on to a one-point lead minutes
from the end when Roscommon were awarded a close free. Jimmy
Murray handed the ball to the ever reliable free-taker, Donal Keenan,
happy in the knowledge that a replay was inevitable. But horror of hor-
rors, for once the noted marksman shot wide. Galway won 2-6 to 0-11.
There were no recriminations over that miss. The game was to prove a
very useful learning process against a more experienced Galway side,
who were subsequently beaten by Dublin in the 1942 All-Ireland final.
Roscommon got a timely reminder that a lot of hard work goes into
winning the blue riband of Gaelic football. Jamsie Murray, reflecting on
the defeat by Galway, was more convinced than ever that the margin
between his aspiring team and other leading contenders was not that
great.

Roscommon had already captured All-Ireland minor and junior All-
Ireland honours and the big push for the elusive senior crown was the
immediate target at the start of 1943. It was to be a momentous year for
the Roscommon team and their captain Jamsie. They reached the

Connacht final again with keen rivals Galway and achieved victory by
2-6 to 0-8. Thus did Roscommon win the coveted Connacht title for
the first time since 1919. Seldom was such jubilation seen in St
Coman's Park as the players were chaired off the field and hailed as true
champions.

Louth posed a lot of problems for the Connacht men in the All-
Ireland semi-final before the westerners emerged victorious by 3-10 to
3-6. Liam Gilmartin, who had replaced the injured Frank Kinlough in
the Connacht final against Galway and who played brilliantly against
Louth, was retained at midfield for the All-Ireland final against Cavan.
The first part of Murray's dream had come true—to reach an All-
Ireland senior football final. It was now up to the team itself to achieve
the dream of outright success.

The Cavan team bristled with big names: Big Tom O'Reilly, Simon
Deignan, Mick Higgins, T. P. O'Reilly, Joe Stafford and John Joe
O'Reilly. Roscommon and their captain Jamsie were facing a mammoth
task. The players were very edgy. But not so Liam Gilmartin. Jamsie
said: 'We used to often remark that Liam was so relaxed before a game
that he could lie down and sleep in the dressing room and then go out
and play a blinder.'

For the first time in Roscommon's history the county had qualified
for an All-Ireland senior football final. It was to be the biggest occasion
ever for Jimmy Murray and the rest of his side. There was a lot of
tension in the dressing room, which was natural for first timers. There
was a loud roar from the Roscommon followers when Jamsie led his
team out on to the field before an attendance of 68,023. As I viewed the
scene on that occasion, I was surprised to notice that Roscommon didn't
engage in any pre-match kick-about. The team simply stood around in
a group, waiting for the band to form up for the match parade.

Cavan did a bit of a kick-around and the usual running and passing
the ball to each other before they eventually joined Roscommon for the
parade. Cavan took command from the start and quickly got into their
stride while Roscommon looked all at sea. By the time Roscommon
had an opening point from Liam Gilmartin, Cavan had scored a goal
and a couple of points. Slowly Roscommon responded and at half-time
they trailed 1-4 to 0-3.

Minutes after the restart Jimmy Murray gave his team the boost they
so badly needed. A Brendan Lynch free came soaring into the Cavan

defence, the ball broke down into the waiting hands of Jamsie Murray, who turned quickly and crashed the ball to the Cavan net. At the end of the second half it fell to John Joe O'Reilly to save the Breffni men with an equalising point, 1-6 all. Roscommon were glad to get a second chance.

The replay took place before a reduced attendance of 47,193, but wartime restrictions prevailed at the time and getting to Croke Park was always a big problem. The replay produced exciting enough football, but Roscommon appeared to have shrugged off a lot of the mediocrity which had assailed them in the drawn match. They led 2-2 to 2-0 at the interval. Roscommon laid the foundation for victory early in the second half with Donal Keenan points, and captain Jamsie was seen to great effect laying on another point for Frankie Kinlough. Phelim Murray knocked over a point and tempers became frayed at that stage. In a goalmouth mêlée referee Paddy Mythen was assaulted. The offenders were severely punished by Central Council after a lengthy investigation weeks after the game. Roscommon won the match 2-7 to 2-2.

Jamsie Murray recalled that great achievement when he stated: 'It was my most fond memory. We got great receptions at every station on the way home. They had torchlight processions on the platform at Knockcroghery and a big bonfire at the station gate. For months afterwards, we attended victory receptions all over the county. It's something that we will never forget.'

My near neighbour Liam Gilmartin, Roscommon's 6' 4" midfielder who ably partnered Éamon Boland against Cavan's great combination of Simon Deignan and T. P. O'Reilly, enjoyed the exchanges and the sporting battle for midfield control. He told me: 'It was a very enjoyable contest all through the game. Éamon and I had our periods of control and we used it, I thought, wisely. Jimmy Murray was always on the prowl and he was always available for a pass. We won that All-Ireland because we had got over any nerves that had militated against us in the drawn match. Murray was a very good captain. He always commanded the respect of the players and if he saw some flagging in efforts of the play he would give a shout, "Come on lads, don't let the side down", and we always responded.'

The fact that the team was relatively young was to stand to them when they opened their defence of their Connacht title in 1944. Roscommon were now the team to beat in terms of an All-Ireland honours quest. They retained their Connacht title with an easy win over Mayo, then easily disposed of Cavan in the All-Ireland semi-final.

Croke Park was packed with 79,245 spectators for the Roscommon-Kerry final. Jamsie Murray had the notable distinction of once again captaining the reigning champions. In one of the best All-Ireland finals ever, victory went to the Roscommon men by 1-9 to 2-4. In his victory speech Jamsie told the cheering crowd: 'To beat Kerry in an All-Ireland final is every team captain's dream and I'm delighted that this Roscommon team has achieved it. It is well known that no team can be regarded as true champions until they beat Kerry in a final.'

Jimmy Murray's All-Ireland winning credentials have still remained intact. His record of having shared in the unique honour of captaining his county to win back-to-back All-Ireland titles still stands, while his record of leading his county team on five occasions in the All-Ireland parade has never been bettered.

34

JOHNNY NEVIN

Carlow dual star Johnny Nevin may never, as a player, have sampled the joy of All-Ireland hurling or football final days in Croke Park, but he and fellow Carlow man Joe Hayden do share a unique piece of GAA history as the only players to win All-Ireland senior B medals in both football and hurling. The old Leighlin footballer and Naomh Bríd hurler was a member of the Carlow team which lifted the All-Ireland B football title in 1984 when beating Westmeath in the final at O'Connor Park. Playing at centre forward, Johnny Nevin scored 0-2 in Carlow's 2-10 to 1-11 win over the Lake county.

Five years earlier in the summer of 1992, Johnny was a key defender, anchoring the team at centre back as the Barrowsiders defeated London by 2-15 to 3-10 to win the All-Ireland B hurling title. Today Johnny may be closer to 40 than 30, but he still retains all the enthusiasm of youth, continuing to play senior club hurling and football. Indeed, earlier last year Johnny won a Kehoe Cup senior hurling medal with his native county, and he has by no means given up on having a future role to play with his county senior footballers.

They say that good goods come in small parcels. Johnny Nevin is the living proof of that. Although small of stature, he is a great-hearted player who has always given 100 per cent to club, county and province, be it hurling or football. And while Johnny gives his all for the cause, he is known throughout his native Carlow and indeed outside the county as being a genuine sportsman who seldom, if ever, earns censure from referees. Over more than two decades he has inspired many a club and county team to success by imposing himself on the proceedings and showing the way for his colleagues.

The man from Closutton, Leighlinbridge, has played a phenomenal total of 330 games at senior competitive level in the yellow, green and red of Carlow—174 for the county footballers and 156 with the hurlers. Despite the ongoing demands of both codes, he has rarely suffered a serious injury. His only one of note was a broken thumb in football training which kept him out of the game for about a month. As a Gaelic promotion officer with the Leinster Council of the GAA, Johnny is constantly on the go, imparting his skills to primary school children throughout County Carlow. He is also involved with the county football and hurling development squads at under-14, under-15 and under-16 levels. For the affable Johnny, working with these young players in the sporting codes to which he is so dedicated, is indeed a labour of love.

Johnny attended Leighlinbridge National School and Presentation De La Salle College in Bagnellstown. He first played with the local John Tydall's under-14 footballers and later minor football with Michael Davitts. He made his first impression when lining out for Carlow under-16 hurlers when they reached the All-Ireland B Centenary Year final against Down—a game the Mourne county won. The following year he was part of a strong Carlow minor football team which beat Laois and Wexford in the Leinster championship, before losing out narrowly to Offaly.

Having claimed a special All-Ireland under-21 hurling medal with Carlow in the early 1980s and played with the county under-21 footballers, Johnny went on to make his Leinster senior football championship debut against Laois in 1988 at Dr Cullen Park and scored the game's first point. Carlow beat their neighbours that day courtesy of a late goal from Joe Hayden. Around 1989 Johnny found himself in demand for both the county senior footballers and hurlers and answered the call from both. A firm favourite with Carlow supporters, the man from Closutton went on to have distinguished careers in both codes. In 2004 he was named 'Sports Star of the Week' in the *Irish Independent* after Carlow shocked Longford in the Leinster championship in Tullamore. As a result of that display Johnny was also named 'Vodafone Footballer of the Month' for May 2004. In 2002 he claimed an O'Byrne Cup medal when Carlow defeated Wicklow in the final at Dr Cullen Park—the Barrowsiders had beaten Dublin in the semi-final.

That good Carlow team was captained by Andrew Corden, the outstanding O'Hanrahan's defender, who was later to lose his life in a tragic accident. Johnny was also honoured with Railway Cup selection in hurling for Leinster and was by no means out of his depth when mixing with the household names of the small ball code. However, he nominates a club victory as his most cherished career memory to date.

That was when Old Leighlin won the club's only county senior football title in 1997. Although rank outsiders, the men from close to the Kilkenny border beat Palatine in the final, with Johnny playing a pivotal role in that famous victory. It was the proudest day in the history of the wearers of the blue and white. Much of Carlow gaeldom rejoiced that Johnny Nevin now had a football medal to go with his senior hurling championship won the previous year when Naomh Bríd—an amalgam of Leighlinbridge, Ballinabranna and Old Leighlin—won their first hurling crown with a shock win over red hot favourites St Mullins.

In 2004 Johnny won a second county championship hurling medal when Naomh Bríd overcame Ballinkillen in the final. He continued to play in the half-forward line for Old Leighlin and at full back for Naomh Bríd in the 2006 Carlow senior championships of both codes, in which he was an inspiration to his club colleagues and a role model for young players.

He is adamant that the day of the dual inter-county GAA star is over, and says the time is not far off when a man lining out in football and hurling for his club will come under threat. He cannot see any player of the future achieving what Cork's Teddy McCarthy did in 1990—winning All-Ireland senior hurling and football medals in the same year. It is not possible, Johnny asserts, to combine the two codes nowadays. The number of competitions dictates that a player who hurls and plays football with his county must make a career decision and opt for one code or the other.

He states: 'If a player seeks to play both games he will find himself training five to six nights a week, with nothing left in the tank for a Sunday game. The situation will be quickly reached whereby one team manager will put it to the player that he has to make a choice between hurling and football.' So to the Carlow man's mind, there will be no more Jimmy Barry Murphys, Liam Currams or Teddy McCarthys coming on the scene to claim Celtic crosses in hurling and football. He is also of the opinion that the stage is also being reached whereby club players will have to make a choice between hurling or football because of the dedication being demanded by managers to their particular code. In his estimation dual status at club level is now quite definitely a threatened species.

Born just a few miles from the Kilkenny border, Johnny has great admiration for the hurling style of the Cats. He has an affinity with the black and amber as his mother Margaret Drennan is a native of Paulstown. The Carlow and Kilkenny colours fly proudly outside the Nevin household beside the N9. Had he been born on the Kilkenny side of the border, no doubt Johnny would have made a strong bid for hurling glory with the Cats. But he is a proud Carlow man and his loyalties lie with the men of the Barrowside. He has no hesitation opting for football over hurling in terms of personal preference. Hurling was never the big ambition in his sporting career that football was.

Outside of the GAA, Johnny has a keen interest in horse-racing—not surprising really, when one considers that the Willie Mullins-trained Hedgehunter, the winner of the 2005 Aintree Grand National, is from the townland of Closutton. When Hedgehunter stormed home to that thrilling win, he was not only carrying jockey Ruby Walsh but also Johnny Nevin's money. He follows Derby County in soccer, without knowing why.

A true, dedicated sportsman, he plays the game as it should be played, demonstrating the commitment and leadership that has kept him at the top for so long, even though now in his late thirties.

35

DERMOT O'BRIEN

There were six minutes remaining and Cork were hanging on to a narrow one-point lead in the 1957 All-Ireland senior football final at Croke Park. Louth captain Dermot O'Brien was in possession of the ball as he soloed goalwards. He quickly changed direction and punted a short pass to Séamus O'Donnell, who cracked a rising shot towards the Cork goal, but it was deflected out for a 50 by the Cork goalie Liam Power. Kevin Beahan took the 50 and sent it straight and true into the Cork parallelogram. The lion-hearted Paddy O'Driscoll rose high in the goalmouth, gained possession and lashed the ball out over the sideline to safety. Beahan, one of the best free-takers in the business, was again called into action. Beahan flighted the ball beautifully to the left-hand goal post. Up went Seán Cunningham and fisted the dropping ball to the Cork net. That left Louth ahead 1-9 to 1-7. There were still a few minutes left to play. With the seconds ticking away, Paddy O'Driscoll led a Cork rally. A Cork forward crossed a ball from the left wing, it bounced across the Louth goalmouth, and there waiting for it was Louth's Jim 'Red' Meehan, who caught it, moved out with the ball and kicked it upfield as the final whistle sounded.

The wee county had regained the All-Ireland title after a lapse of forty-five years. And the captaincy honour had rested on the shoulders of Dermot O'Brien. It was his first and only All-Ireland senior football medal, but he treasures it to this day.

As Dermot related to me after that epic victory for my *Evening Press* report of the match: 'I was asked to take over the captaincy when my St Mary's Ardee club mate Patsy Coleman was injured during the Leinster championship. Patsy recovered and during a training session both of us were asked to sort out the captaincy situation. I offered to step down, but we were told to toss a coin for it and I won.'

Dermot's inability to gain entry into Croke Park on the day of the 1957 All-Ireland final still remains a vivid memory. 'I stayed behind in the hotel to get a pain-killing injection for an injured shoulder I picked up against Tyrone in the All-Ireland semi-final. When I got to Croke Park there were thousands of spectators clamouring to get in. I couldn't get near the entrance stile. I went to the back of the Hogan Stand and with the help of a Garda convinced the stile man to let me cross the field to the dressing rooms.' A very distraught Jimmy Mullen, the County Board chairman, none too happy about his missing captain a few minutes from the start of the All-Ireland final, was a very relieved man when Dermot made his appearance. Mullen was a far happier man subsequently when Dermot brought the Sam Maguire Cup into the dressing room and handed it to him. He accepted it with tears in his eyes. It was a very emotional occasion for everyone in the crowded room.

Dermot was glad in a way that the hiatus involved in getting into the ground on that famous day banished any of the pre-match nerves he would normally have experienced. He was more concerned about getting to the dressing room and togging out. Said Dermot: 'Imagine the dramatic scene there before I entered . . . twelve minutes to the throw-in and no captain on hand to lead the lads out . . . I had no trace of nerves as we came out through the tunnel and on to the pitch to a massive roar from the crowd. That near miss took all the pre-match tension away.'

Dermot and Kevin Beahan were members of the Ardee St Mary's club and they were vital cogs in the Louth attack. Both had experienced the trials and tribulations of the All-Ireland atmosphere when they played and lost to Kerry in the 1953 All Ireland semi-final. Said Beahan: 'Out there you are all alone. In an All-Ireland final there is no pity. I mean, you have arrived at the day on which all hopes are pinned. Unless football is in you, when you get to that stage, no one can tell you how to play it. You have got to know what to do without being told. Winning an All-Ireland medal is the greatest thrill. I personally will know no greater sporting thrill. All my hopes and aspirations had been built on the achievement of that goal.'

Dermot O'Brien won his first senior county championship title with St Mary's in 1951 at the age of 19. Two years later he won his first Leinster senior football championship medal when Louth beat

Wexford 1-7 to 0-7 in the Leinster final, and that gave him a major boost. He was selected at right half-forward on the team which faced Kerry in the All-Ireland football semi-final that year. His immediate opponent was Kerry's brilliant Seán Murphy, probably one of the best defenders ever to grace the Croke Park pitch.

Dermot confessed that he wasn't doing very well against the experienced Murphy and was moved to the corner. As he took up his position, his marker, Jas Murphy, stuck out his hand and said, 'How are you, you creatur?'

All the action was confined to the Louth defence and in a fifteen-minute spell the Kerry forwards turned on the style to shoot three great goals and take a commanding lead in the match. Indeed, Kerry would not have been flattered had they added a few more goals to their winning tally. Louth paid the price for indifference that day, and they lacked the necessary balance which was so essential in a battle for supremacy on a major occasion.

There was one redeeming feature for the Louth men which lifted the gloom of their defeat. An unnumbered substitute was introduced by Louth in the second half. Fr Kevin Connolly from Ravensdale was brought in at midfield. He played under his mother's name, McArdle. Being a cleric, he was not supposed to play in physical contact sports. Kevin Connolly was a brilliant all round athlete, an All-Ireland sprint champion and a 440 yards winner. Connolly's entry very nearly changed the whole trend of the game. His high fielding and midfield dominance brought Louth back into the game. His solo runs were brilliant and Kerry had no one to either match him or catch him. The Louth players responded too and at the end Kerry were happy to record a five-point victory, 3-6 to 0-10. It could have been much more but for Kevin Connolly.

Dermot O'Brien learned a very valuable lesson after that defeat. He made up his mind that there were facets of that defeat at the hands of Kerry which could have been avoided. All that was needed was a greater emphasis on team work and far more commitment. Dermot also learned that football at All-Ireland level needed a special effort, and that misdirected passes and wild kicking were no basis for winning matches. They were perfectly capable of making amends as the team contained talented footballers. Louth were therefore well prepared when the Leinster championship started in 1957. No stone was left unturned in order to improve the quality of their football and remove the weaknesses which had dogged their efforts against Kerry in 1953.

Jimmy Quigley was now the team trainer. He had played a lot of football himself. There was only one objective—to bring the Sam Maguire Cup back to the wee county. Discussions had taken place and analysis had pinpointed the faults that led to the defeat in the All-Ireland semi-final against Kerry three years earlier. But Dermot O'Brien's inter-county career suffered a rare set-back. Late in the semi-final against Kerry in 1953, he fell over the shoulder of big John Cronin and landed on his back. He burst a blood vessel and was badly concussed. That kept him out of football and he did not play for Louth from 1954 to 1956. He did play for Ardee St Mary's, and early in 1957 a Louth selector asked him, 'If we pick you, will you play? We don't want to be picking players if they don't want to play.' Dermot's answer was equally blunt. 'If I'm picked, I'll play.' His first outing in the red jersey was against Dublin in the National League.

Dermot was chosen at centre forward and found himself up against one of Dublin's greatest defenders, Jim Crowley. They had a great battle and O'Brien had the distinction of scoring two very good goals against a formidable foe. When the Leinster Championship got under way in 1957, Louth defeated Carlow in the first round at Navan.

Dermot takes up the story: 'Of the six forwards that played in Navan that day, I was the only survivor in the Leinster final. Little by little it came together: Séamus O'Donnell was brought on; Jim Roe got his chance and took it; Jimmy McDonnell came back out of retirement and went to full forward and had a brilliant year; Frank Lynch was taken on and he was only 18.' The Louth team was taking shape much to the delight of all concerned. They beat Wexford, and Kildare followed next, but the big bogey was still Dublin whom they met in the Leinster final.

The heavens opened on Leinster final day before an attendance of 30,234. Despite all that Dublin threw at Louth, the visitors' defence of Tom Conlon, Jim Meehan, Jim McArdle and Stephen White were rock-like. The noted Dublin forwards were never allowed to express themselves and Louth went on to win 2-9 to 1-7.

Their defeat of Dublin came as a great relief because the city men had always been the dominant force in the province. Louth's next big task was against Tyrone in the All-Ireland semi-final, and what an intriguing contest that turned out to be! Tyrone's defeat of Derry before an attendance of 36,000 was one of the most exciting Ulster finals in years. Louth had every reason to fear Tyrone's supreme stylist, Iggy Jones. I remember refereeing a colleges inter-provincial semi-final at Croke between Ulster and Leinster and Iggy Jones stood out like a beacon. His speed on the ball, his solo runs and his unquestionable skills singled him out as a player with a lot of talent.

So on 18 August 1957, Tyrone and Iggy Jones were back in Croke Park, still hoping to go one better than the previous year when they were beaten by Galway 1-10 to 2-6. It was a super goal by Seán Purcell which sank Tyrone on that occasion. Dermot watched the 1956 Tyrone-Galway clash and rated the Ulster champions as the finest, most spirited and courageous challengers he had ever seen coming out of Ulster. 'We knew what to expect. The Tyrone team was a very well balanced one. They had strength in all the right places: full back Jim Devlin, centre back Eddie Devlin, left half-back John Joe O'Hagan and forwards like Jackie Taggart and Iggy Jones. We had prepared team tactics, but we also had far greater belief in ourselves on that occasion, knowing the big prize that lay ahead.'

Tyrone didn't waste much time getting into their stride in the All-Ireland semi-final. They were now battle hardened and they had the potential to end the Louth dream. They got away to a flying start and though creating at least five goaling chances, led by only 0-5 to 0-2, a margin which didn't flatter them. Disaster struck Tyrone at the end of the first quarter. Jody O'Neill suffered a leg injury that left him a virtual passenger from the end of the first quarter onwards. He had been in brilliant form and Tyrone were looking certain winners at that stage.

By half-time Louth had forged 0-6 to 0-5 in front. Within two minutes of the restart, the brilliant Tyrone wing back Seán Donnelly soloed upfield and shot over a cracking point to level the scores. The play was exciting with both teams battling for the upper hand. The lion-hearted Kevin Beahan, one of the deadliest sharpshooters from frees and placed balls, started a Louth revival with a point from a thirty-five yard free. Jim McDonnell and Jim Roe added a brace and the Wee county were in command.

Tyrone moved their best forward Jackie Taggart to midfield to curb the influence of Beahan and Dan O'Neill (the latter was a great all rounder). Chance after chance was missed by the Tyrone forwards and that was to prove their undoing. Three points from Jim McDonnell, Jim Roe and Kevin Beahan left the final margin Louth 0-13, Tyrone 0-7. Louth team captain Dermot O'Brien, while delighted to beat their valiant opponents, acknowledged the fact that the poor marksmanship by the Tyrone forwards cost them dearly. 'Three factors swung it in our favour. The Tyrone selectors failed to address a number of areas where we dominated. They had the winning of the match but failed to put away at least five goaling chances; added to that was the injury to Jody O'Neill. He should have been replaced; he was struggling from the end of the first quarter onwards,' said Dermot.

The Tyrone match was soon forgotten when Louth resumed training for the 1957 All-Ireland against Cork. O'Brien's recollection of the final was quite clear. As he was battling his way to get to the Hogan Stand for the cup presentation, his arm was grabbed by his immediate opponent during the match, Paddy O'Driscoll, who, instead of going to his own dressing room, went out of his way to follow Dermot to shake his hand—a real sportsman. Dermot and the Louth team didn't reach Ardee until three in the morning. But the town was packed and the team, standing on the back of a big truck, received a tumultuous reception. Standing beside Dermot on the truck was Tom Conlon, the full back who had played a masterful role in the team's success. He turned to Dermot and said, 'Isn't this something else?' Dermot agreed. Tom said, 'You know, it's good for you but I saw the two days and it's far better for me.' Tom was on the beaten Louth team that played Mayo in the 1950 All-Ireland final. Like all winning All-Ireland captains, Dermot O'Brien savoured the 1957 success when he brought the Sam Maguire Cup back to Ardee after a lapse of forty-five years and carved his name in the annals of Louth football history. He told me, 'To win an All-Ireland title is the fulfilment of a dream, and to captain a winning team while doing so is the icing on the cake.'

36

KEVIN O'BRIEN

Wicklow still remains one of the weaker football counties who have yet to make the big breakthrough at championship level. But over the years Wicklow players have been selected on Leinster inter-provincial teams, rubbing shoulders with some of their more illustrious colleagues with All-Ireland titles to their names. Over the years since the inter-provincial series was launched in 1927, Wicklow players have represented their county with remarkable distinction. Three Wicklow men, Jim Rogers, Gerry O'Reilly and Kevin O'Brien, however, have left an indelible imprint during their stints in the Leinster colours. All three played on successful teams, as indeed did other great Wicklow players going back over the years. Kevin O'Brien from the Baltinglass club is a prime example. I include him in this book on the strength of his great industry and remarkable, tireless energy in pursuit of the successes he did achieve.

Renowned Dublin star Kevin Heffernan, who with seven Railway Cup medals, a record for the province, had only the height of praise for Wicklow's O'Brien. He said: 'Kevin gained his place on Leinster teams primarily for his ability to win the ball and score. I always admired him for his loyalty to his county and his amazing capacity to measure up to the demands of a stiff contest. He worked like a beaver whenever he was selected for Wicklow or Leinster and was a very unselfish performer on the field of play. I would compare him with Declan Browne of Tipperary who fills a similar role with Munster and Tipperary.'

John O'Leary, Dublin's star goalkeeper of 1983 All-Ireland final fame, first encountered a young Kevin O'Brien when the Leinster selectors decided to have a few trial matches before selecting the panel for the Railway Cup series. He hadn't even gained the honour of being chosen for his native county for the Leinster championship.

But he was a vital cog in the Baltinglass club team which was one of the dominant forces in Wicklow football. John O'Leary was soon to be thankful for the presence of O'Brien in the Leinster attack. And John was not surprised later that year when Kevin was chosen on the Ireland team for the International Rules matches against Australia.

O'Leary insisted that O'Brien was one of the greatest forwards of his generation; he even rated him ahead of Kerry's Pat Spillane, quite a remarkable tribute, which O'Leary explained in his book, *Back to the Hill*. The Dublin captain said: 'People might think I'm mad putting him ahead of Spillane, but I'll stand by my judgment on this one. Let's put it this way. O'Brien would have been a resounding success with the great Kerry teams of the 1970s and 80s. How good would Spillane have been with Wicklow?' O'Brien was chosen on the Leinster team in 1986 which beat Ulster in the Railway Cup semi-final in Breffni Park and figured prominently at centre forward.

Kevin recalled the occasion very well: 'It was a fierce cold day and my feet were freezing. After ten minutes I caught this ball and tried to kick for a point. My feet were so cold that my effort dropped short, but somehow it looped into the net over the head of goalie Brian McAlinden. It was a pure fluke. But it must have looked good from the sideline because the papers the following day credited me with chipping the goalkeeper. If only!' Kevin was picked for the final on St Patrick's Day and played a blinder in a roving role and knocked over some vital points. He was named man of the match the following day. He had thus joined the elite band of Wicklow players who had won Railway Cup medals, and he was on a high.

Three months later I was at Aughrim doing a radio commentary on the Wicklow-Laois Leinster senior football championship match when all hell broke loose. Some months earlier Laois had beaten Monaghan 2-6 to 2-5 to win the National League title and were very determined to make a good start in the championship. The meeting of Wicklow and Laois is now history, but it earned the tag the 'Battle of Aughrim'. It started with true championship fervour and continued in that vein. Gradually the exchanges led to a number of stoppages. A major row broke out involving players from both sides. The end result was that three Laois players got their marching orders, and one from Wicklow. When the game concluded, Wicklow had achieved a remarkable victory, the shock of the Leinster campaign that year.

One of the heroes for Wicklow was Kevin O'Brien, who shot two goals and two points, apart from his industry in creating scores for the other Wicklow forwards. One of the goals came from a penalty award which Kevin described as one of the worst he had ever taken. 'Normally I slot them to the right or left of the goalie, but on that occasion I shot it straight at the Laois goalie who saved it, but luckily for me it bounced out and I got in to finish it to the Laois net. That gave us a great boost and we went on to win the match by four clear points.' Sitting below me in the stand seats was Niall Quinn of Arsenal fame. I interviewed him on air at the interval. He was home for the season's break and was holidaying in the Garden county. Niall claimed that there was more action in that championship clash than you would have got in an English soccer game.

However, Wicklow didn't build on that success and made their exit in the next round. Their conquerors were the men from Meath who showed them no mercy. They were hammered by nine points.

Kevin's great regret is the fact that the county is still one of the Cinderellas of Gaelic football. They haven't yet won a Leinster senior football title. He told me: 'I would dearly have loved winning a Leinster championship medal at senior level, and that would have given me the chance to play in the All-Ireland semi-final. I did win an All-Ireland club medal with Baltinglass and we are still the only club in Wicklow to have achieved that honour.' Kevin firmly believes that the basis for all great triumphs at club level stems from the effort and commitment shown by the players.

On the way to capturing the 1990 All-Ireland club title, they disposed of Longford Slashers, Ferbane (Offaly) and Thomas Davis (Dublin). They beat Castlehaven of Cork, who were led by Larry Tompkins, in the All-Ireland semi-final and finally beat Clann Na nGael (Roscommon) in the All-Ireland final by 2-7 to 0-7. The following year in the Leinster final, Baltinglass were held to a draw by Dublin rivals Thomas Davis, and in the replay at Newbridge the Dublin champions defeated them 1-8 to 0-8.

Having won thirteen county senior titles with Baltinglass, the victory in the All-Ireland club final was another step up the ladder for O'Brien. But the Leinster championship medal continued to elude him. He contested three Leinster semi-finals but failed to advance to the final stage. Perhaps the clash most eagerly anticipated was the quarter-final stage against Meath in 1991. It was the time when Dublin and Meath met in the first round of the Leinster championship. This led to the famous and never to be forgotten four fantastic matches, which Meath eventually won at the fourth attempt.

It took great commitment and stamina on the part of Meath to emerge successfully from the four gripping games. But for Wicklow, Meath's next opponents, it looked the perfect situation for Kevin O'Brien and his colleagues to achieve the shock of the championship. The Wicklow challenge, in the eyes of the Meath opposition at the time, didn't constitute any great problem. Many people viewed the outing as a romp for the Meath men.

Meath survived the challenge of the gallant Wicklow men, but only just. It was simply heart-break for Wicklow. Kevin really believed that his team had the beating of Meath in that drawn match. 'We had trained very hard,' he told me. 'Even during the game we were matching them man for man, score for score, but that little bit of important luck seemed to fall to Meath every time. They were feeling the exertions of the four games against Dublin, but that little extra push we needed to edge them out just didn't materialise. We had our chance to make history but we left it behind us in the drawn match. It was a far different Meath we came up against in the replay. We never produced the same form again,' said the ageless O'Brien.

Kevin is a fitness fanatic and spends a lot of time in the gym working out and when necessary will train an extra day or two to help maintain his fitness level. During the course of writing this piece, I phoned him at home. He had just finished packing his bags for an early flight to Australia to play in the International Masters series. He had been training very hard for that particular trip. The Baltinglass star is no stranger to Australia. He was chosen on the International Rules panel under Eugene McGee's managership for the home games in 1987 and the away trip in 1990.

Shrewd Eugene McGee had the height of praise for O'Brien's contribution on both occasions that he was in charge. 'There is no doubt in my mind about Kevin's prowess. He is one of the best forwards of his generation and worthy of his place on any of the top teams in the country. I would have him on any representative side. In the Rules series he was always looking for the action and if there was a sniff of a scoring chance, he would take it. His ability to take on defenders in quest of the ball made him a forward to fear. He was a great team player. He didn't look for glory and hated the trappings of publicity accorded to him by the press,' said the affable McGee.

While major national honours were not to be his, an All Stars award was attainable should his performances with the county or the province capture the attention of the All Stars selectors. It may have been wishful thinking on his part, but driving to work one morning to the Wicklow County Council offices, he nearly crashed his car. RTÉ had just announced that Kevin O'Brien of Wicklow had been chosen on the All Stars football team. A missing link had just dropped on his playing career CV. It was the one he had always dreamed about; now it had arrived. His selection on a coveted All Stars football team was greeted with unanimous approval countrywide, and especially by his legion of supporters.

Kevin has suffered over the years as a result of injuries picked up throughout his playing career. He is a much-travelled performer once Wicklow make their exit from the Leinster championship. When I was in Chicago on a holiday visit some years ago, the name of Kevin O'Brien ranked very highly with the Wolfe Tones club, with whom he played. It was the same with the Leitrim club in New York. He was an instant success in the Big Apple. Now in his forties, Kevin is still addicted to football and still available for his club Baltinglass. He was courted by Kildare and Dublin clubs in his earlier years and promises of jobs were readily available. He shunned all such offers even though they were very tempting.

After fourteen years of service to club and county, the name of Kevin O'Brien ranks with the best in the game of football. He is indeed one of the greats among that august band.

37

PADDY O'BRIEN

Paddy O'Brien was born in the football stronghold of Skyrne, Co. Meath. He was always very keen on football in his early childhood days, and football was a constant topic in the house where he lived. And when they ran short of local heroes to praise, they would list the achievements of Joe Norris, the peerless O'Tooles and Dublin star of the 1920s. Joe was an uncle of his by marriage. There were seven boys in the family, and one sister Carmel. He was the second eldest and two of his brothers, Séamus and Cyril, wore the Meath jersey. And just for good measure his first cousin, the tireless and tenacious 'Meehawl', was to accompany him at corner back right through his football career. Indeed I must say, the Meath full back line of Mícheál O'Brien, Paddy O'Brien and Kevin McConnell was the finest defensive line to grace the football scene at that time.

It was Brian Smith, his teacher (no relation to Brian the footballer), who struck the spark and enkindled his enthusiasm by praising some achievement of Tony Donnelly on the Meath county team. Tony Donnelly was his hero and he felt very privileged to be playing beside him for Meath, more so than any other football decoration.

Paddy was chosen on the Meath juvenile team when his schooldays were over. They were paired against Dublin. There were three boys from Skryne on the Meath team: Tom Brown, Mick Devine and Paddy himself. Dublin won that game in Navan and Paddy was very impressed with the style and skill served up by the city visitors. He was pleased with his own performance at midfield, a berth he was to fill later in his senior career. He was also thrilled at being congratulated by shrewd judge, zealous official and one-time football star Father McManus of the Meath County Board.

Competitions were almost at a standstill when Paddy O'Brien was leaving school at the start of World War II, so he had no chance of playing minor grade. But his progress to the senior ranks was accelerated, and though, as he said, he did not immediately shine, 'the selectors had patience with him'. He subsequently got his chance in the Leinster league and finally established himself in the Cairnes Cup final in 1944. His love of football remained undimmed despite the lack of opportunity. The spread of the dreaded foot and mouth disease severely restricted even local traffic in Meath, and for a time all football competitions were suspended. He vividly remembers cycling twenty miles to Croke Park as a youngster to see Meath play Kerry in the All-Ireland final in 1939, and now can hardly recall that first ever visit to the GAA's national stadium. He does, painfully, recollect the long cycle home to the farm in Skyrne.

There was amazing enthusiasm for football in the Skryne parish around that time. They reached the county final in 1944 against Parnells of An Uaimh. After three wonderful games, two of which were drawn, the Skryne men emerged victorious.

At the time, the National League had been suspended because of foot and mouth disease, but a new competition was introduced, the Leinster league. The league was divided into four sections, which kept football very much alive in the province through the non-championship months. Louth were Meath's group opponents and the teams met in Dundalk. Paddy O'Brien was picked at midfield. He joined the group which was bringing Matt O'Toole, Jackie May and Tony Donnelly to Dundalk. Outside Drogheda a black cat dashed in front of the car, and Paddy claimed it was his good luck charm.

As it was his first inter-county game, he was extremely over-anxious in his approach and that did not help. He could do nothing right. Soon he was 'on the move'. From centrefield he was shifted to the forty, from there to the wing, and then to full forward. But the other members of that side, Frankie Byrne with his excellent points from frees and play, ably assisted by Peter McDermott, Jackie May and Paddy Meegan, reduced Louth's lead to three points. With a minute left, that black cat must have been keeping a close eye on things. A dropping ball to the square was well fielded by Paddy O'Brien, he turned and the ball was in the net. That goal gave Meath the crucial draw and the section honours.

The following Sunday, Meath faced Cavan in the final of the 'Three Counties League' in Virginia with O'Brien again at full forward and Meath won 3-8 to 1-8. They were out again the following Sunday in a

challenge game against Down at Newry, but in the course of the
match he collided with a Down defender and had to be replaced. His
next outing was against Louth in the Cairnes Cup in November 1944.
He knew he had to make a deep impression if he wanted the selectors
to keep him on the team. On that occasion he was at midfield,
partnered by Paddy Meegan, which was to prove a very successful
pairing. It helped in no uncertain manner in beating the wee county
4-4 to 2-2. From then on Paddy O'Brien was a regular member of
the Meath team and that was due to his display in the middle of the
field. He was described as having 'an inspired performance which
pointed the way to victory for the well balanced Meath men'. There
were high hopes in the county when the Leinster championship
started in 1945, but that dream came to a sudden halt when Meath were
beaten 1-8 to 0-5 by an inspired Offaly team in the Leinster semi-
final. The only consolation was their victory in September against
Carlow in the Leinster League final at Croke Park. The margin of
victory was one point.

In 1945 Paddy O'Brien came to Dublin and joined the famous Seán
McDermotts club, spending ten happy years with them before he
retired. In 1947 he captained 'Seans' to win the Dublin senior champion-
ship title. They were among the strongest club teams playing in Dublin.
The bulk of the team was drawn from the best inter-county players of
the time, including Meath's Christo Hand, Clare's Noel Crowley, Dick
Bradley, Jack Morrihy, the peerless Eddie Boyle of Louth, Willie Adams,
Paddy McEntyre and Joe O'Connor of Offaly, all involved in that
victory, as were Tom Langan, Vincent Brown and Tommy Acton of
Mayo.

'Seans' were beaten by Garda in 1948 and the St Vincent's club
became the kingpins in Dublin, dominating the football scene for the
next decade. Paddy O'Brien makes no secret of the fact that his ten-year
spell with the famous Seán McDermott club was the happiest of his
playing days in the capital.

When the National Football League commenced in the autumn of
1945, Meath were determined to make amends for their disappointing
championship display against a formidable Offaly team. True, they had
won the Leinster League, but a championship or a league title would sit
better on the Meath sideboard. Their first league game was against
Fermanagh in Enniskillen. There had been heavy rain for days preceding

the match. Not alone was the pitch nearly ankle deep in mud, but flood water came up almost to the pitch itself.

When any player kicked the ball too hard or too wildly in one particular part of the field, the leather would go sailing away into the nearby Lake Erne. The ball had to be retrieved by a man in a boat, who sat there for that purpose. Sometime during the game Paddy elected to take a penalty. As he ran up to take the kick, the surface at that particular spot was so soft that his boot stuck in the mud and he fell over the ball. Meath won the match easily enough, but his most lasting impression was the truly phenomenal goal-kicking of the Fermanagh full back Al Breslin who, despite the almost impossible conditions, got tremendous distance into his deliveries. All thirty mud-covered players dashed to their hotel and rushed every bathroom on the premises. Twenty minutes later there was consternation. So much mud was washed off the players that it clogged the pipes, and the hotel was in danger of being flooded too!

Through the winter and spring of 1945/46, Meath continued a winning run in the league campaign. They beat Monaghan, were held to a draw by a good Longford team and were pleased to get over near neighbours Louth. In their next outing they beat Cavan by 3-9 to 2-5. Paddy was marking the strong Simon Deignan and he had a great battle of wits against a very sporting competitor.

In 1947 Meath won the Leinster senior football championship for the first time in six years and qualified for the All-Ireland semi-final. The significant feature about the 1947 championship was that the two finalists would play in the Polo Grounds, New York. All the championship contenders had their sights set on an American trip. In that respect Meath were no different from all the other provincial competitors. They were going all out to earn that lucrative prize.

A first-round win over Wicklow proved a good start, followed by victory against Westmeath. Paddy and Christo Hand missed the Westmeath game because both players were assisting their club, Seán McDermotts, to win the Dublin senior football championship at Croke Park. Next up in the Leinster championship were Louth, a team that always appeared to bring out the best in Meath. Wind assisted in the first half, Meath were struggling a bit before a record Croke Park attendance. They were leading 0-4 to 0-2 a few minutes before half-time when Paddy Meegan was fouled. Frankie Byrne pointed the free. But from the kick-out Louth broke away and scored a goal. The real battle had commenced. Louth put over two more points at the start of the second half and were looking good. For a spell it looked like 'Farewell, New York' for Meath. But in stepped Frankie Byrne with his accurate right boot to knock over two more points and Meath were back in tune. Paddy O'Brien landed a long-range point that levelled the match, and Paddy Meegan and Frankie Byrne had closing points to give Meath a deserved victory. Frankie Byrne scored six of Meath's nine points.

Another record crowd turned up at Croke Park for the Leinster final between Meath and Laois. The O'Moore county were the provincial title-holders. But in spite of the presence of the great Tommy Murphy and the lion-hearted Bill Delaney, Meath won the day 3-7 to 1-7. So, after a six-year wait, Meath were again Leinster champions. They were in the All-Ireland semi-final, only one step away from those New York skyscrapers and the Polo Grounds.

It was a long step—Kerry were their next opponents. Not only had Kerry, as usual, the greatest name in football, they were also the reigning all-Ireland champions into the bargain. But Meath were more than hopeful when they fielded out against the great Munster champions. Paddy O'Brien had Victor Sherlock as his midfield partner. Paddy was eagerly awaiting his duel with Kerry's superstar Paddy Kennedy. Kennedy was nursing an ankle injury that began to affect his play right from the start and he had to retire. The odds appeared to favour Meath. But Kerry introduced Eddie Dowling as a midfield replacement for Kennedy. The Kerry transformation that followed was unbelievable.

Dowling and Teddy O'Connor took over complete control in the centre of the field, consequently the Meath backs began to feel the pressure. Score after score went sailing between the Meath posts, and with every score visions of the New York skyline grew more and more feint. The final tally was Kerry 1-11 Meath 0-5. When the last whistle sounded, a leg-weary and very disappointed Meath team trooped off the Croke Park pitch. As Paddy O'Brien viewed it, the defeat was the most spirit-crushing set-back he was ever involved in. The rest of the players attested to that fact as well. Meath lost out to Louth in the Leinster championship in 1948 and they went on to win the provincial title. They were later to fall to Cavan in the All-Ireland semi-final.

Mayo swept through Connacht and confounded all the critics by hammering Kerry in the other semi-final by 0-13 to 0-3. Mayo were pitted against Cavan in the All-Ireland final that year. Paddy had a special interest in that game because his midfield partner of the previous year, Victor Sherlock, had returned to his native Cavan and was now filling one of the Cavan midfield roles. The Croke Park gates were closed as a huge crowd packed inside the ground and outside, when Paddy and a friend arrived. They went around to the back of the Railway end, crossed the tracks and sought a vantage point on the railway wall. That unofficial stand was already full, but they managed to secure a precarious seat directly over the scoreboard. It wasn't a very comfortable perch. A couple of youngsters down on the railway line showed remarkable business initiative by pulling big handfuls of long grass. A bundle of grass provided some slight protection for their posteriors against that granite stone wall. The youngsters did a roaring trade, charging sixpence a bundle. Paddy O'Brien's partner of 1947, Victor Sherlock, was playing a blinder for Cavan at midfield. He got possession on the left wing, side-stepped his way through the Mayo defence very neatly and cracked a left-footed drive to the roof of the Mayo net.

Though Paddy applauded Victor's great score, at the same time he was a trifle jealous. Twelve months before, he had looked on Victor as his junior partner in the middle of the field. Yet here was Paddy O'Brien, precariously sitting on a tuft of grass on top of the railway wall, a mere gatecrasher at the All-Ireland final, while down below on the green sward the brilliance of Victor Sherlock was thrilling the huge crowd. At that particular moment, Paddy wondered if he would ever win that coveted All-Ireland medal. With the teams level in the closing minutes, the accurate boot of Peter Donohoe put Cavan ahead. Then came Pádraig Carney's scorable effort from a forty yard free, which was rushed by Mick Higgins and cleared. In fairness to Carney and Mayo, Paddy thought the free should have been retaken.

Three months later O'Brien, entirely by accident, found himself starting an almost completely new football career, for he was suddenly transformed into a full back. Meath were to play Cavan in a National League game at Breffni Park. A car bringing Paddy Meegan, Matt O'Toole and Billy Halpenny broke down and they failed to make the match on time. Meath had to call on an army man, Lt Rooney from Carlanstown, to make up a team. It was a disastrous day for Meath. They had to be completely reshuffled and Paddy was shifted to full back. Cavan won the match easily, 3-10 to 0-3. Paddy had the very rare distinction of holding the Cavan star forward Peter Donohoe scoreless from play.

In 1949, Meath cruised through the Leinster championship, winning their six outings to qualify for an All-Ireland semi-final with Mayo. The weight of the odds against Meath clearing that hurdle made Paddy O'Brien and the Meath players fully determined that Mayo would earn their tickets to the All-Ireland final. Everyone outside of Meath didn't give them a hope, but Meath had other ideas. First of all they were lining out with the best full back line in the game in Mícheál O'Brien, cousin Paddy and Kevin McConnell, a full back line created in a moment of inspiration by the Meath selectors for the Mayo match. The partnership, begun that day, lasted for more than six years. Time and again the whole line was chosen by Leinster, and all three of them, though never all three together, wore the Irish jersey.

The All-Ireland semi-final against Mayo was a brilliant affair. It took one fortuitous score to finally clinch it for Meath. Early in the second half Meath's left half-forward Matty McDonnell, backed by the wind, lobbed the ball into the Mayo square. It fell between the fourteen yard line and the square. The Mayo goalie Byrne hesitated for a moment, then dashed out and dived in an attempt to smother the ball as it fell. He missed and the ball hopped into the net. The game was Meath's from then on.

And so to the most exciting day of Paddy O'Brien's life—and his first All-Ireland final—against near neighbours Cavan. He remembered sitting in the dressing room before taking the field and one of the team saying to him, 'Paddy, if you don't stop running your hands back through your hair, you'll be bald before the game ever starts.' This was to be his big moment, his dream, and that coveted All-Ireland medal. Meath achieved it. Their marvellous defence contained the Cavan forwards, with the O'Brien, O'Brien and McConnell full line brilliant. The great veteran Jim Kearney from Oldcastle and Paddy Connell took over control at midfield, with Frankie Byrne, Peter McDermott, Brian Smyth and Paddy Meegan doing what they did best in attack. O'Brien remembers with pride that occasion and the subsequent victory bonfires of 1949 that blazed from Clones to Oldcastle and from Bettystown to Kinnegad, and on every hill and in every town and village square of the Royal county.

Before Meath and Kerry met in the 1954 All-Ireland final, they had not met in a competitive game since the Kingdom hammered them in the All-Ireland semi-final in 1947. Six Meath players were on the 1947 side and there were eight on the 1954 team that had beaten Kerry in 1949. A week or two before the final, Paddy Meegan got married and promised he would be in the dressing room in time for the match. Paddy O'Brien had other worries. Some days before the final he developed a carbuncle on the back of his neck, and by Thursday he was in bed chock-full of penicillin. He was still ill on Friday but woke up on Saturday morning feeling in the pink.

A brilliant one-handed save by Patsy McGearty in the Meath goal proved a great morale booster going in at half-time. Meath had Kerry's measure in the second half. Seven years before, Paddy O'Brien galloped round midfield while Kerry were knocking over point after point to shatter Meath's New York dream. In 1954 he was able to stand in front of the Canal goal and watch Brian Smyth, Michael Grace, Paddy Meegan, Mattie McDonnell and Peter McDermott (captain) inflict the same fate on the Kerry side. When McDermott punched a ball high over the bar to put Meath seven points ahead, he knew the medal and the All-Ireland trophy was finally his.

Having had the pleasure of refereeing the 1952 All-Ireland semi-final between Meath and Roscommon, I can honestly say that Paddy O'Brien was, in my estimation, one of the finest and most sporting full backs I have ever seen. He was my choice at full back in my 'Best Ever GAA Team'.

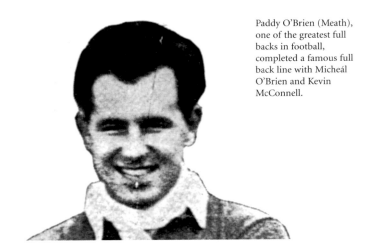

Paddy O'Brien (Meath), one of the greatest full backs in football, completed a famous full back line with Micheál O'Brien and Kevin McConnell.

November 1981: Seán Óg (*right*) with P.J. O'Dea (Clare) in Croke Park before the 2004 All-Ireland football final.

Mick O'Dwyer, later the famous Kerry trainer, in action at Croke Park (*right*) against Dublin's Johnny Joyce.

Kerry manager Mick O'Dwyer urges his players on from the side line in the final minutes of the 1985 All-Ireland final against Dublin. (*Inpho*)

The great Wexford four-in-a-row team of 1915–18, captained by Seán O'Kennedy. *Front row, centre*: Seán O'Kennedy holding the cup.

Seán O'Neill of Down, a truly wonderful footballer, and All-Ireland medal winner in 1960, 1961 and 1968.

Gerry O'Malley and the Roscommon team of 1953, beaten by Armagh in the All-Ireland semi-final. *Front row:* C. Garvey, P. Kearns, M. O'Regan, Batt Lynch, Bill Jackson, G. O'Malley, E. O'Malley, G. O'Donoghue, F. Kelly, J.J. Breslin. *Standing:* J. Finnerty, M. Rogers, G. Casey, A. Brady, E. Boland, S. Scanlon, M. Shivnan, P. English, E. Beegan. Gerry O'Malley says that, of all the Roscommon teams he played in, this one most deserved to win, and was good enough to win an All-Ireland.

Gerry O'Reilly, *front row, third from left.* The Wicklow team defeated by Meath 1-9 to 1-8 in the Leinster senior football championship of 1954. *Front row, left to right*: Tom McCauley (St Patrick's), Shem Furlong (St Patrick's), Gerry O'Reilly (Donard), Tommy Cooney (Ashford), Frank Keenan (Roundwood), Ger Mahon (Valleymount), Jimmy Byrne (Laragh). *Back row, left to right*: Tommy Doyle Selector (Rathnew), Joe Fitzpatrick (St Patrick's), Johnny Kenny (Baltinglass), Jim Rogers (Donard), Andy Phillips (St Patrick's), Paschal Deering (Dunlavin), Larry Redmond (Dublin club), Joe Timmons (Annacurra), Joe Carroll (Wicklow).

Seán Purcell (Galway), one of football's all-time greats, prepares to shoot for goal, with 'terrible twin' Frankie Stockwell awaiting the outcome.

Noel Roche (Clare), in possession, is tackled by Dublin's Jack Sheedy in the 1992 All-Ireland semi-final. (*Inpho*)

Larry Stanley (*right*), renowned footballer and athlete, who won All-Ireland senior football medals with Kildare and Dublin in the 1920s. (ʀᴛé *Stills Library*)

Larry Stanley with a few
sporting trophies.

Mick Tynan, Limerick's dual performer in
action against Wexford's Jim English.

Munster Railway Cup winning team, 1972. Jim Wall, Waterford and Munster full back, is third from left in the back row. *Standing, left to right*, Ray Cummins (Cork), Denis Coughlan (Cork), Jim Wall (Waterford), Billy Morgan (Cork), Mick O'Dwyer (Kerry), Michael 'Babs' Keating (Tipperary), Mick O'Connell (Kerry). *Kneeling, left to right*: Seán Fitzgerald (Kerry), John O'Keeffe (Kerry), Frank Cogan (Cork), Donal Hunt (captain, Cork), Tom Prendergast (Kerry), Kevin Ger O'Sullivan (Cork), Eamonn O'Donoghue (Kerry), Donie O'Sullivan (Kerry).

38

MICK O'CONNELL

L ike all great football teams, Kerry could claim to have had three of the game's most brilliant midfield players in Paddy Kennedy, Mick O'Connell and Jack O'Shea. I had the privilege of watching all three perform in the testing competitive atmosphere of an All-Ireland final in their respective decades. I can truthfully say that each of the three stood out like a beacon, displaying all the artistry needed to control the situation. Each of the three stars had his own distinctive style. Let me summarise each of them.

Paddy Kennedy, just tipping the six foot mark, never flinched from a challenge for a high ball. He was strongly built, he was forceful in his rise for a ball and rarely lost possession. I remember him most for his drop-kicking of a ball and the distance he could achieve. Mick O'Connell was the most polished of the three. He had a style and grace which outshone his other great qualities. Jack O'Shea, of a much later vintage, was a far more industrious player. He travelled the whole field in quest of the action. A great carrier of the ball after gaining possession, he created vital scores from his shrewdly placed passes. He always popped up to relieve defensive pressure and was at hand to avail of a scoring opportunity. He had the courage of a lion.

Yet, putting all three in proper perspective, I must say that Mick O'Connell's whole demeanour on the field has stayed fresher in my recollections. He possessed a brilliant football brain. He could rise from a static position to gain possession and had a very telling lift in order to outreach an opponent. Dublin's Cathal O'Leary had a similar gift in that regard. Both had great sporting qualities and marvellous sporting duels ensued whenever their teams clashed.

Mick O'Connell was born on Valentia Island, Co. Kerry, where he spent all his life apart from a term studying engineering at UCC but left after one year. He was a brilliant student and the college kept writing to him to complete his studies for his degree, but to no avail. In 1959 he became the first member of the local Young Islanders football club to win a senior All-Ireland medal with the Kerry team, which he also captained. He added to that first All-Ireland medal by winning All-Ireland titles in 1962, 69 and 70.

He collected a couple of National League medals and was the sports-writers and Caltex award winner in 1962. Living on his farm on the island was his way of life. He loved fishing and spent a lot of time bringing visitors to the island and to the fishing grounds near the Skelligs Rock.

Mick did not set the heather blazing in his first three years of inter-county football, nor were there any great successes or trophies won. In fact he got a valuable lesson on what to expect in his first senior Munster final against Cork in 1956. On rising to make his first catch of the ball, his midfield partner John Dowling accidentally clobbered him. O'Connell came off worse and it affected his display for the remainder of that match. It ended in a draw, but Cork had the winning of it but for a lack of finishing by their forwards. O'Connell was placed at right half-forward for the replay in Killarney, where he was opposed by the great Mick Gould, a good fielder and kicker of the ball. Though the Valentia man played a solid game, his clever passing wasn't properly utilised. He had several good chances of taking scores himself, but the fear of missing them pressured him into passing the ball to a colleague instead who was no more advantageously placed.

Mick O'Connell made his Croke Park debut in the National League semi-final against Cavan on 7 April 1957. He was chosen at midfield which pleased him. He liked the freedom of that berth. He was partnered by Tom Long against the very imposing Cavan pairing of Victor Sherlock and Tom Maguire. It was a great Cavan team containing highly reputable star players: Phil 'Gunner' Brady and Noel O'Reilly in defence, Jim McDonnell and the Gallagher brothers, at full forward was Mick Lynch, a very slick score getter, who went on to make his name in soccer.

O'Connell's versatility and all-round masterful play helped Kerry to qualify for the final against Galway. There was not to be any joy for the Kingdom; they lost to the Tribesmen 1-8 to 0-6, and more disappointing was the fact that a trip to America, a big bonus for winning the league, was denied the Valentia man.

There was worse to follow, inter-county wise. In 1957 Kerry met Waterford in the Munster championship, a game Kerry were firm favourites to win. But in one of the greatest upsets in the provincial championship series, Waterford defeated the mighty Kerry. This was humiliation in every sense of the word. Adding insult to injury was the fact that one of the stars of the Deise team was former Kerry player Micksie Palmer. It was said in Kerry that the coach carrying the Kerry players back home was delayed to avoid the wrath of the Kerry football fans. Micko's attitude to that set-back was clear and simple. It followed the age-old adage: nobody has a God-given right to expect to win every game. The Kerry mentors offered the excuse of being without their regular goalkeeper, who failed to make the trip. The replacement, an outfield player, had no experience of the position and failed to stop two easy shots at goal.

Mick was always his own greatest critic. He concentrated all the time on improving his free-taking, using various difficult angles from which to drive the ball over the crossbar on his local pitch. His sportsmanship was a feature of every performance and he became the perfect model for all aspiring midfield players. In time he was to become a cult figure admired by friend and foe.

Micko's first All-Ireland semi-final at Croke Park was against the Ulster champions Derry in 1958. Kerry had defeated Cork in the Munster final thanks to two opportunistic goals from corner forward Garry McMahon, one of the goals coming from a lobbed delivery from O'Connell. It was another O'Connell—Seán—who spoiled his name-sake's gallant effort for a place in the All-Ireland final. The stylish Derry star shocked Kerry when he beat Marcus O'Neill with a cracking goal near the end of a thrilling game to pip Kerry by a single point.

Derry were denied the Sam Maguire Cup when they were subsequently beaten in the All-Ireland final that year by Dublin. Kerry got a mead of revenge when they beat Derry in the 1959 National League final. But O'Connell's quest for that All-Ireland medal still remained unfulfilled, though the Valentia man made no great fuss about trophies. His greatest reward was when he played his best football, which in turn led to Kerry successes. That was reward enough for him.

The great rivalry between Kerry and Cork was proving to be an annual event at Munster final time, and 1959 was no exception. Kerry won the day, 2-15 to 2-8, by no means a football classic on the part of either side. Mick, by now firmly established as a regular midfielder, trained harder than ever before. And more important for him was the fact that he was team captain as well. But, as he once told me, the captaincy aspect never bothered him in the least. He still played his own stylish brand of football and he expected the same response from the other members of the squad. He would always argue that spoiling football was a defeatist policy. He pitched his own endeavours at the highest level and rarely allowed them to weaken.

The meeting of Kerry and Dublin in the 1959 All-Ireland semi-final brought an attendance of over 70,000 to Croke Park to watch two great rivals battle for a place in the final. O'Connell made no secret of the fact that the Dublin opposition always brought out the best in him. He named Dublin as one of the few counties who liked to express them-selves through their own distinctive brand of free flowing football. This had always been the characteristic of Dublin teams down through the years, perhaps even more so in the 1970s.

O'Connell was none too happy with the Kerry defence in the Munster final against Cork and he felt that a few changes were needed. He wasn't alone in that way of thinking. Filling the midfield position gave him a good opportunity of appraising the defence. The Cork forwards were constantly on the move, if a little over-anxious in their marksmanship. The Kerry forwards did enough to grind out a 2-15 to 2-8 winning scoreline. It was perhaps coincidental that Dublin had a similar winning margin over Laois in the Leinster final; their winning margin was also seven points, 1-18 to 2-8.

The 1959 All-Ireland semi-final between Kerry and Dublin lived up to all expectations. The Kerry defence was reshuffled. Niall Sheehy was a surprise choice at full back, his first major contest. Mick O'Dwyer was moved to corner back to the exclusion of Tim Lyons. Another new face, Moss O'Connell, played at wing back.

It was a cracker from start to finish. The highlight was the midfield duels between Dublin's Des Foley and Johnny Joyce and Mick O'Connell and Séamus Murphy. While Murphy lacked the height of the three other midfielders in aerial combats, his positional play was excellent. He frequently found space to receive the well-placed pass from O'Connell. That proved very valuable for Kerry in their build-up for scores. Both teams produced outstanding bouts of fast, open football which kept the capacity attendance on tenterhooks all through the match.

The Kerry midfield partnership of O'Connell and Murphy, two very experienced performers, had the edge over their Dublin opposites, and that was the cardinal factor at the end, with Kerry the victors, 1-10 to 2-5. It must be said that Kerry had survived a gallant battle in one of the finest displays of top-grade football seen at Croke Park for some years.

In the other semi-final Galway defeated Down by 1-11 to 1-4. But the Ulster men laid down a marker as a future force to be reckoned with, and as they were to prove subsequently.

Mick O'Connell's dream had come true. He often wondered what it would be like to lead a Kerry team around Croke Park as captain. That wish was fulfilled on 27 September 1959. It was his first All-Ireland final, but fate was to deal him a cruel blow. He had trained diligently from the start of the year. He had escaped injury and was eagerly awaiting the start of the championship season. His form was never better and his fitness level was higher than it had ever been. He was fully tuned up to meet the greatest challenge of his career and his ardent wish for a first All-Ireland senior medal.

The 1959 All-Ireland final between Kerry and Galway was, as usual, very well contested, but Kerry had obviously learned more from their win over Dublin than Galway had when ending Down's hopes by nine points in their respective semi-finals. Down were coming off a high after winning their first Ulster crown. Such was O'Connell's eagerness to produce his very best form on the big occasion that he increased his training schedule above the normal. It was not a wise move. After a promising opening quarter, Micko rose to collect a high ball. On the way down he twisted his knee badly.

Only he knew the extent of the damage. After some attention from the medics he was brought to the sideline, only to be asked by the selectors to move into the attack, the idea being that he might cause unease among the Galway defenders. He tried to run for a ball, but the knee buckled and that was that. He limped off and watched Kerry achieve a nineteenth All-Ireland success. Though in much pain from the injury, O'Connell walked up to the presentation area in the Hogan Stand where he accepted the Sam Maguire from GAA President Dr J. J. Stuart.

On leaving the Hogan Stand he was immediately grabbed by the jubilant Kerry supporters and chaired across the pitch. The trophy disappeared from his hand and he assumed one of the players had taken it. After a shower he dressed and left the grounds. Nursing a very sore knee, he struggled on his way to the train station. He never bothered about receptions after matches. His main worry was getting back to Valentia Island. In spite of the terrible pain, he rowed the short distance across to his home.

He was ordered to rest the knee injury, which he did. A week later he heard the sound of a band. It was a jubilant procession of islanders, bearing aloft the Sam Maguire Cup. He had only grasped the trophy for a short period on the Hogan Stand prior to crossing the Croke Park pitch. It was now in the hands of the Valentia Islanders, who were now celebrating its arrival for the first time to south Kerry. This proved a very emotional gathering of friends and well-wishers from the mainland.

It was to be Mick O'Connell's finest moment, one which had been crammed into a memorable year of unforgettable successes for the 'King of Valentia Island'.

39

P. J. O'DEA

I include P. J. O'Dea of Clare in this publication, not on the basis of All-Ireland football successes with his native county, or even provincial or National League honours, but simply because of a reputation built up in the late 1940s and 50s with Munster Railway Cup teams when he represented his native county. P. J. O'Dea was an extremely gifted forward of his time and appeared on the Munster team in the early 1950s along with Éamon Young (Cork), Jim Brosnan (Kerry), Packie Brennan (Tipperary) and fellow Clare star Noel Crowley. P. J. played on the Clare team in the Munster championship in 1948, a Clare team which included Joe Power of O'Tooles (Dublin) fame.

P. J. O'Dea was probably one of Ireland's best-known sporting ambassadors when the Kilrush-born star took off on the emigration trail, which led to him lining out with over forty teams in eleven cities, and with a couple of continents thrown in. A student in his local Kilrush CBS, he collected his first silverware at juvenile level with county honours in football in 1939, 40 and 41. While hurling played a secondary role to football in the west of the county, P. J. played the game from an early age. He collected a minor medal in 1944 when he was selected for the county. Three years later a Cusack Cup winner's medal followed in the Kilrush jersey at the expense of Miltown. However, with the repressed economic environment after World War II, work was scarce, forcing P. J. and others to leave their native hearth.

P. J. headed for Ennis and played football and hurling with the Faughs and the Old Mill Street Ennis Rovers. His display with the Faughs against Doolin in the 1949 championship was considered one of the best of his career. He lost out on a 1949 junior hurling medal against Ruan after a stirring replay. He moved on to Limerick where he joined

Treaty Sarsfields and helped them to win the coveted double of senior
hurling and football titles. He caught the Clare selectors' attention and
made his senior debut in 1946 against Kerry in the Munster championship when Clare ran the Kingdom to a solitary point at the Show
Grounds. In 1949 he had the distinction of holding the famed Kerry star
Batt Garvey scoreless from play and that ensured his inclusion on the
Clare team thereafter.

Fate played a cruel blow on P. J. in the 1949 Munster football
semi-final against old rivals Kerry at Cusack Park when the home
county lowered the mighty Kingdom's colours. But P. J. wasn't on duty.
He played soccer and suffered suspension after being reported by the
vigilance committee for playing 'foreign games'. For his crime he
missed out on the junior hurlers' progress to the All-Ireland final
against London at Cusack Park that year as well.

P. J. has many claims to fame, not all of which are connected with the
playing fields. I know of no other individual who would have the
audacity to lock a noted and indeed a distinguished member of the bar
out of his bedroom the night before P. J. turned out to play with Clare
against Kerry in a National League game in Tralee. P. J. takes up the
story: 'It was in 1950 and I was accompanied by a friend James Griffen
of Kilrush. We went to the Limerick Greyhound track before driving to
Tralee. I met Des Hanrahan, then a Limerick journalist and later chairman of Bord na gCon. Thanks to the tips I got from Des, I won over
£200, which was an awful lot of money in those days. When we got to
Tralee I was feeling very tired and went straight to bed, locking and
bolting the bedroom door on account of the large sum of money I had
in my possession. About 2 a.m. I was awakened by a lot of hammering
on the bedroom door and calls to open it up. I refused. I told whoever
was doing the knocking to go away, even though he was pleading with
me to give him out his pyjamas.' After further pleas had been rejected,
the late night caller left.

The next morning there was consternation in the hotel when P. J.
entered the dining room for breakfast. The manager approached P. J.
and told him that the room he had slept in was the one booked by
Judge Barra Ó Briain, who was the Munster circuit judge. P. J. had taken
the wrong room and had made matters worse by refusing even to give
the angry judge his own pyjamas. He apologised profusely for his error,
explaining his tiredness, the major coup at the dogs, the winning bets

and the room mix-up. Needless to say he ate his breakfast quickly and left the hotel.

P. J. earned automatic selection on the Munster teams of 1951 and 52 where his duels with Roscommon and Connacht's Éamon Boland were memorable. The great Jim Gallagher of Donegal and Ulster paid P. J. the supreme compliment by numbering him among the great forwards of his time, along with Éamon Young (Cork) and Kevin Armstrong (Antrim). The roving P. J. moved on to Cork where he joined the Fermoy and St Nicholas clubs. Later wanderings brought him to Dublin where he togged out with the great Seán McDermotts team which included such stars as Paddy O'Brien of Meath, Leitrim's Packy McGarty and Kevin Beahan of Louth. In 1954, he took the boat to England. The Holy Rosary club in Birmingham quickly signed him for a spell.

He moved to London and threw in his lot with Tara's and the west Clare combination called St Senan's, a football club. Canada beckoned and he used money he had saved from his various jobs in London to fly to Toronto and stayed there for a spell until he moved to New York and met the famous GAA figure-head John 'Kerry' O'Donnell.

His reputation as a very accomplished footballer and hurler had preceded him, and John 'Kerry' persuaded him to play for Kerry in football. He also turned out for his native Clare in a hurling championship match in Gaelic Park against a former Cork star who was well into the autumn of his hurling career. All through the game P. J. was getting plenty of stick from the Cork man, who kept pushing him and pulling at his jersey every time he attempted to play the ball. P. J. still managed to pick off some neat points and indeed scored the clinching goal for the Clare men. When the game ended, P. J. turned to his Cork opponent and said, 'Well, Tom, that's that, but I'll tell you something now. If they ever hang you for being a hurler, they will be hanging one innocent man.'

P. J. had the distinction of making an appearance with the late Noel McNamara, an exiled Kilrush Shamrocks player who had played for the Clare footballers against Wexford in the 1917 All-Ireland final. John 'Kerry' O'Donnell paid him while he turned out for Kerry. In 1957 he offered him an extra twenty bucks to be night watchman at Gaelic Park. The place burned down while he was sleeping, he told me. 'I left New York over that. I was very embarrassed. Everybody thought I set fire to the place, but I didn't smoke at all. I never smoked,' he said.

Ever on the move, P. J. next turned up on the west coast of America, where he soon became a household name in San Francisco and Los Angeles, starring with Cork and Kerry. His roving days came to a conclusion when he travelled to Chicago and got a job tending a bar at the Holiday Ballroom. It was there that he met his wife, the charming Mary Fives, a native of Tuam, Co. Galway.

Between them they make a perfect team, not only promoting the games, the language and culture of Ireland, but also espousing many Irish causes such as immigration, peace and reunification in Ireland. P. J. turned in star performances with Erin's Own and St Mel's in football, and Shannon Rangers in hurling.

He played his last game there on 17 May 1987 during the Bank of Ireland All Stars visit to the Windy city. P. J. scored a goal and two points for the Press and TV against a team of GAA officials, a happy end on the playing pitch. Pat Hennessy, brother-in-law of the late Paddy Grace of Kilkenny, writing in the Chicago *Irish American News,* recalled how another Clare man was instrumental in founding the GAA a little over 100 years ago. He wrote: 'Cusack was the man who coined the phrase "Bring the hurling back to Ireland", and he was the one who worked for its promotion. And yet, perhaps, in his wildest dreams he could never picture the tremendous good that this association would do at home and abroad. It would become the premier organisation in Ireland, the largest amateur organisation in the world and it would spread its wings through its sons and daughters all over the globe. Men and women from the 32 counties of Ireland would emigrate to distant shores and would bring with them love of God, of Ireland, its games, language and culture. One of these is another Clareman, P. J. O'Dea from Kilrush, destined also to become a legend of the GAA.' Pat Hennessy concluded his contribution: 'Today the great gael from Kilrush is as dedicated as he ever was in the promotion of Ireland's national games. Unassuming despite his many honours, P. J. O'Dea exemplifies the meaning of a true gael in the mould of his country-man—Michael Cusack.'

P. J. is the liaison to the Irish community for Cook County Sheriff Michael Sheahan. He returns to Ireland every September for the All-Ireland football and hurling finals. He brings a letter from Mayor Daley each year to the Mayor of Dublin. Should the GAA ever contemplate setting up a special 'Hall of Fame' award for its overseas ambassadors,

P. J. O'Dea, Clare man extraordinaire, will surely be a prime candidate for inclusion in that august body of Gaelic greats.

40

MICK O'DWYER

Mick O'Dwyer has a very impressive cv: winner of 4 All-Ireland senior medals; 8 National League medals; 12 senior provincial medals; trainer/manager of Kerry senior team in 10 All-Ireland finals (won 8); played in 10 senior All-Ireland senior finals (including one replay); 3 county championship medals; one Railway Cup; and trainer of Kerry under-21 team in four consecutive All-Ireland finals (won 3 in a row). The list is endless. No other individual in the history of the game could come near him. His greatness coincided with the appointment of what was to be his keenest rival, Kevin Heffernan of Dublin. Both former players were chosen by their respective county boards in 1973 to take charge of their senior football teams. It was an extraordinary quirk of fate and one that would revolutionise the game of football.

Both men took over their respective appointments at a time when morale was at its lowest ebb. Kerry were still smarting from a Munster final drubbing by Cork, while Dublin had not won a Leinster title since 1965. Mick O'Dwyer was under pressure, but Kerry lost out again to a great Cork team in 1974.

Heffernan used the league campaign to build up a team which he felt was needed to compete at top level. He believed the answer lay in a physically fit team capable of measuring up to the strongest opposition. Kevin had figured prominently on Dublin teams in previous years who were cut down to size by more physically endowed opponents. When he took over as the Dublin manager in 1973, he vowed that he would reverse that trend. He did—thanks to sheer physical force, superb athleticism, stamina, speed and a never say die spirit.

Mick O'Dwyer was taking note. Dublin's rise from the ashes became the focus of attention from the media generally and that rankled with

O'Dwyer. He had a dream too. He searched the Kingdom looking for young players who were willing and able to learn. He knew from his own experiences over many years on Kerry teams that a new approach was needed. The old ways had to be banished but not the traditional style of football which was sacrosanct. In 1975 Mick O'Dwyer faced his moment of truth when his young side was pitted against the pro-fessionalism of a Dublin team basking in the glory of a coveted All-Ireland title won the previous year.

Naturally, Dublin were the popular favourites defending their title against an up and coming young Kerry team still lacking the necessary big match experience—or so it seemed. But Dublin hadn't reckoned on Micko's motivational qualities; nor had they believed the stories that emanated from the Kingdom, that the Kerry team were trained to the hilt. Speed, hunger, stamina and aggression awaited the Dubs.

This was to be a battle of two great minds. The protagonists were Kevin Heffernan (Dublin) and Mick O'Dwyer (Kerry). Heffo had gained much media attention on the strength of his achievement in restoring Dublin to the top bracket of the football game in 1974. O'Dwyer set about putting the matter straight. He was Kerry's answer to the arrogant Dubs. O'Dwyer knew going into that 1975 All-Ireland final against Dublin that a defeat could well prove a poison chalice and would not be accepted by Kerry, who were still without an All-Ireland title since 1970. O'Dwyer had every reason to be apprehensive. After all, his was a young team pitted against a much more experienced Dublin side.

Mick also knew that this Dublin team that his squad faced would be trained to the hilt. Heffernan would have his charges motivated and eager to dispel any notion of cockiness at the sight of a Kerry jersey. For O'Dwyer's part, he had studied videos of Dublin's performances and noted facets of their games and where, to his experienced eye, weaknesses could be exploited. And there were some notable dis-crepancies laid bare in the Leinster championship games against Wexford and Louth.

Mick O'Dwyer noted one fundamental flaw in the Dublin defensive make-up and that was down the central line. He immediately drew up his battle plan. To maximise his attack he instructed his flankers in attack to hug the touchlines, making it impossible for Gay O'Driscoll, Robbie Kelleher, Paddy Reilly and Georgie Wilson to perform their normal sweeping roles in defence. O'Dwyer was also aware of the great strength of the Dublin midfield partnership of Brian Mullins and Bernard Brogan; that needed addressing too. He instructed his centre-field pairing to adopt a more defensive role, thus creating the added room for their own fast forwards. Breaking the ball down, rather than catching it, was introduced to the Kingdom's armoury.

It was the Kerry sharpness and alertness to that break-down of the ball which added immeasurably to their shock third-minute goal that eventually led to Dublin's downfall. Mick O'Dwyer's exhaustive analysis of the Dublin style of play had paid off. He knew that a couple of the Dublin weaknesses which had appeared from time to time had not been repaired and that they were ripe for exploitation. That early Kerry goal in the opening minutes was a gift from the gods. A combined Kerry attack along the left wing opened up a lane in the Dublin defence. The ball was punted forward towards John Egan, it was fielded instead by his marker, Gay O'Driscoll who, in a momentary lack of concentration, fumbled the ball unexpectedly. Egan nipped in, grabbed possession and shot past Paddy Cullen in the Dublin goal.

Kerry's victory in that 1975 All-Ireland final was most comprehensive, 2-12 to 0-11. The standard of football did not reach the heights expected. A more physical element appeared in the quest for the ball, but Dublin lacked the fluency they had perfected in their earlier contests. At the end of the day, Kerry fully deserved the honours and Mick O'Dwyer's tenure as manager had passed the test.

But there was another side to the managerial feud between the two coaches which became very apparent. It is accepted practice, when the last whistle sounds after a game, that the respective managers exchange a few words of praise on one side and sympathy for a lost cause on the other. Mick O'Dwyer always seems to find the proper level of praise which he extends to the opposition, whether he is on the winning or losing side. The Kerry team mentor's praise for a beaten team comes easily to him, because it does not mirror his inner thoughts. Heffernan's stance was quite different. He acknowledged a brief hand-shake or a brief word with the opposing team official—but that was all. I don't think that O'Dwyer or Heffernan ever exchanged pleasantries after matches. Heffo disliked media attention, preferring to let Donal Colfer and Lorcan Redmond, his fellow selectors, deal with after-match comments.

Both managers shared a common belief—to win at all costs—but that was attributed more so to Kevin Heffernan when he started out on his mission to restore Dublin to its proper place at the top. Mick O'Dwyer was pointed in that direction too when he took over the reins in Kerry in 1973. The 1975 All-Ireland final gave him his chance to show the football world that Kerry football was very much alive and well. Kerry's victory over the Dubs was acclaimed throughout the length and breadth of the county, and Micko became 'King of the Kingdom'. He had moulded the youngest team ever to represent the county, average age 25, and changed their traditional style of catch and kick into the new mode which had been very much favoured by Heffo. While Kerry were not as physically endowed as the title-holders, their running style, swift ball distribution and telling accuracy from well-planned attacks completely upset all Dublin's pre-match plans. Mick O'Dwyer had set out his stall: heaven and earth were not going to stop him achieving his greatest objective, a reputation-building dismissal of Dublin, the current arch rivals and big crowd pullers. Micko wanted glory and public attention and he wanted to be revered as the possible saviour of Kerry football.

It was a great stroke of luck and timing, then, for Mick O'Dwyer that he took over control of the Kerry team when he did. For one reason, the players under his command were comparatively young, and having spent nearly twelve months putting a shape on them, he realised their potential. Dublin's defeat certainly opened up new horizons and the victory achieved silenced many critics in the county not too enamoured with the change that the new style had brought. Kerry, topping the honours roll of All-Ireland football successes, had grown familiar with winning the Sam Maguire trophy. Losing an All-Ireland final is anathema in a county where victory is always expected.

The whole picture was to change for Mick O'Dwyer following Dublin victories over their great rivals in 1976 and 77. A ground swell of criticism erupted following those set-backs and, of course, the blame was laid on the shoulders of the manager, which I felt was totally unfair. They didn't believe in the old adage concerning sport in Kerry—you win some, you lose some. It was most surprising that the trainer who had changed the whole face of Kerry football, replacing it with a more revolutionary style, rarely got the praise he deserved. On the eve of the 1976 All-Ireland final between Dublin and Kerry, none other than

Kevin Heffernan paid Kerry a veiled compliment in *The Irish Times*. He said: 'The modern evolution of football can be traced back through the Dublin teams of the 50s, the Down teams of the 60s, the Galway team and "even" the Kerry team. It is the creation of space and the speed at which players with space can switch the play around.'

Switching play around was much desired by O'Dwyer in his quest for glory. The only snag was that Kerry had not adopted the new style of play as well as Dublin did in 1976 and 77. For Mick O'Dwyer, the 1976 defeat came as a bitter disappointment; it tended to wash some of the gilt off the previous year's success. But at least the Kerry maestro had a measure of satisfaction when Kerry beat the Dubs in the National League final the following year. It must be said that following the defeats in 1976 and 77, the bond between O'Dwyer and his players was never deeper. They had made many sacrifices both on and off the field. No manager could have asked for more. Yet forty-eight hours after beating Cork in the 1977 Munster final, the Kerry players were put through the most gruelling training session they ever experienced.

Now the emphasis was on skill, speed, mobility, sharpness and strength. Mick O'Dwyer made no secret of the fact that beating Dublin in the championship was Kerry's top priority. He said: 'At every training session, the same message was being hammered out. Beating Dublin was very much on our minds. Yes, you could say that we were definitely gunning for them in 1977.'

Three weeks before the 1977 All-Ireland semi-final against Dublin, star Kerry midfielder Seán Walsh twisted his ankle in training. It was a recurrence of an old injury and it was to have major repercussions for the Munster men. Walsh was one of the best footballers on view in the county and he was a 'moveable feast'. He could play anywhere, full back, centrefield and full forward. The cast came off his ankle only five days before the Dublin match. He was Micko's greatest worry and his absence would tell a sorry tale. O'Dwyer's rapport with his squad never weakened. He was known to be ruthless in his application of discipline—not unlike his opposite number, Kevin Heffernan.

Before selecting the side for the Dublin clash, Kerry staged a trial match in which Pat McCarthy played a blinder at midfield, but he hadn't measured up to events in 1976. The selectors, on a split vote, decided to leave him out and picked Jack O'Shea and Paudie O'Shea at midfield, a very ambitious decision and one that failed to pay dividends.

Dublin's defeat of Kerry for the second successive year in an All-Ireland semi-final has been well chronicled. Paddy Downey in his report of the match in *The Irish Times* wrote: 'The giants of Gaelic football clashed in fierce combat and at the end of a spectacular All-Ireland semi-final, the huge attendance was left almost speechless with awe and admiration The second half was truly a titanic struggle.' Padraig Puirseal in the *Irish Press* commented: 'Tony Hanahoe and his Dubliners are not only alive, they never lived more gloriously than they did at Croke Park yesterday, when they played possibly the most effective football of their careers to beat Kerry fairly and squarely in one of the best games of football staged at headquarters in twenty years.'

Mick O'Dwyer was devastated and disillusioned, having suffered the ignominy of defeat in successive years by Dublin. He knew that his critics within the county would again be seeking his head. He was so right. A move was already afoot in Kerry to have him replaced. Some ex-county players had been canvassing against him. That heave fizzled out. Micko knew that in Kerry there is little respect for past achievements. You are as good as your last match. But the word 'failure' had no place in O'Dwyer's vocabulary. He was back at the helm in 1978, ready and willing to atone for the disappointments of the previous years. The results were mind-boggling: All-Ireland victories over Dublin in 1978 and 79, and over Roscommon in 1980 and Offaly in 1981.

In 1982, the all conquering Kerry team was deprived of an unparalleled fifth in a row All-Ireland success, when a late goal by Offaly substitute Séamus Darby denied them an unbeatable record. It also deprived Kerry manager Mick O'Dwyer of a personal first ever five in a row All-Ireland victories, a feat never achieved before or since. Remarkably, Micko never made anything of the alleged Darby 'push' on Tommy Doyle, which led to Darby scoring the winning goal. But the Kerry manager was scathing in his condemnation of referee P. J. McGrath for handing Offaly two very dubious frees which Matt Connor pointed near the end of the game.

When Mick O'Dwyer stepped down from the Kerry manager's job after a very fulfilling career, he added further to his laurels by taking over the coaching of the Kildare senior footballers. He led them to a Leinster crown in 1998 for the first time since 1956 and on to a first All-Ireland final appearance since 1928. Moving on to Laois, and again success attended his coaching efforts when Laois captured Leinster senior honours in 2003 for the first time since 1946.

Seán Ó Siocháin and I stayed in Micko's Strand Hotel in Waterville on golfing holidays. I asked him once why he never sought the Ireland manager's job for the International Test series in Australia. His reply surprised me, 'I was never asked or considered.' Mick O'Dwyer made no secret of the fact that one of his greatest regrets was not being given the opportunity of managing an Ireland team for the internationals against the Aussies. I encountered many twists and turns in my efforts to seek an answer to this startling omission. It was mentioned that O'Dwyer may have stepped out of line by arranging sponsorship from leading business firms for his players, without getting proper GAA approval. His sound business sense and popularity broke down barriers in obtaining the best deals for the Kerry players. Apparently that did not go down too well with the GAA hierarchy, and thus he was ostracised as a result. It was also mentioned that candidates for the Ireland manager's job would have to come from those who had no county commitments at that time. If one turns back these pages and reads the opening paragraph again on Mick O'Dwyer, it could well be argued that there has never been a more illustrious candidate or one better suited with the qualifications for the job.

Owen McCrohan, writing in his 'no holds barred' authorised biography of Mick O'Dwyer, stated: 'A whole generation of young people have now grown up who know little or nothing about O'Dwyer and Heffernan in the arena where they first won fame and acclaim. The unprecedented hype that followed them and the teams they led from 1974 onwards would ensure that a new and more glorious dimension had been added to their earlier playing careers. It may be a contradiction in terms, but both men are, today, better known than they ever were during that golden age when they ranked among the best footballers in the land.'

41

SEÁN O'KENNEDY

Pádraig Kehoe, the Enniscorthy poet, wrote in tribute to Seán O'Kennedy after his death:

In him the Nore and Barrow met
To fashion a frame that we'll ne'er forget
A frame through whose every fibre glowed
A passionate love of the Gaelic code
An open hand and an open heart
A tongue that rallied—but left no smart
Gallant and gay and unafraid
He played the game as it should be played

Seán O'Kennedy was one of the greatest and most skilful dual captains that the GAA has ever known.

Sportsmen of the older generation in the Model county are quite convinced that he was the best all rounder ever to don the purple and gold. His record on the playing fields certainly shows that he was in a class apart.

A native of New Ross, O'Kennedy was one of the heroes of Wexford's senior hurling win of 1910. He later went on to captain Wexford to win the first three of their four successive All-Ireland senior football titles from 1915 to 1918 inclusive, while his fellow townsmen, his brother Gus and Patrick J. Mackey, both won four football medals. Mackey was also in the 1910 hurling side.

Those early years produced many brilliant footballers and hurlers, and yet those are decades of which little is written. Even so, the name Seán O'Kennedy has remained synonymous with the game, not just in the Model county but throughout the land.

Seán O'Kennedy's record on the pitch was something special. Few more picturesque figures ever graced Irish playing fields, for his natural aptitude for games made him equally skilful at both codes. He also had a great sense of leadership and of seeing early on weak points in the opposing side. During those early years when Wexford were well established as a football stronghold, O'Kennedy was a boyhood hero of the stature of Rackard, Ring, Mackey and Langton.

The O'Kennedys were one of the great Wexford GAA families of that time. Seán played in the 1913 All-Ireland final when Wexford lost to Kerry, and captained the senior football team in 1914 when hopes were again ended by the Kingdom that year in a replay.

Having had an insight into the cauldron of bubbling talent then at the disposal of Wexford, O'Kennedy was mainly responsible for instilling belief into the players and formulating the plans to ensure that, despite those two defeats, Kerry could be beaten.

Seán continued to develop his skills, but his greatest moment arrived when he captained Wexford to All-Ireland success in 1915, the first major breakthrough for the county on the national football stage. The young man from New Ross went on to prove one of the brightest stars of that great run of All-Ireland triumphs.

It was during those years and right through to the 1940s that the standard of football was so high compared to hurling, days when crowds turned out for football but not for hurling. During that 1915–18 period Seán O'Kennedy would often cycle fifty miles from the Barrowside town to places like Castlebridge, Wexford and Enniscorthy to train the teams, direct their plans of campaign, and his word was always law.

O'Kennedy started his career in Dublin with the Rathmines team, an offshoot of the Gaelic League, and, stretching in inches and avoirdupois, was in first-rank condition when he returned to his native county.

He demonstrated an art that has long since disappeared from Gaelic football. He specialised in drop-puck clearances of prodigious length in hurling, and established a kind of vogue in that style in the big-ball game.

His direction of the field in front was masterly, his half-time instructions deadly and to the point, and his switches of positions led to many victories.

Seán was a delightful companion and a pleasant singer of Irish ballads. A fine type of Celtic manhood, he played his full part in the Sinn Féin movement and was imprisoned more than once.

O'Kennedy was a leading officer in the GAA in the county and was Wexford county secretary in 1910 and county chairman in 1913, as well as filling positions in higher councils. A Leinster Railway Shield player in hurling and football, he also acted as officer of district committees before going on to become county team hurling manager from 1940 to 1945. That position was later held by his son-in-law, Billy Kielthy, in 1951, when Wexford re-emerged as a championship force in hurling, and who was named by the late Paddy Grace of Kilkenny as the best hurler he had encountered in a long and distinguished career.

Taken all round, Seán O'Kennedy had few equals either on the field of play or in the GAA councils.

42

GERRY O'MALLEY

For a period of eighteen years from 1947 to 1965, the heart-beat of Roscommon football was Gerry O'Malley. He gave hope in the latter years of the 1950s and the early 60s. While Roscommon had many fine footballers during that era, the one name that echoed the length and breadth of the Gaelic football world was that of O'Malley. Not only did he represent his native county with distinction in both football and hurling, but he was a central figure in a great Connacht team when the Railway Cup was a highlight of the Gaelic games calendar.

In the 50s, the five Connacht counties probably had their greatest ever individual footballers. Galway had Seán Purcell; Leitrim had Packie McGarty; in Sligo it was Nace O'Dowd; Mayo was spoiled for choice; and in Roscommon it was Gerry O'Malley. The Roscommon man played for thirteen years with Connacht, winning three medals in 1951, 57 and 58 in the golden age of the Railway Cup. The hope always was that O'Malley would achieve his just reward and win an All-Ireland senior football medal. Though he came close, having appeared in the All-Ireland final of 1962 and semi-finals in 1952, 53 and 62, he did not achieve the ultimate accolade.

He was later feted in 1984 in the Sunday Independent/Irish Nationwide Centenary team, representing the 'greatest players never to have won an All-Ireland senior medal'. Naturally, he was also selected in both the Roscommon and Connacht selections of the century. While an All-Ireland senior football medal eluded O'Malley, he did win an All-Ireland medal in hurling in 1965, when Roscommon beat Warwickshire in the All-Ireland junior final.

Gerry came from Brideswell near Athlone in south Roscommon and went to school in the Marist College, Athlone. He later progressed to UCG and UCD for his agricultural science studies. In university he participated in the Sigerson Cup, the universities' senior football championship, which he regards as 'the toughest competition I was ever involved in'. His native area is now represented by one of the county's top GAA clubs, St Brigid's, whose emergence in the early fifties was in part due to the prowess and inspiration of O'Malley. He just missed out on the great period of Roscommon football in the forties, arriving on the scene in late 1947. That was the year of the All-Ireland senior football final between Cavan and Kerry at the Polo Grounds in New York. Roscommon lost the semi-final that year to Cavan. Perhaps the inclusion of a young O'Malley might have tipped the scales otherwise.

O'Malley quickly rose to stardom and was a substitute on the Ireland team of 1950 for the inaugural series of annual games against the Combined Universities. Those were really the All Stars of the time and the Roscommon ace was selected a record eight consecutive times, from 1953 to 1962, when the series ended.

When one defines greatness in a player, it is not just the occasional great performance that must be considered, but a consistency over a long period laced with exceptional performances. A large number of O'Malley's displays had the sportswriters reaching for the superlatives, such as the Connacht finals of 1953, 61 and 62. Perhaps the most etched in the folk memory is the Connacht final of 1962. This is aided by the linkage to a particular incident which resulted in this decider becoming known as 'The Broken Cossbar Final'.

The Mayo dominance of the late forties and early fifties was broken by an O'Malley-inspired Roscommon in the Connacht summit of 1952. There was a newspaper strike at the time and legend has it that such was the scepticism with the result submitted that the Radio Éireann sports department held back until it could be confirmed. The result was Roscommon 3-5, Mayo 0-6. In a very good team performance the hero of the hour was O'Malley. He gave one of the greatest displays ever seen in a Connacht final, similar to Purcell in the 1954 decider. The Mayo *Western People* was generous in its praise of O'Malley as the match report described: 'He gave a display so outstanding that no praise of mine would give him due merit! Four great Mayo players, Carney, Mongey, Langan and Irwin, all tried their luck on him, but to no avail.'

Roscommon were unlucky to be beaten by Meath in the All-Ireland semi-final. Gerry regards that side as the best he played on. The side had a mix of fine new players such as Kelly, Batt Lynch, Scanlon, English and O'Malley's close friend Eamonn O'Donoghue, with some of the great players from the county's golden era such as Nerney and Jackson. There was more disappointment for Roscommon against Armagh in the 1953 All-Ireland semi-final. But accounts of the county's championship games throughout the following disappointing years are dominated by the performances of O'Malley. He was regularly referred to as 'the great-hearted' and 'the lion-hearted' warrior of the primrose and blue.

The latter years of the fifties were dominated by Galway. It was not until 1961 that Roscommon turned the tables in 'a gripping affair', as the *Irish Independent* reported. Disappointment followed with defeat by the great Offaly team of the time. Roscommon reached the National League semi-final earlier and O'Malley was selected as Gaelic football 'Sportsman of the Year' by the Association of Gaelic Sportswriters in an eventful year. If the 1961 Connacht final was regarded as a high point for Roscommon at the time, few could have predicted that it would be surpassed by the even more dramatic 'broken crossbar final' of 1962.

The Roscommon goalkeeper, Aidan Brady, swung on the bar and it broke. Galway were leading comfortably at the time. After the necessary repairs, O'Malley, from midfield, took the game by the scruff of the neck and inspired all around him. Roscommon drew level and it looked as if a remarkable draw had been salvaged. In a last surge, O'Malley powered his way upfield through the heart of the Galway defence, past bewildered rivals and team mates alike, the crowd in a frenzy. An amazed Roscommon support willed him on; a shocked Galway support feared the worst. This was an image of a sporting battlefield in slow motion. Finally, O'Malley released the ball to put Des Feeley in possession, and he calmly made an angle and dropped the ball neatly between the uprights.

The ball was kicked out and the game was over. Roscommon had come back from the dead. There was pandemonium, Roscommon euphoria and stunned disbelief from the Galway supporters. There was no rush to the exits as people tried to absorb it all. The sports doyens did their best but realised that even their best superlatives fell short. Donal Carroll (*Irish Independent*): 'The unsurpassable Gerry O'Malley has done it again. His was a masterly exhibition.' Jack Mahon, in the *Gaelic Weekly*, reintroduced the term 'the lion-hearted O'Malley', while in the *Roscommon Herald* it was 'the incomparable O'Malley'.

Having overcome Cavan in the semi-final, the All-Ireland decider was to have been 'O'Malley's final' as so many hoped that he would finally reap his just reward. Overall, there was too much pressure resting on one person's shoulders. Alas, an early injury necessitating hospitalisation meant he was not the necessary influence and was eventually forced to retire as another great, Mick O'Connell, dominated for the victorious Kerry side. Gerry looks back on this as 'the greatest disappointment of my life'. He was to continue until 1965, but the great new Galway side emerged as Roscommon declined.

O'Malley served many units of the association with loyalty and commitment. His first club was the famed St Patrick's of Knockcroghery, with Jimmy Murray and many members of the great Roscommon team of the forties. They lost the 1947 county final to their great rivals of the time, Tarmon, from outside Castlerea, run by GAA President of the time Dan O'Rourke. This was followed by victories in 1948 and 49 over another power-house of the time, Elphin. While those victories were sweet, they faded into the background when his own parish of Brideswell and Kiltoom (St Brigid's), emerged to defeat Elphin in 1953. After losing to the same opposition in 1957, St Brigid's put titles back to back in 1958 and 59. A feature of those wins was that the same line-out appeared in both years. O'Malley's last county final victory was in 1963. He continues to follow the fortunes of St Brigid's and regularly attends their games and functions. He is a great believer in the position of the club as the bedrock of the GAA and is a very willing and visible inspiration to clubs who call on him.

Gerry O'Malley, who has lived in Swords in Dublin for a number of years, was also an excellent hurler, having been introduced to the game by his national school teacher, Master O'Sullivan. He played with the Four Roads club where his mentor was Johnny Mee. He helped them to their first title in many years at Easter 1946 for the 1945 title. He was only a youngster then. He was a member of five further county championship-winning teams with Four Roads and was also the major figure in a good county hurling side in that period.

As well as winning an All-Ireland junior medal in the code in 1965, he was one of a few Roscommon hurlers to play Railway Cup with the Galway-dominated Connacht sides.

It is somewhat unsatisfactory simply recording mere statistics of O'Malley's long and illustrious career as many of his displays are intertwined with an emotive response nurtured by such games as the Connacht finals of 1952 and 53. His unquenchable spirit shone through those games and will never be forgotten by those privileged to have seen the lion-hearted Gerry O'Malley in full flight.

43

SEÁN O'NEILL

Seán O'Neill was a bright jewel in a very talented company of footballers from Down, who were associated with momentous and emotional moments in Gaelic games—moments in 1960 that saw the county make breakthroughs in the National League and All-Ireland senior championship.

Down beat Cavan before a then record attendance for a National League football final of 49,451 at Croke Park in May to capture the title for the first time, 0-12 to 0-9. Even better was to come the following September. No team from the Six Counties had ever won the All-Ireland senior football title as the Mourne county lined out for their Sam Maguire Cup debut against title specialists Kerry in the 1960 summit.

The final newcomers, aided by goals in the second half from centre half-forward James McCartan and left full forward Paddy Doherty from a penalty, turned the long-held dream of many into a reality by scaling the heights with a 2-10 to 0-8 win.

O'Neill played his part in that success with his intelligent football, and a year later scored one of Down's goals in their successful defence of the title against Offaly before a record attendance for any Irish sporting fixture at a tremendous 90,556.

The year 1968 was another memorable one for Down, who again completed the big double in football of the National League title and the All-Ireland senior championship. Those were also campaigns in which Seán O'Neill provided further evidence of his gift for finding the goal in expert style—and at the highest level and in a tension-laden atmosphere.

The league match was twenty-eight minutes old when O'Neill took a pass from right half-forward John Murphy, and in a free-flowing movement that was completed in a twinkling, he dropped the ball to his toe and shot home a gem of a left-footed goal. That was a striking example of the speed of thought and action of the Down ace.

Later in the year Down were bidding against Kerry to regain the All-Ireland title after seven years. O'Neill was one of four survivors from the winning sides of 1960 and 61. The half was only six minutes old when the first goal arrived. Right full forward Peter Rooney got through the Kerry defensive screen. His shot for goal looked like it would go inches wide, but instead it hit the upright and bounced back into play. The ever alert Down full forward was in the right place at the right time to collect the ball and in a flash slot it home with the inside of his boot. A lucky score? Far from it. It was O'Neill's quick-thinking, his ability to size up a situation quickly and take full advantage that turned the half-chance into a score.

The Newry Shamrocks club man's concentration and single-mindedness, so evident in that moment, allied to his mastery of all the arts of the game, and particularly when it came to banging in goals, made him without question one of the all-time greats.

Seán made his mark in the minor grade and won an Ulster medal at under-18 in 1958 at midfield. Not long afterwards he helped to write a bright new chapter in the Sigerson Cup (the then universities' senior football championship). Queen's, Belfast, and UCD played a draw at Fahy's Field in Galway in the final in November 1958. The replay did not go on until February 1959 at Ballybay when the Belfast side, with O'Neill to the fore at left half-forward, rallied from arrears of five points at the interval to win by a point for a first-ever title. He won a second Sigerson Cup medal in 1964.

O'Neill's senior inter-county career began in 1958 and he went on to win every major honour in the sport in a busy 285 games, including All-Ireland senior medals in 1960, 61 and 68, three National League souvenirs, and he was full forward in each of the first two All Stars selections in 1971 and 72. He also put his many talents on parade at centres outside this country—Wembley Stadium in London, San Francisco, Chicago and New York.

In his early days in the big time he played in the half-forward line, but later took over at full forward to bring a new and wonderful dimension to the berth. He could get up for the high ones with the best of them, had the ability to leave an opposing defender standing with a brilliant swerve, and could also create the chances for his team mates with his incisive and imaginative football.

The Down man is entitled to rank as one of the greatest Railway Cup footballers of all time. That competition (now known as the M. D. Donnelly inter-provincial) has lost a lot of the pulling power it enjoyed during the time the brilliant Down forward was parading his many gifts in such exciting style. In those days the Railway Cup hurling and football provincial finals were regular attractions on St Patrick's Day. There were some top-class matches during O'Neill's long reign in the Ulster jersey. Long reign? Believe it or not he made twenty-six appearances for Ulster! That says much for his consistently high standard of play over a lengthy period. Along the way, too, he established a number of inter-provincial records. In 1968 he became the first Ulster man to play on six inter-provincial football title winning teams. Three years later he carved out an even more impressive ranking as the first in any province to win eight Railway Cup medals. His successful years were 1960, 63, 64, 65, 66, 68, 70 and 71.

Impressive? Without a doubt. But it is a measure of the talent of the man that this proud record does not reveal the complete story. He had the amazing distinction of being chosen for every single Ulster team in the series from the 1960 semi-final up to and including the 1974 semi-final. The North lost that semi-final, and when the competition came around a year later, the Down forward was, unusually, among the substitutes. But his talents were not to be left on the bench for the entire match. It came as no surprise when he was eventually sent into the game and played his part in forging a win over Connacht.

Nor could anyone have been surprised when he was retained for the final against Munster. However, a goal-scoring performance to remember by the then 20-year-old Jimmy Barry Murphy (Cork), who helped himself to four, ended Ulster's hopes.

Despite that defeat, O'Neill's years in the Ulster jersey contributed to one of the most illustrious eras ever for the province in the series. That is further emphasised by the fact that he scored a splendid 9-26 (53 points) in his engagements.

In 1979 Ulster regained the Railway Cup after an interval of eight years and once more O'Neill was a key figure—but this time in a contrasting new role. He was a selector and team trainer. So, the Down man has a record in the inter-provincial football championship that is unequalled by any other and one that strikingly underlines just what a deep imprint he has made in football. Few then could have been surprised when he was chosen at centre half-forward in the Centenary Team—the side chosen in 1984 as part of the GAA Centenary Year celebrations.

Incidentally, Seán O'Neill was no stranger to a title-winning role as a manager when he guided Ulster to that 1979 success. Less than two years earlier he played a big part as coach in blue-printing Down's All-Ireland minor title win.

Seán O'Neill, then, was a footballer of many talents who has left his mark on the history of football in general and in Ulster in particular.

44

GERRY O'REILLY

It was something Kevin O'Brien said some years ago about football standards in Wicklow. He said there were great football people in the county but they needed to change their attitude. The problem in counties like Wicklow is that not enough people believe. They had no tradition of winning, so each generation of footballers is starting from scratch. He always believed the breakthrough could be achieved, but too many people in the county look for excuses instead. He said that not enough was done to build on the solid base laid down in the 1989–91 period. Too few people in the county actually believed in the county team, an attitude that infuriated him. Yet down through the years I have been watching Wicklow perform, there were always the star players who stood out but were battling a lost cause because of a lack of belief in others on the field. That observation does not apply to the Garden county alone; there are other counties in the country that suffer from the same malaise.

Writing in the *Sunday Independent* in February 1977, GAA columnist and former Galway football star Jack Mahon stated authoritatively: 'Half-back was my own favourite position. If I were to pick the best half-line from footballers I had seen, I'd have to consider men like Stephen White of Louth, Seán Quinn of Armagh and last but by no means least Gerry O'Reilly of Wicklow, the best inter-provincial footballer I ever saw.' He went on to say that the half-backs are the powerhouse of the team, though they seldom get the glory. I would be inclined to disagree with him on this.

During Gerry O'Reilly's period of service on Leinster teams, he was repeatedly accorded the man of the match award. It must be stressed that one of the great tests of a player's ability is when he is chosen on a team comprised of players from seven or eight other counties in the province. Gerry's test resulted with a man of the match award. He regularly filled that role during his glory days with Leinster and Wicklow. In 1984 he was chosen on the Centenary football team in centenary year and received his gold medal when he was fittingly honoured for his outstanding achievement for county and province. The other fourteen players also received gold centenary medals. The GAA president at the time, Paddy Buggy, was responsible for putting the scheme in place. It was a fitting gesture to those players in football and hurling who never won major championship titles with their respective counties. Gerry travelled from Rhyl in Wales to receive this honour. 'This is the proudest moment of my life,' he said, as he accepted his gold medal with his name inscribed and the years 1884–1984.

Former great Mayo star Éamon Mongey, in a series he penned for the *Sunday Press* in the mid-1950s, made this observation: 'Whenever in a boxing broadcast W. Barrington Dalby is called on to explain the horizontal position of the "British boy", he invariably offers as his opinion, that "a good big 'un can always beat a good little 'un". To that I say that he must never have heard of Leinster's little 'un, Gerry O'Reilly, or as many call him, Gerry the giant-killer.' He went on to say that for his size, Gerry could produce more pressure per square yard than any other player he knew.

He was an irresistible force who had never met an immovable object. He was a human dynamo. He was a law of the lever all unto himself. How he performed as he did, he wasn't sure, but perhaps what Joxer Daly said to Captain Boyle in *Juno and the Paycock* could be applied to him—'He's a Wicklow man, and that explains everything!'

Though starting his football career as a corner forward, later moving out to wing forward, it was as a half-back that Gerry O'Reilly exploded on to the GAA scene. And it was as a half-back that he became one of the most feared defenders in football.

The Donard-Glen man had been playing football with his club and with the county for six years, but apparently had never been discovered by the Leinster selectors. He came to their notice for the first time in 1951 when Wicklow played Dublin in a league game in Croke Park. But I had already singled him out as a very powerful performer when I refereed a National League match between Wicklow and Louth at Aughrim. O'Reilly was easily the star of the game, which Wicklow won. Billy Lawless was Wicklow county secretary and he had a stentorian voice which boomed out all over the pitch. I wasn't spared either. I stopped the match and marched over to him on the sideline. I told him if he used 'Open your eyes, ref' one more time, I would put him outside the railing. I carried out my threat five minutes later, but he still continued to boom out instructions from his new vantage point.

Gerry got his first big assignment when he was chosen at right half-back on the Leinster team to play Connacht in February 1952 in Ballinasloe. Éamon Mongey was picked at centre forward on the Connacht team and he made this comment about the Wicklow man: 'I must say that I have rarely seen such a display of attacking half-back play as he produced that day. To say he justified his selection would be the understatement of the Gaelic year.' Nobody could touch him on that occasion. He brushed aside all attempts to stop him once he gained possession. He was so effective that the Connacht selectors moved their best man on him, Seán Purcell. The Tuam Stars player was to suffer an injury and had to retire. Gerry O'Reilly never let up and in the closing minutes, with the honours even, it was from a great attacking run that the Wicklow man created the opening for the fisted point that won the match.

During Gerry O'Reilly's best years he was never overlooked by the provincial selectors. Indeed, he was virtually an automatic choice at wing back. Although small in stature, the much-honoured Wicklow man has not been at any apparent disadvantage with taller opponents. His wonderful zest, stamina and football skill have always confounded both players and onlookers alike. His speed to the ball was cultivated very early in the year, before serious competitions got under way. When I contacted him at his home in Wales, he immediately asked me about his friends who worked with him in the Guinness brewery, especially members of my former hurling club Eoghan Ruadh. Nothing had changed as regards his fitness levels. He was just going out for a three-mile walk.

During his playing days he would walk at least six miles, spend a couple of hours during the week playing football, and doing long-distance running apart from playing local league matches. One of his big disappointments was in 1956 when Leinster were beaten by Munster 3-4 to 0-9 in the Railway Cup semi-final. It was the first time Gerry had figured on a beaten Leinster team, having won provincial medals from 1952 to 1955. He was a great favourite with the spectators, friend or foe.

John D. Hickey, writing on the Leinster-Munster game in the *Irish Independent* on the following day stated: 'A feature of the game was the magnificent display of the loser's right half-back, Gerry O'Reilly, who outplayed Munster's Tadhgie Lyne to such an extent that the Kerry man was switched into the corner.' Continuing, he wrote: 'As the hour progressed it was something to marvel at when the Leinster player beat his rival. Not content with neutralising the danger man of Munster, the Wicklow player made some daring sallies upfield but his marksmanship was not on a par with all other aspects of his game. And I heard even Munster folk express regret that his efforts were futile.'

Gerry never won All-Ireland or even Leinster championship medals, but it was a measure of the player's greatness that he commanded a huge following at inter-provincial level. Once a game commenced, all eyes watched the Wicklow pocket dynamo in action. Padraig Puirseal, in his write-up of the match in the *Irish Press*, said: 'For Gerry O'Reilly the Leinster jersey retains all its old magic. Once again he proved that he can play better in inter-provincial football than in any other grade. Time and again he sallied right up the field, shaking off the tackles of a half a dozen Munster men. But on each occasion he chose to shoot and never succeeded in finding the range of the Munster posts.'

While O'Reilly is best known for his industrious displays at provincial level, fate has been none too kind to him at club and even county level. That was due to the numerous injuries he suffered from time to time. His litany of injuries reflects his efforts in all kinds of challenges. Three broken ribs, a dislocated shoulder, torn ligaments in the ankle, wrenched knees and torn hamstrings are only some he has suffered during a busy career. The worst was a groin strain he suffered in training three weeks before a championship game against Dublin. He spent four weeks out of work and another four before he could play again.

I had the privilege of refereeing the inaugural Ireland versus the Combined Universities exhibition match in 1950. The Ireland team featured a galaxy of star players, and yet there was no room for one of the greatest Railway Cup players of all time, Gerry O'Reilly of Wicklow. Had he been from any of the so-called prominent counties, he would have walked on to the team on merit. One of Gerry's favourite stories concerns a challenge game which was to be played on a certain Sunday. When the teams arrived the pitch was completely under water. Was the game abandoned? Certainly not. The players, helped by officials, removed the goal posts and brought them to an adjacent field and they fulfilled the fixture there.

One of my fellow scribes working for the Dublin *Evening Press* was the great Joe Sherlock. He wrote a column for that now defunct paper and made frequent comments about the wasteful forwards playing in the Munster-Leinster Railway Cup final which Munster won. He wrote two columns on the game itself, and kept the best of the piece till the end. 'But, lest you may be thinking that I have been mesmerised by Munster's victory yesterday, and can only see virtue in the team that wins, I am going to leave the best to the last. In other words I thought the outstanding player on the field was on the losing side—Gerry O'Reilly, of Wicklow and Leinster. The impression I got was, that O'Reilly, knowing he was up against Tadghie Lyne, was determined not to be outwitted. A sturdy broad shouldered "little fellow"—well, in height, if not in girth—he looked "little". Gerry, whether in defence or attack, was the inspiration of his side. He got into Tadghie's ribs, and Tadghie got into his and in a fair, if robust combat in which both gave and took without squealing, the Wicklow player came through with colours flying. All in all, he gave a masterful performance. It was a pity he had to finish on the losing team.'

That was how Joe Sherlock viewed the performance of a man who had never won an All-Ireland title, or a Leinster crown, or was even considered for an Ireland jersey. Yet in my book, he was one of the most inspirational figure-heads in the game of football during his very impressive career.

45

SEÁN PURCELL

They were known as the 'terrible twins' of Gaelic football; they lit up the scene during their brilliant days in the 1950s; and they are still remembered to this day. But it was really in the 1956 All-Ireland football final that Seán Purcell and Frankie Stockwell demonstrated the remarkable influence they wielded at football's top level—it was brilliance personified. Seán Purcell was a player extraordinaire, having during his remarkable career accomplished the rare feat of filling important team positions at full back, centre back, midfield, centre forward and full forward, and in each specific role produced a display of the highest calibre.

He became a feared opponent like his counterpart from Meath, Paddy O'Brien, who in a football sense was a gentle giant and a sportsman par excellence. I remember that Galway-Cork 1956 All-Ireland final particularly well. I was Gaelic games writer for the newly launched *Evening Press* at the time. I had never witnessed a performance to equal that served up by Purcell and Stockwell.

The Galway captain that day was goalkeeper Jack Mangan. He, Purcell and Stockwell all lived in Bishop Street, Tuam. Not alone did success attend their efforts but Frankie Stockwell scored a personal tally of two goals and five points, a record for a sixty-minute final. When Jack Mangan, who gave a superlative display between the posts, accepted the Sam Maguire trophy from GAA president Séamus McFerran (Belfast), he was the last player to receive a trophy in the old Hogan Stand, which was later taken down and re-erected in the Limerick Gaelic Grounds. I wrote on that occasion that I had never seen such a gigantic display as that served up by the Purcell-Stockwell combination. It was devastating stuff.

Yet in the years leading up to the ultimate success in 1956, Galway football was at a very low ebb. In 1951 they went down to a shattering 4-13 to 2-3 defeat at the hands of Mayo at a time when Mayo were ruling the roost at the top of the football ladder in Connacht. Mayo went on to add back to back All-Ireland successes in 1950 and 51. In 1952 a new look Galway, captained by Seán Purcell, beat Cork by five points in the league. The team was reorganised with particular emphasis on those who would perform a central role, Gerry Daly, Jack Mahon, Seán Purcell, Tom 'Pook' Dillon, Frankie Stockwell and Gerry Kirwan. If my memory serves me right, Kirwan was the only minor player promoted to the Galway senior squad during the league campaign from the successful Galway minor side which beat Cavan in the All-Ireland final I had refereed a few months earlier.

They beat Mayo in the league, Stockwell getting all three goals, 3-3 to 1-6, but they were later to lose out to Kerry. In the 1953 Connacht championship, after winning against a Packy McGarty-led Leitrim team, Galway went down to a strong Roscommon team in McHale Park, Castlebar (4-4 to 0-3), but they came back strongly in 1954 to beat Sligo in a controversial Connacht final, after leading by nine points at half-time.

The Sligo hero was Nace O'Dowd at centre back, who inspired his side to slice the Galway lead to three points. Jack Mangan saved Galway blushes when he brought off a master save in the closing minute. Sligo claimed the ball had crossed over the goal line. One of the Sligo forwards ran in, grabbed the green flag and waved it furiously, but the referee wasn't impressed. He consulted his umpires and immediately gave a free out instead to Galway for a foul on Mangan.

Kerry showed their mettle in the All-Ireland semi-final when they beat the Galway men 2-6 to 1-6 but not after Kerry got the fright of their lives. At half-time Galway's prospects looked decidedly bleak. But the old war horse selector, John 'Tull' Dunne, had other ideas. He berated the team for the sluggish form they had displayed in the first half, gifting Kerry unlikely scores. He castigated his team for their dismal approach which was not acceptable, he told them.

With 'fifteen Galway men are as good as fifteen Kerry men any day' ringing in their ears, Galway strode out for the second half in a far different frame of mind. Switches were made at the break. Seán Purcell was moved to midfield and that quickly had its effect. The weather took a turn for the worse, but gradually the Galway forward division, with

Frank Evers and Billy O'Neill very prominent, began cutting away at the Kerry lead.

It was a far cry now from the insipid first half offering from the Connacht men. Purcell started a great Galway offensive and Mick Greaney got inside the Kerry defence to produce a smart goal. Only three points now separated the teams.

Alas, time was the enemy. A gallant last ditch stand was foiled when the final whistle sounded with Galway still attacking the Kerry defensive lines. Jack Mahon apportioned much of the blame for the defeat on pre-match nerves. 'The occasion simply got to us and that was reflected in our first half showing. Nothing we attempted succeeded and Kerry punished us time and again. I felt we showed greater spirit in our second half efforts, but by then it was too late,' he said.

The set-backs of the early 1950s were offset by the heart-warming victory in the 1956 All-Ireland football final in which Purcell and Stockwell produced a brand of combination play, the likes of which had never previously been witnessed at GAA headquarters. The splendour of the football served up by both teams enthralled the attendance of 70,772, but all eyes were on Seán Purcell at midfield for Galway. Every time he got possession spelt danger for Cork and the Leesiders knew it only too well.

There was an added dimension supplied by Galway captain Jack Mangan, who was like a virtual rock between the posts, so in effect the three Bishop Street school mates were by now masters of all they surveyed. In spite of the supercharged atmosphere of the combat, the conduct of the contestants was exemplary. As the play developed, the standard of football was inspiring as well, even if the tension of the closing period was gripping.

One might employ a litany of superlatives to emphasise the co-ordination and excellence of the terrible twins in their quest for scores. Purcell's fielding at midfield was immaculate and his directional passes were reminiscent of a school teacher (where he was the master) giving lessons to pupils in the schoolyard, rather than in the cauldron of an All-Ireland final. When Purcell delivered a ball in that All-Ireland decider, the recipient of the pass, Frankie Stockwell, was watching and already moving into the space intended by Purcell; he had read Purcell's mind and intention. Stockwell's marker read the danger too late and looked on helplessly as the Galway corner forward flashed the ball over for a vital point. Stockwell simply applied his own tactics which he had developed with Purcell's assistance. Both had that sixth sense or anticipation that is characteristic of all great players. They make it look easy because they are invariably in the open space a split second before the opposition. That gambit worked like a charm every time Purcell got possession.

It was not generally known that Purcell went into that 1956 All-Ireland final nursing a slight groin strain. He was suffering a lot in the closing quarter and while it affected his customary speed, it did not inhibit his brain or his skill. His plan was simple. He juggled with the ball hand to toe until Stockwell began moving into position. From Purcell's pinpointed cross the ball reached the waiting Stockwell outside the square and he coolly punched it home for the crucial goal.

Ironically, when I caught up with Frankie Stockwell years later when I was interviewing him about his county's prospects for the 1963 televised All-Ireland final, the conversation turned to the famous 1956 final. I asked how the famous combination between himself and Seán Purcell came about. The question brought a smile and then a chuckle from Frankie. 'You know, we never had a plan that was so much talked about at that time. Purcell was such a great footballer, the most natural player of all time, that I had only to move to the right spot and he would place the ball perfectly for me. There were a number of great players who had that ability, but Purcell with his pure natural skill could make his feet do what his head dictated any time he wished.'

In another book of mine, *Tall Tales and Banter*, I relate a story told to me about Purcell. Seán, who was academically brilliant, qualified as a teacher and became known as the 'master'. A function took place in Galway to mark the 1956 All-Ireland victory. Seán as usual enjoyed the function and celebrated with the rest of the players.

Later that evening Seán was seen standing at a bus stop near the hotel in great form, hoping to get a bus to his home in Tuam. A city bus going to the depot, as it was now approaching midnight, suddenly screeched to a halt. The driver had recognised Purcell, so he opened the door of the single decker bus and asked, 'Master, is it yourself that's in it? Are you OK?' to which Seán replied, 'I want to go to Tuam.' 'No problem, step on board', and his grateful passenger acknowledged the gesture. 'Fair play to you, driver. I appreciate it.'

The bus was nearing Oranmore when a bus inspector, heading back to the depot after his last inspection, noticed the city bus travelling out of the city at 12.20 and signalled the bus to stop. 'Hold it, hold it. Where do you think you're going at this time of night?' The driver replied, 'Tuam.' The inspector asked, 'What the blazes is bringing you to Tuam?' The reply was immediate. 'Take a look inside and you'll know.' The inspector stepped inside and espied the passenger and in reverential tones said, 'Master, is it your good self? I'll never forget that '56 All-Ireland. You made me feel proud to be a Galway man. You were brilliant. You took them apart. It was one of the greatest displays of football I have seen, fair play to you.' Said Seán in a sleepy voice, 'I just want to get home to Tuam.' The inspector didn't mince any more words. 'No problem, master. Leave it all to me', and turning to the bus driver he said, 'Bring this bus back to the depot and take out a double decker. The master might like to have a smoke on his way home to Tuam.'

Frankie Byrne, the former Meath All-Ireland football star, also a teacher, always held Seán Purcell in very high esteem. He told me that Purcell had no parallel in Gaelic football: 'His versatility was incredible. He filled all five central field positions during his long playing career and received rave notices in all five departments. Seán did not possess exceptional speed, nor was he a tall man, standing about 5' 9". But he was sturdily built and was very strong on the ball. In fact, I cannot remember him being dispossessed once he had gained possession. He had a very good side-step which, combined with a feint and swerve, left opponents floundering in his wake. Purcell was a natural leader on the field and his passing from hand or foot was quick and accurate. Seán was a very shy person and for one on whom many accolades were heaped, a very modest and unassuming man. It was a pleasure to have watched him.'

In my opinion, he was the most talented footballer I have ever seen.

46

¡NOEL ROCHE

In any list of outstanding footballers, the name of Clare's Noel Roche is sure to get a mention. A regular in the county senior side from the late seventies until the mid-nineties, the St Senan's Kilkee club man is one of only a few Banner county footballers to have been nominated for an All Stars award. He played on many occasions for Munster and has the rare distinction of being on the Irish team for four consecutive Compromise Rules series against Australia. A devoted Kilkee man, he steered his club to a number of county titles at all levels including senior, and when his playing days ended he turned his attention to management and trained St Senan's to county success at under-21 and senior levels.

On the inter-county front, Noel was more successful than most who have given their all for Clare over the years. He was a vital cog in the Clare side on that never to be forgotten Sunday in July 1992 when they lowered the colours of mighty Kerry in the Munster senior final in Limerick. It's a success that is still talked about throughout Clare.

From a young age, the talents of Noel Roche as a footballer were evident, and it was no surprise when he was drafted into the county senior side. Throughout a distinguished career he played in a variety of positions for Clare, but he is probably best known as a wing back, the position in which he made most of his illustrious inter-county appearances.

One of the problems, in the view of several members of senior selection committees for Clare football, was a lack of scoring power, and because of that Roche found himself switched to the attack. Indeed, he was a regular up front during that memorable campaign of 1992 when Clare were so unlucky to lose out to Dublin in the All-Ireland semi-final in Croke Park. There was an electric atmosphere at headquarters on that

August afternoon, but the Dubs managed, with the help of a few lucky breaks, to make it through to the final, where they lost out to Donegal.

Few people were more deserving of that 1992 Munster success than the great Kilkee man who had been part and parcel of every Clare senior football panel for well over a decade at that stage. Incidentally, the Clare manager then was Mayo man John Maughan, who continues to be one of the leading coaches in football. His appointment as the Clare boss in 1991 was his first with any county team, and it proved to be a very wise decision on the part of the GAA powers that were in office at that time.

Indeed, Roche almost captured further Munster honours when inspiring his club team to the provincial final of the club championship, only to be beaten by O'Donovan Rossa (Cork).

In a province where Kerry and Cork have dominated football pretty much throughout the history of the association, winning selection on the provincial team is a rare feat for players from counties other than the 'big two'. It didn't prove to be any problem for Roche, who was a member of the Munster Railway Cup team in nine successive seasons. That fact alone speaks volumes for the talent and football skill of the great St Senan's player, something that was recognised by a succession of provincial committees. Given how highly rated he was within the province, his selection on the Compromise Rules team did not come as any great surprise either.

Such were his outstanding displays for Ireland on one of their trips to Australia, that he was named as the player of the series. He made history back then when he was the only player to be chosen on the Irish squad for four consecutive series and he justified his selection each time with outstanding performances on all occasions.

When his inter-county days ended, Roche continued to play for his club, and when his playing days were over, he turned his attention to coaching. In 2005 he trained his club team to the Clare senior title and to an appearance in the provincial final where they were narrowly beaten by Nemo Rangers (Cork).

Like many GAA players, he has taken up golf, and, not surprisingly, is proving to be as competitive and as successful. For Clare sports fans he will always be remembered as one of the county's greatest ever footballers.

47

LARRY STANLEY

He was born one of seven sons in Blacktrench in the parish of Caragh, a parish always divided when it came to football. Some parishes are tailor-made for two clubs and the parish of Caragh is one. The Caragh club ground and clubhouse are located in bustling Prosperous, while Raheen's complex is in tiny Caragh. Over the years the more urban club has struggled, while the rural one prospered. Blacktrench were the forerunners of Raheen.

His catching and ability as a jumper and holder of the ball led to Larry Stanley being acknowledged unreservedly as the greatest footballer Kildare has produced, and probably the greatest of all time. He trained himself to kick accurately by chipping a football into a bucket hung from the rafters of a barn at home.

He described the hours of practice: 'I started by taking shots close in and getting them over the bar. Then I would move out slightly until I had mastered every distance and angle.' It was not his kicking alone but his high jumping that distinguished Larry Stanley as a footballer. A high jumper of international standard, he broke the Irish record and was a member of the first Irish side represented at an Olympic Games in Paris in 1924. In the same year he won the AAA championship in Stamford Bridge, while in the inaugural Tailteann Games at Croke Park he fought a terrific duel with the newly crowned Olympic high jump champion, Harold Osbourne of the USA, pushing the American to an inch.

His interest in athletics started almost by accident. Larry was waiting around one day at sports in Two Mile House. A football game would follow the track and field events. A friend named Martin Murphy suggested that he 'have a go' at the high jump. The rest, as they say, is history.

He captained Kildare to a great All-Ireland victory in 1919. Indeed, it happened somewhat by accident. Blacktrench and Caragh had come together to win the Kildare senior football championship under the Caragh banner. The captain of that team was a boy of 19, Mick Buckley, the grandfather of Kildare All Star Niall 'Knuckser' Buckley. Mick Buckley decided that the more experienced Larry should have the honour of leading the Lilywhites. Exploiting the hand-pass to deadly effect, Kildare swept aside the Galway challenge by 2-5 to 0-1 in a one-sided final.

One of Stanley's finest hours was against Dublin in the 1919 Leinster final, and it made him an overnight hero. He captained the team against a powerful Dublin team which included the McDonnell brothers, Johnny and Paddy, Joe and John Synnott, Paddy Carey, Paddy Burke and Frank Burke, Brendan Considine and Joe Norris. One of the highlights of the game was the terrific midfield duel between Paddy McDonnell and Larry Stanley, the respective captains. Kildare's swift hand-passing was the key element in the Lilywhite victory. One of the stars in their attack was George Magan, a brilliant wing half-forward, who scored the winning goal for the Lilywhites.

A newspaper report describing the Kildare-Dublin game stated: 'Larry Stanley is the finest footballer to grace a Gaelic pitch. Notwithstanding his hard pace, his performance from beginning to end was brilliant. Not once did he fail to capture the leather with that extraordinary spring and one-handed grasp, for which he has become noted—it has been said with truth that it would take three men to mark the Kildare captain.'

Although closely associated with Kildare, it was surprising to learn of the few occasions he played for the county. In a sixteen-year period he played just seventeen times for the Lilywhites. During that time he also played for Dublin, winning an All-Ireland with them in 1923, and for Belfast Celtic. He was unavailable for many years of his playing career because of commitments to athletics.

An uneasy relationship with the powers that be didn't help either. Not long after that marvellous victory of 1919, Kildare played Kerry in a benefit challenge for a Kerry 1903 All-Ireland player who had lost an arm. Kildare won a low-scoring game with a team which included six of the All-Ireland winning side. By all accounts a number of the Kildare players—including Larry Stanley—were very much off their game. The following February, the amazing announcement was made that 'Larry Stanley is suspended pending his supplying a satisfactory explanation to the Kildare county committee of his conduct in the Kerry-Kildare benefit match played in Croke Park on October 26th.' Stanley was given no opportunity to defend himself and was understandably very disappointed at the treatment meted out to him by the Central Council—not the Kildare County Board. There was a real danger that this great talent would be lost to the GAA as Larry proceeded to have a quite successful association with Belfast Celtic soccer team over the remainder of their season.

The Kildare players released a statement placing 'sincere and thorough confidence in Larry Stanley'. However, the sad fact of the matter was that he was not to be seen in championship action with the Lilywhites for another seven years. While undoubtedly lost to Kildare when in his prime, Larry Stanley was not lost to the GAA.

As a Garda based in Dublin, he threw in his lot with his adopted county, winning All-Ireland honours with the metropolitans in 1923. Three years later he was back with Kildare as the Lilywhites and the Kingdom embarked on a series of games from 1926 to 1931 that were to popularise Gaelic football. Six times they clashed in All-Ireland finals, Kerry winning four times, Kildare once, and one game drawn. It was in the drawn final of 1926 that Larry Stanley scored one of the finest points ever seen in Croke Park, from out near the corner flag. Kerry, however, came with a late goal to draw the match.

The replay left something of a sour taste in Kildare, with Stanley coming in for some pretty rough treatment and never being allowed to perform to his potential. The Kerry midfield pairing of Con Brosnan and Bob Stack were comparatively small men for the position—both of them well short of six foot. Years later when questioned about the incident, one of them explained it away with a typical Kerry man's answer: 'Larry Stanley was six foot tall and could jump six foot one. Sure, we had to do something.'

When Kildare won the 1927 All-Ireland and retained it the following year to win the first Sam Maguire Cup with the same fifteen, Larry Stanley was conspicuous by his absence. He was not seen again in a Kildare jersey until the Leinster final of 1930 when he came out of semi-retirement to score a goal and two points in their 2-6 to 1-2 defeat of Meath after a replay. They were subsequently beaten by Monaghan in the All-Ireland semi-final. That was the last time this marvellous footballer turned out for the Lilywhites.

Larry passed away, having won almost as many awards after his retirement as he did on the field of play. In 1980 he won the GAA's 'Hall of Fame' as an all-time great player award, while in 2002 he was selected on the all-time Garda football team, on the occasion of the eightieth anniversary of the foundation of the force. In 1984 all the living All-Ireland winning captains were paraded at half-time in the All-Ireland final—Kildare's 1919 skipper was the oldest surviving captain.

Undoubtedly Kildare's finest footballer and one of Ireland's great athletes, the quietly spoken Caragh man was also one of the county's most enthusiastic followers right up until the time of his passing. I remember in 1980 when he received his Hall of Fame award, I recorded an interview with him for my programme on radio. He told me about his sporting life: 'I loved sport and all sports. If I had my life to live all over again, I wouldn't change one bit of it. I played with some great Kildare footballers and winning an All-Ireland was the biggest achievement in the GAA in my time. Winning an All-Ireland doesn't come easy. A player has to sacrifice a lot of things and be prepared to fight to the last kick to achieve the objective. It takes dedication, fierce commitment and extreme fitness to meet the challenge that present day football demands. We should never give up the chase until we finally climb the barrier to greatness, and that Kildare spirit still abounds in the county.'

48

MICK TYNAN

Mick Tynan's greatest hour in the Limerick colours was in 1965 when he lined out at full forward against Kerry in the Munster senior football final. Limerick lost that one, but the lion-hearted Tynan played a magnificent role in the attempt to beat the Kingdom.

Mick had already gained provincial recognition in 1958. In 1963 he was chosen on the Munster team and again in 1966, 67 and 68. The 1966 final was against Tyrone, again highlighted by Tynan's performance. He worked in New York for a time, but his stay was short as he was back in the Treaty city with his club and county a year later.

His devotion to the sport he loved was recognised by the Limerick branch of the Variety Club of Ireland when he was awarded the 'Sportsman of the Year' honour. He was the first Limerick man to get the award. His part in Claughaun's county senior hurling successes in 1957, 58, 68 and 71 will always be remembered with great pride and admiration. To those he added county football titles won in 1955, 67, 70 and 71. Be it football or hurling, Tynan was a towering figure in the glory days of Claughaun. In the 1970 football final against Oola at the Gaelic Grounds, he shot two opportunist goals and found the target between the uprights on five occasions. At administrative level he served as chairman of Claughaun and as assistant secretary of the Limerick County Board.

It was back in 1950 when Mick came into prominence while playing hurling with Sexton Street CBS. Figuring with him on the famed school team was Dom Lipper, from a well-known family in the world of politics. Other Claughaun players on that team were Martin Clancy, Seán McDermott, Niall Day, Paddy O'Connor and Ralph Prendergast. In 1954 he was selected on the CBS team crowned Dean Ryan Cup hurling winners, ably assisted by Tom McGarry, Jackie Quinlan, Ralph Prendergast, Liam Moloney, Paddy O'Connor and Joe Sherlock.

Prior to that—1950 to be exact—Mick was on the CBS team that captured Spillane Cup honours in football. On the Keane Cup winning team and runners up in the Harty Cup were Tynan, Mick Whelan, George Ryan, Niall Day, Ralph Prendergast, Liam Moloney and Paddy O'Connor. In a classic 1957–58 National Hurling League final against the winners, Wexford, 5-7 to 4-8, Mick Tynan excelled against the renowned Nick O'Donnell, the Wexford full back. In Gaelic Park, New York, both Mick Tynan and Ralph Prendergast won New York championship medals. His first Limerick senior football award came in a one-sided victory over Treaty Sarsfields on a scoreline of 5-4 to 0-1. Mick completed the Limerick county senior double in 1971.

By the time he came to the end of his playing days, he was remembered for his great fighting qualities, and in football for his excellent fetching of the ball. Football experts in Limerick like Billy O'Connor and Pa Joe Cussen from Galbally always gave him their number one when talking about the best to come out of the county.

Going back to 1963 when Mick won a first team place on the Munster Railway Cup side, the entire Munster football team is worth mentioning: Johnny Culloty, Niall Sheehy, Tim Lyons, Seán Óg Sheehy, J. Flynn, Mick O'Connell, C. P. O'Sullivan, T. O'Sullivan, Mick O'Dwyer, Séamus Murphy, M. Queally, Tom Long, Babs Keating, P. J. Kennedy, Mick Tynan, Noel Lucey. He also played football in the august company of such stalwarts as Paddy Harrington (Cork), Senan Downes (Clare), Dave Geaney (Kerry), Billy Morgan (Cork), Patsy Dawson (Tipperary) and county colleagues Pat Murphy and Tony Fitzgerald. Selection on the provincial team was in recognition of his qualities as a top football competitor.

In the Munster final of 1965, Limerick had been playing at junior level for some years. The decision was taken to compete at senior level when they defeated Waterford in the first round of the provincial championship. The pundits were impressed with their 4-10 to 0-6 performance in Tipperary town.

Though not given much of a chance against Cork in the semi-final, which was played in Killarney, the Mick Tynan-led Shannonsiders were to create their own bit of football history when they shocked the Leesiders in a well-contested game. It was on to the final, then, against

Kerry and there was great support for the challengers on home soil at Limerick Gaelic Grounds. It was the first time the counties had met in a provincial final since 1934, which Kerry won. Dual stars Eamonn Cregan, Bernie Hartigan, Tony Fitzgerald and Mick Tynan were to the fore for Limerick, with Cregan and Tynan figuring prominently on the scoring sheet. Limerick led 2-5 to 0-6 at the interval and the holders looked in trouble. Kerry, however, pulled up their socks and took the game to the home side and gradually wiped out the Limerick lead. Johnny Culloty in the Kerry goal saved two great goaling efforts from Cregan and Tynan before the holders claimed the honours.

The Limerick team lined out as follows: Joe Meagher (Oola), Liam O'Shaughnessy (Ballysteen), Séamus Cox (Old Christians), Timmie Woulfe (Athea), Basil Fitzgibbon (Ballysteen), Bernie Hartigan (Old Christians), John Aherne (Clanna Gael), Davy Quirke (Oola), Eamonn Cregan (Claughaun), John Mullane (Athea), Tommy Carrig (Ballysteen), Pat Reidy (Ballysteen), Mick Tynan (Claughaun), Pat Murphy (Old Christians).

Mick Tynan will forever rank among the greats of Gaelic football in Limerick.

49

JIM WALL

In recent years Waterford's senior footballers have been going through a lean time, but in the late 1960s and early 70s they were a force to be reckoned with. They competed on merit in Division I and it was probably the county's best ever period in senior football competition in modern times.

While many names come to mind, one player who definitely shone on the local and national stage was Jim Wall, from the Nire club in the west of the county. A defender who had the respect of all the top forwards of his day, Jim was the last Waterford footballer to be selected for the Munster team during the era when such games were so popular they regularly attracted crowds of 40,000 spectators.

Wall broke into the Waterford team in 1967 at the age of 22, having played a starring role in the Nire team that was beaten in the county junior final that year by Windgap. Totally dedicated, he became a permanent fixture on the senior panel. He played in every game and attended every single training session until a bad knee injury ended his inter-county career in 1974.

From Knockanffrin near Ballymacarberry, Jim made his last Railway Cup appearance in 1973 and during those games more than held his own in the company of such household names as the legendary Mick O'Connell and Mick O'Dwyer.

While retaining a vivid recollection of most of the games he played in, Jim particularly remembers Waterford playing exceptionally well to draw with Galway in the league at Fraher Field, Dungarvan, just months after the westerners played Offaly in the All-Ireland final. He also remembers playing against Dublin at Croke Park in the league, a game Waterford should have won, but too many of the players were overawed by the venue and they eventually lost by five points.

Jim always played at full back for his club and for Waterford, and while he faced many worthy opponents, he singles out three forwards in particular as being outstanding players, Ray Cummins (Cork), Babs Keating (Tipperary) and Paddy McCormack (Offaly). McCormack, known as the 'iron man from Rhode', normally played at full back for his county, but in games against Waterford he was brought upfield in an effort to match the towering presence of the Ballymacarberry man. Jim's wife, Ann (née O'Meara), is a proud Tipperary woman from Moyglass, near Killenaule, and he recalls that she particularly enjoyed his tussles with the famous Babs.

Keating also remembers his battles with Jim and is generous in his praise of his old friend and opponent: 'A big, strong man and a wonderful footballer, he would surely have won a number of All-Ireland medals had he been born in any one of the stronger football counties,' he said.

Looking back, Jim is quick to sing the praises of other Waterford footballers of his time, such as Monty Guiry, Tom and Ger Mooney from Kill, Jimineen Power and the three Walsh brothers from Kilrossanty, Tom, Pat and Noel. He reckons the midfield partnership of Pat Walsh and John Hennessy, from Ardmore, was an outstanding combination. They both represented Munster in the Railway Cup.

In more recent times, Jim rates small Pat Walsh from the Nire and Jimmy Maher from Kilrossanty as excellent exponents of the game. Gary Hurney, from Ballinacourty, who was recently selected for the Munster All Stars, also stands out in his opinion. The Nire man also acknowledges the fantastic achievement of the Stradbally club that won five senior titles in a row from 2001 onwards.

Though he won a county intermediate title with the Nire in 1971, Jim's playing days were over when his club enjoyed a golden era and won four senior championship titles in 1993, 94, 97 and 2000.

Despite the dominance of hurling in Waterford, Jim still regards football as his No. 1. He believes there is talent in the county, but most are playing hurling. As an example, he points to the current hurling star Michael 'Brick' Walsh. Jim believes that Michael could be one of the best footballers in the country, yet he has never played the game at inter-county level beyond the under-21 grade.

Former county chairman Paddy Joe Ryan considers Jim Wall to be a player with a deserved national reputation and without question 'one of the most outstanding players ever to wear the Waterford shirt'.

Mount Sion's Séamus Grant, the longest serving county secretary in the country who occupies a better position than most to offer an informed opinion on the man from the Nire, says that Jim was a 'sterling defender of the highest calibre, who genuinely enjoyed the respect of his peers in Munster and in other provinces'.

Jim maintains his interest in club football and currently coaches some of his club's under-age teams. He stepped down as a selector for the Nire's senior side when his sons, J. J., Brian and Diarmuid, broke into the team. Brian played for the Waterford senior football team in 2006 and was on the county senior hurling panel in 2005.

Jim was a selector for the Waterford senior team in the early nineties when the St Saviour's stalwart and former Carlow footballer, Michael Brophy, was in charge. Michael referred to Jim as 'a gentle giant fully committed to the ethos of the GAA'. He also says that Wall is very knowledgeable about the tactics of the game and regards him as having a good football brain. 'He is a great man to read a match and imparts his advice in an unobtrusive way. He is also a good motivator who gets on well with players, especially his own club members who can sense his fierce love for the Nire and the GAA club.'

BIBLIOGRAPHY/SOURCES

— Carthy, Brian, *All Ireland Football Captains*, Dublin: Wolfhound Press Ltd, 1993.
— Dublin GAA Annuals (1975–1983), Dublin: Gaelic Sport Publications.
— Mahon, Jack, *The Game of My Life*, Tallaght: Blackwater Press, 1993.
— Ó Ceallacháin, Seán Óg, *Tall Tales and Banter*, Dublin: Costar Associates Ltd, 1998.
— O'Connell, Mick, *A Kerry Footballer*, Cork/Dublin: Mercier Press, 1974.
— 'Sean', *Six Glorious Years*, Roscommon: Roscommon Herald, 1944.
— Smith, Raymond, *The Complete Handbook of Gaelic Games*, Kildare: Leinster Leader Ltd, 1999.
— Smith, Raymond, *The Football Immortals*, Dublin: Madison Publishers, 1995.
— Walsh, David, 'It's back to the hill', Dublin: *Magill*, 1980.

— Éamon Gaffney (*AngloCelt*)
— *Mick O'Dwyer* (Owen McCrohan)
— Jim Carney (*Tuam Herald*)
— John O'Connor (*Waterford Star*)
— Philip McGrath (Longford)
— John Guiton (*Tipperary Star*)
— Séamus Hayes (*Clare Champion*)
— Charlie Keegan (*Carlow Nationalist*)
— Brendan Furlong (*Wexford People*)
— Paddy Flanagan (Westmeath)
— John Roddy (*Kildare Nationalist*)
— Jack Nolan (Portlaoise)
— Eddie Rogers (Tullamore)
— John O'Shaughnessy (*Limerick Leader*)
— Tommy Moran (Ballinamore)
— Gerry Buckley (*Westmeath Examiner*)
— Liam Burke (*Kilkenny People*)
— Tony Conboy (Boyle)

INDEX